KICK-ASS
BUSINESS & MARKETING
SECRETS

KICK-ASS

BUSINESS & MARKETING

SECRETS

HOW TO BLITZ YOUR COMPETITION

BOB PRITCHARD

WILEY

John Wiley & Sons, Inc.

Published by John Wiley & Sons, Inc., Hoboken, New Jersey.
Published simultaneously in Canada.

For general information on our other products and services or for technical support, please contact our Customer Care Department within the United States at (800) 762-2974, outside the United States at (317) 572-3993 or fax (317) 572-4002.

Wiley also publishes its books in a variety of electronic formats. Some content that appears in print may not be available in electronic books. For more information about Wiley products, visit our web site at www.wiley.com.

ISBN 978-1-118-03508-5 (cloth); ISBN 978-1-118-11345-5 (ebk);

ISBN 978-1-118-11344-8 (ebk); ISBN 978-1-118-11343-1 (ebk)

Printed in the United States of America.

10 9 8 7 6 5 4 3 2 1

Contents

Preface

Despite its title, this Preface is a total *after*thought. I dictated it well after the book was completed, while relaxing after a lovely massage and a couple of glasses of red wine. It is amazing just how clearly one can see this mysterious subject of marketing when one is in a totally objective state.

Although the world has been changing frenetically since advertising began, traditional marketers and advertisers have stuck to strategies based on four tried-and-true laws: brand awareness to create recall and drive sales, the attributes of the product, the price, and satisfied customers. In fact, research shows that some 87 percent of all marketing and advertising is focused on either one or a combination of these four elements.

Yet advertising and marketing effectiveness has decreased dramatically over the past decade. In fact, Bob Kuperman, CEO of advertising agency Chiat Day, was quoted in a *Time* magazine article claiming that "95 percent of all advertising does not work." Although this might seem to be an exaggerated generalization, this research was supported by numerous other studies—including the Levi study in England—all of which produced advertising failure rates of 87 to 95 percent.

What? So 95 percent of what we're doing doesn't work . . . and we keep doing it?

Studies in 2002, conducted by the University of Toronto, even throw some serious doubts on the long-held, widely accepted "fact" that repetition increases an advertisement's effectiveness. The university's research suggests that repetition does not necessarily increase brand awareness, and, in fact, may actually *confuse* consumers. When respondents were asked to match up tag lines and products after watching advertisements, less than 50 percent were able to do so. The more the advertisements were shown, the worse the recall became, falling to 35 percent after just three viewings.

It has long been accepted that recall depends on frequency and that most people experience an exponential jump in their ability for recall after seven exposures of a given fact/image. So where did these "facts" come from? Did someone just make them up once upon a time and they happened to stick?

If the rest of the business world had been so complacent about modifying and updating its rules—particularly such obviously inaccurate or ineffective ones—we would all still be driving horses and buggies and sending smoke signals.

There is nothing wrong with the communication vehicles we are using as a conduit for the marketing message. Despite the extraordinary proliferation of communication mediums in recent times, each have their own applications in which they are effective to varying degrees.

> Rather, there are two essential causes of most companies' lousy marketing performances today, both of which lead back to a combination of the complacency of the marketing industry and the almost inconceivable gullibility of the corporations that employ their services.

In what other discipline would it be acceptable for leaders to claim that their applications are only 5–10 percent effective—and still keep their heads in the sand and go blithely on spending, spending, spending? You would think that they would have gotten the message 20 years ago when the expression "50 percent of advertising is wasted . . . the only problem is we do not know which half" was in vogue. What does it take to ring alarm bells? The acres of marble foyers in advertising agencies may be down to quarter acres, but there is still an incredible lack of accountability and performance.

The marketing evolution (or is it the revolution?) is occurring very rapidly and the marketing and advertising industry is struggling to keep up. For example, there is a disconnect between the excellent results being produced by the literally hundreds of effective social networking sites—the better-known ones including Twitter, LinkedIn, and Facebook—and traditional marketing and sales managers' (and their advertising and marketing advisors') inability to understand this new media. Fortunately, an increasing number of the world's top brands now have social media marketing specialists in their departments.

The media environment is undergoing a revolution the likes of which has not occurred since the very inception of advertising. The first television advertisement was broadcast on July 1, 1941, prior to a Brooklyn Dodgers and Philadelphia Phillies game—and it took a couple of decades to advance from the Bulova watches 10-second slot (which featured a still image of a clock and a voiceover) to more sophisticated advertising. This has been a steep learning curve. The so-called new media of mobile, short message service (SMS), online, sophisticated voice-web interaction, in-game, and a host of other technologically driven tools, have been with us only a relatively short while, and all but a few of the cutting-edge agencies have been caught flat-footed in their attempts to adjust to the new technology. Most agencies and their clients are just complacently doing what they have been doing for over 60 years.

Let's look at marketers' performances over the last 10 years by considering the following facts:

- According to Harvard Business School studies, 45 out of 51 categories of businesses are commoditized. This means that the customer does not differentiate between various competitors on anything except price—which is a guaranteed recipe for disaster.
- Corporate boards are now controlled by financially minded executives; most boards do not have a marketing person in sight.
- Despite common knowledge that long-term success, brand building, and developing loyal customers requires long-term planning, most of these financial people force marketers into three-month performance cycles.
- Marketers are also forced to approach people in financial roles for marketing budgets. The problem with that is that most of these "money people" do not understand what marketing is, far less why it would be necessary to implement a particular strategy at a particular time.
- Marketing is seen by most outside the profession as a nonexact science, if not just plain mumbo jumbo.

> It seems fair to say that marketers have lost respect and influence in both the business marketplace as a whole as well as with consumers.

Why has this happened? I believe there are four major reasons. First, marketers do not take responsibility for the real elements within the marketing portfolio. Let's begin with a fundamental question: What is marketing?

> My definition of marketing is this: Every action taken by the company, by anyone who works for the company, or by any other business or agency representing the company that in any way comes in contact with a potential or current client.

This includes not only advertising; PR; direct, online, and other traditional marketing disciplines, but also the performance a potential customer encounters when he or she walks into reception, phones the company, applies for credit, receives a delivery, makes a service call, and so on.

Do marketers take responsibility and produce return on investment (ROI) figures for *all* these facets of business? Unfortunately, most do not. What's even worse is that very few marketers seem to have even determined what all these customer touch points are; and there are literally dozens of them in most industries. For that reason, most financial people see marketers simply as advertising people, or worse, as sales and advertising or sales and marketing people. They're not considered to be marketers, highly skilled business professionals who can control the long- and short-term destiny of a corporation.

Marketers *are* the future of business; after all, every business transaction starts with a sale, and marketers drive business growth. Does the business community see them this way? Sadly, no.

Why? Because marketers' overall performances have been pathetic!

The second reason that marketers have lost respect is because they do not talk the language of business. The corporate world talks in terms of investment, ROIs, and yields, terms that have both qualifiable and quantifiable values. Marketers still talk about reach, frequency, CPM, and hits, most of which is absolute crap that means nothing to anyone besides fellow marketers.

Third, despite the fact that today's technology provides us with the ability to measure pretty much everything we do, marketers are primarily unaccountable. They don't even provide measurements for any form of advertising's actual audience—much less measure their efforts' actual sales results. Of course, audience size means squat; the only thing that actually counts is resultant sales. However, something about the ability to claim that 23 million people saw a particular advertisement makes marketers feel secure. In reality, 23 million watched the program, but far fewer actually *saw* the advertisement—and we have no idea who purchased as a result. Therefore, because marketers can't complete these relatively simple tasks, it is not surprising that they don't measure the results of the literally dozens of other forms of interaction between a company and its potential customers.

Fourth, research clearly shows that the majority of marketing and advertising does not work. Marketers can't be taken seriously when the majority of the profession delivers poor performance. They don't get respect because respect has not been earned. Until marketers perform more effectively, *no one* is going to take their efforts seriously.

So If These Are the Reasons, What Are the Causes of This Malaise?

There Are Three Primary Causes. Most Marketers:
1. Have forgotten the basics of marketing.
2. Do not do their homework and know very little about the potential client.
3. Do not measure everything they do.

In a wonderful June 2006 article in the *Financial Times*, Maurice Saatchi—founder of renowned advertising agencies Saatchi and Saatchi—claims that the death knell of advertising occurred because the "digital native"—those who learned the digital language as effortlessly as they learned their mother tongue—has a differently wired brain that responds faster, sifts out, and recalls less. Day-after recall has fallen from 35 percent in the 1960s to less than 10 percent today. Saatchi goes on to explain that brands today need a one-word CPB (Consumer Purchasing Benefit) which will come before all actions, in all media, at all times. It will be possible for only one brand in each category to own one particular word. The challenge for organizations will be defining the characteristic or the emotion that you are trying to make your own in just one word.

For example, Search is now owned by Google, Apple owns Innovation, Royal Bank of Scotland owns Action, Britain's Labor Party won three elections with New, America's one-word equity is Freedom.

This kind of one-word equity is the most priceless asset in the world of new technologies. There are 750,000 words in the English language. Which one is yours?

Most communication programs still have a limited and simplistic approach to their target groups. Meanwhile, these groups have moved on to another level because most businesses/advertising and marketing agencies are still anchored in traditional marketing methods. What most marketers describe as cutting edge is not cutting edge at all. Cutting edge is not more inventive stunts, creative ideas, better copywriting, or more testing; these are merely the basic minimums of any marketing these days.

In today's marketing world, we need to consistently build customer relationship data mining and multichannel approaches that continuously:

♦ Enhance knowledge of the potential customer.
♦ Increase the dialogue between the advertiser and the consumer.
♦ Improve the lifestyle connection.
♦ Build a bridge in every communication between the trigger for an emotional desire to buy and the pragmatic need to see the data as it applies specifically to the purchaser.

These claims are true whether you are using traditional vehicles—such as print, radio, TV, outdoor, or digital media. For instance, variable data multi-channeling (DM) enables data to talk individually to people using any channel. It allows for highly complex and creative direct mail packages to be fully personalized, with names, dates, an individual's usage information, savings, graphs, even photos and such in headings, and all body copy can be totally customized to every specific customer within a normal print run. One example of this is a recent program for a fixed-line phone carrier who received a 22 percent response rate from a print DM using one-to-one variable data technology to over 340,000 customers, as opposed to a traditional DM response rate for a similar program of 1.7 percent.

Selecting the Correct Media Mix Is Complex

Digital technology is only one element that is stretching marketers to actually think about the kind of message they need to convey to specific audiences and their media placement. Key product and service offerings are becoming increasingly similar, and response times to market change becoming shorter. Yet, not nearly enough direct marketers are using their skills to identify the communication channels that are having the most positive effect on influencing customer acquisition, buyer behavior or decision making, and customer loyalty and retention. Even fewer are providing advice; education and specific-instance comparisons tailored to specific customers, as opposed to hitting them with yet another creative message.

The first problem is selecting the communication vehicle. Marketers are not putting enough emphasis on choosing the correct vehicle—or more accurately, the mix of vehicles—to cost effectively impact and motivate the target market to buy. This is largely due to the lack of effective measuring systems being implemented and a lack of understanding of social media.

For example, it is ludicrous to measure the audience for television programs and then dissect it every which way in order to establish the target audience and advertising rates for slots in various programs. Why not just measure the viewing audiences directly for the advertisements? It is just as easy to do as measuring who watches the programs. However, there is a simple answer to this question: The advertising industry and its indirect masters—the media owners—have seen extensive research that claims that there is no one in the room in over 60 percent of the time advertisements are playing, and that a substantial percentage of the remainder of people are seriously distracted.

The chain-reaction effect of establishing advertising rates that actually *reflect* the viewing audience actually watching is too horrific to contemplate. Production budgets for shows would collapse, making most of them even more unwatchable than they are now. Sports coverage would drop from 30 cameras to 5, and broadcast rights would drop from billions to millions. Superstar athletes and entertainers would have to live on hundreds of thousands of dollars a month instead of millions; advertising agency commissions would drop, fewer Ferraris would be sold, and all of a sudden we would have a red wine surplus.

Reality in advertising would be a dreadful thing! It could be the end of the world as we know it. It is, therefore, much easier for corporate executives to continue to fall for the great stories spun by those extremely smooth but sneaky ad guys. Of course, the only true measure of advertising success is how much product is being sold or how many people are using the service being marketed. So why on earth don't we use this as the measure of marketing performance across the board?

That is certainly a worthwhile question to contemplate.

The second problem with most marketing and advertising is the structure of the message and the way it is conveyed. Most companies are, naturally, driven by the company's image and their product—as are the messages they use to try to communicate with potential customers. Both of these messages should, therefore, be driven by their customers. It is in the development of the product and the machinations of building a business that the blood, sweat, and tears have been expended; most organizations are under the impression that this is what the customer will also be interested in. At the very least, they want the customer to know what they have gone through. However, these companies fail to realize an important truth.

> The customer doesn't give a damn about them or, in reality, their products or services. The customer only cares about solving their own problems or meeting their needs.

In today's global marketplace, everything must begin and end with the customer. They are, in truth, *all that counts*. Customers can screw up all the hard work that went into creating products and building businesses in a heartbeat—simply by buying from a competitor.

Yet how many companies realize this and operate in a truly customer-centric manner? Probably fewer than 1 percent. Research shows that the public believes that the level of customer service is at an all time low, despite the daily mantra of "service, service, service," chanted by corporate executives around the world.

Customer service has improved an estimated 300 percent in the past decade, yet customer dissatisfaction is at an all-time high. The acceptance of satisfied customers as a success benchmark is, in my view, one of the reasons for the poor word-of-mouth that most organizations endure. Someone who buys a product or service is entitled to quality assurance; it is their right, and what they are paying for. They should be guaranteed good products, substantial range, effective warranties, excellent customer service, necessary information, and so on.

However, brands will never build customer loyalty and the increased profitability and decreased marketing costs that word of mouth provides by merely giving people what they are entitled to. Today, you have to knock your customers' socks off. There are four levels of service: basic, expected, desired, and unexpected. If you deliver only the first three, your customer base will erode, although at a decreasing rate as service improves. Only by providing the unexpected will you attain significant repeat business and enjoy positive word of mouth.

The benefits to a business of extraordinary customer service are very significant.

> A 2007 PriceWaterhouseCoopers study shows that customer service leaders in any category can charge 9 to 13 percent more than their competitors for the same product or service.

Perceived service leaders also grow twice as fast as their competitors and improve market share by an average of 6 percent per annum compared with a loss of 2 percent for poor-service-performance businesses. They also have a return on sales 12 percent higher than the average in the category.

You need to really go the extra mile and do something exceptional to get your customers to become advocates. Regrettably, it doesn't take much—because most businesses simply do not do it. Ask yourself, "When was the last time you had a great customer experience?" Now ask yourself an even more important question—"When was the last time I *gave* a customer a great experience?"

The typical answer is "I don't remember"! Therefore, if you are prepared to go the extra mile, if you genuinely care about your customer, if you truly want to give them solutions, not products, it is not hard for you to stand out from your competition.

> It is not about money; the size of your budget is not relevant. It is the size of your *ideas* that count today.

Focusing on product, price, customer satisfaction, and brand awareness just doesn't cut it anymore. Let me ask you some questions.

- ◆ Do you fully understand your existing customers' DNA?
- ◆ How about the DNA of your potential customers?
- ◆ Can you tell me the ROI of the last three campaigns you did for a specific customer and how much this analysis improved each subsequent program as it was rolled out?

◆ How sophisticated are your campaign measurement tools?

◆ How inventive is your in-program data capture? Please do not reply with something like, "Our systems will not accommodate this type of analysis." Without it, you are cheating yourself and your clients—and setting yourself up to lose the account.

In summary: Your target consumer is able to consume and process more information now more than ever. He or she has been conditioned to do so by technological advances. If you think a short–term, seemingly clever stunt, mailer, or communication of any sort can capture and influence this new mentality for more than a fleeting entertainment interlude, then consider that one-on-one, variable data, multichannel communications are performing at response rates in excess of 15–20 percent, not the traditional 1–3 percent levels. Why?

> Because, increasingly, focused personalized intellectual advice is far more effective and motivational over a long period than *any* short-term impact campaign—no matter how clever.

Somehow marketers have lost their way, and the time has never been better to rediscover our true purpose. No other profession has the ability to increase sales. Sure, financial people can improve ROI in the short term by cutting costs, but the true future of business depends on growing sales. So let's get started figuring out exactly how to do this.

Chapter 1

The Need for a New Approach

I constantly hear the following six statements with regard to the business environment today.

1. The e-commerce revolution, the social network phenomenon, and convergence of media have changed the way the world does business.
2. We are dealing in a new commercial environment that requires a fresh approach to marketing our products and services, whether we operate in a bricks-and-mortar business or business-to-business (B2B), business-to-consumer (B2C) or consumer-to-consumer (C2C) transactions online.
3. B2B sales will be commoditized, with global online auctions favoring companies with lower manufacturing costs. Middlemen will disappear, and traditional buyer/seller relationships will weaken. The web will continue to cannibalize an increasing percentage of traditional sales at lower prices.
4. This new economy's consumer thinks and behaves differently. He or she is more educated, more cynical, has access to more information, and is more price conscious than the consumer of days past.
5. The most important keys to success today are a great product, highly competitive prices, strong brand awareness, and satisfied customers.
6. E-commerce represents the greatest advancement and radical change in business history.

In my view, although all these statements contain a sliver of truth, they are essentially wrong.

The new economy has changed the communication mechanism and improved efficiency and speed of transactions. Contemporary technology

1

enables a high quality of business intelligence that allows fast, accurate customer profiling, which enhances sales opportunities. However, successful marketing has *always* been about creating and leveraging the emotional connection with your potential client, whether through advertising, public relations, face-to-face, or any other method.

> Successful marketing has always been about the quality of your brand equity.

As I already established in the Preface, brand awareness isn't worth a damn in today's cluttered, highly competitive environment.

Building real customer relationships by adding value and providing fantastic service with both internal and external customers at every interaction as well as providing customers with a genuine value proposition are simple elements that have always been the true keys to success.

Customers, whether B2B, B2C, or C2C, have not changed. They get elated, enthusiastic, hurt, angry, and upset over the same things they did 10, 20, or 100 years ago. The difference is that, now, an excellent value proposition, identification with the customer, and top-notch service can spread virally across the state, country, or planet in a matter of hours. Think about it: Is the e-commerce revolution a more important or sweeping change than the printing press, steam engine, telephone, or other significant technological advances that we have encountered throughout history? I don't think so.

Each of these changes increased economic growth by around 2 percent, and e-commerce will not prove to be much different. The first half of the 1900s saw monumental change with motor vehicles and highways, air travel, electrification, refrigerators, washing machines, television, and radio, as well as extraordinary medical advances. Has the world really changed *that* drastically in the past few decades?

There is no question that technological change has come rapidly. Just 30 years ago, futurist Alvin Toffler said something along the lines of: "In the future, we will have smart typewriters; letters will be correctable [and] able to be stored on disc or tape; electronic dictionaries will check for spelling errors; we will be able to link these electronic typewriters with phone lines and send written messages to the recipient's screen." How about that?

It is the speed of technological and media change—the drama of dot-coms soaring to extraordinary heights and crashing again, the hype that customers would prefer to buy over the net in preference to traditional sources, and the proliferation of handheld multimedia devices—that fueled the belief that the age-old principles of marketing would not work in this new environment. Most companies these days seem to have confused sales with marketing. They have forgotten—or, more likely, never really appreciated—the real keys to successful marketing.

Although the methodology we use to market our products and services has not changed, there is no question that e-commerce and shifts in communication vehicles have dramatically altered the nature and speed of doing business. The days of supply-driven industries in which a company creates a product or service and hopes the customer will buy are over.

Unless you provide precisely what the customer wants nowadays, you will fail.

This means being able to anticipate the customer's future needs, which requires an ongoing, thorough knowledge of the customer, marketplace, competitors, potential legislation, and other factors.

One thing is certain: There will be two types of companies in the future—those that can lead, innovate, operate efficiently, and respond quickly, and those that go bankrupt.

Today's marketplace is dynamic, as evidenced by the following facts.

- There are 156 million websites covering every conceivable subject.
- *Sony* creates a new product every two hours.
- 50 percent of this year's profits at computer giant Hewlett Packard will come from products that did not even exist 18 months ago.
- The singing birthday card has more computer power than existed just 35 years ago.
- Many of the products we paid for yesterday are free today.
- Companies are dramatically reinventing themselves. For example, NCR has evolved from an office equipment company to a business intelligence company.

◆ There are over 150,000 applications for mobile (cell) phones. They receive video, and can be used for financial transactions. For example, a cell phone can be used for putting money into parking meters and it can function as a boarding pass on airplanes.

The speed of this change is equally extraordinary. Think about the fact that only 15 years ago, fax machines were hot technology. They're now obsolete.

We have moved into an era in which knowledge and information are far more valuable than any product. Consider:

◆ 90 percent of all scientists who have ever lived are alive today.
◆ During the Vietnam War, 17 percent of U.S. soldiers had college degrees. During Desert Storm some 20-something years later, this figure had jumped to 90 percent.
◆ Norway received $17 billion in royalties from North Sea oil in the past 30 years. Amazon.com, with no profits, was worth that in just four years.
◆ Ford paid $6.4 billion for Volvo—plant, equipment, history, the lot. That $6.4 billion would have bought 4 percent of *AOL* at the time.
◆ Silicon Valley at its height produced 67 new millionaires every day.
◆ Technology represents 47 percent of total US growth.[*]

Wow, the Internet and e-commerce really *have* changed everything . . . right? Well, before we say yes, let's look at the facts about Internet companies.

◆ 99.6 percent of all Internet sites fail.
◆ Of the 156 million websites out there, fewer than 500,000 (less than 1 percent) have any real traffic.
◆ Only 280 of 16,000 retail websites are profitable.
◆ 46 percent of people who bought on the web in the past 10 years have gone back to their traditional way of shopping.
◆ Nearly 45 percent of people who have begun a purchase transaction on the web quit before they completed it.

---

[*]Ridderstrale/Nordstrom. Funky Business.

Has the Internet Lived Up to Its Potential?

The Internet hype was primarily developed on five premises, all of which
turned out to be untrue.

1. Being on the Internet will be an inexpensive way to sell product.

    With such a proliferation of websites, the cost of attracting
    people to your site is higher than it is with traditional business.
    Online advertising is no more effective than other forms of advertis-
    ing, and websites do not have the physical presence to drive
    awareness and equity through great service. Utilizing expensive
    traditional media to promote the online site must compensate for
    this. Simply placing an electronic catalog online has resulted in a
    nearly 100 percent failure rate. This makes achieving profitability an
    expensive task.

    The cost of building a customer-friendly, interactive, advanced,
    high volume site can cost millions of dollars. For example, Walmart's
    initial site cost over $110 million. The hardware represents only 10–15
    percent of these expenses, and the software contributes a further 15–
    20 percent. The balance is the price of integrating the site into back-
    end systems.

2. It will be easy to market on the web.

    Building the infrastructure and back-end integration is a *huge*
    job. Let's use Walmart as an example again. The company had 1500 IT
    specialists involved in building the site. Analyzing customer-supplier
    relationships and creating effective distribution and return strategies
    is very difficult and expensive.

    And you thought that the web leveled the playing field!

The reasons for such a high failure rate on the web are usually poor
marketing, a combination of poor design, poor customer-relationship
management (CRM), poor delivery, and poor customer communications.

---

3. E-business will reduce costs by cutting out the middleman.

    This simply will not happen. The middleman adds value to the
    customer purchasing process, education, installation, and repair—
    elements that are usually outside the company's core competencies.

In reality, there are more intermediaries than ever, including lead generators, e-billing companies, market exchangers, virtual distributors (shopping carts), and so on. An increasing number of companies drive web users to retail outlets, often to pacify their current retail partners. For example, Levi Strauss and Stephen King ceased selling online due to the anger of retailers and, in King's case, his publisher.

4. E-business will commoditize markets.

Many people originally believed that the Internet would weaken traditional buyer/seller relationships. They assumed that a lack of physical stores would prompt online prices to represent significant savings, and that customers would switch brands based largely on price.

However, this hasn't happened. The reason is that despite commoditization, only 17 percent of consumers buy based on price. However, 83 percent consider other elements, such as service or ease of use, to be more important.

Internet technology actually encourages business-to-business supply-chain integration and strengthens relationships, creating true strategic partners. This is one reason why traditional companies with integrated e-business strategies are more successful than purely Internet-based companies.

5. The Internet will cannibalize traditional sales.

It was thought that web sales would simply replace traditional sales at lower prices. Clearly, that hasn't been the case at all. For example, publishing division Headland put its Rough Guide travel books online with free downloads. People liked what they saw on the web, prompting retail sales to soar.

Why Do So Many Companies Fail So Badly at Marketing?

In short, too many companies think that they are important. They think their products are important. They think price is important. They think satisfied customers are important. They think brand awareness is important. The executives think they are important.

But they are not.

Customers do not care about the companies or their products, except in very rare cases. The world has thousands of warehouses full of great products from bankrupt companies. Customers only care about themselves.

Low prices simply mean temporary market share until your competitors cut their prices. They lead to decreased profit margins and, therefore, to less competition, which is a recipe for disaster. When customers buy something from you, they are entitled to be satisfied at the very least. According to a Harvard Graduate School study, 62 percent of supposedly satisfied customers do not repurchase from the same source.

> In the vast majority of successful businesses, irrespective of category, four out of every five sales are due to repeat purchase or word of mouth; only one out of five is due to advertising.

Merely satisfied customers are absolutely worthless. You need *advocates* instead—customers who are so delighted with you that they constantly promote and endorse you.

Results from a 2007 Rockefeller Institute study into the primary reason customers stop dealing with companies are extremely revealing.

- ◆ 1 percent die.
- ◆ 3 percent move to a different locale.
- ◆ 5 percent stop using product/service.
- ◆ 9 percent are attracted by competitors.
- ◆ 14 percent leave because they are dissatisfied.
- ◆ 68 percent leave because they felt the company didn't care about them.

Customers do not stop doing business with companies because of poor products or bad service. They cease to be customers because they believe that these companies simply do not care about them. This could be so easily rectified by a little display of attention to show customers that they are important to the companies.

The most important fact that this study highlights is how incompetent most marketers are. The majority of companies, large and small, have advertising budgets, and everyone knows that the purpose of advertising is to attract new business! Any company worth its salt has a database that records all prior customer contacts, sales, and so on, which enables efficient one-on-one marketing to these people, all of which is much more effective than general advertising.

So despite the fact that studies show that only 9 percent of customers will be attracted to competitors because of the competitors' advertising, most companies focus the majority of their marketing on advertising. What about the budget for customer retention? After all, companies will lose seven times more customers through neglect than they will attract by advertising. Unbelievably, most companies have no budget for customer retention.

The best way to grow any business is by one knocked-out customer at a time. Once you get them, make sure you keep them, and then use word of mouth to attract new, high-value, low-acquisition-cost customers.

This study alone makes the brand awareness discussion pretty pointless; however, let's touch on it anyway.

There are a huge number of companies with enormous brand awareness that are still not profitable. Car manufacturer Saab spent $60M a year advertising their cars, with a 97 percent consumer awareness level, only to fail. Having people know who you are and having them buy something from you are two totally different things. If I walked down Fifth Avenue in New York in nothing but a sequined jock strap, I would have great brand awareness. I would be in every newspaper and on every TV news station in the world. Everyone would be talking about me, but would anyone buy anything from me?

The Focus on Price, Product, Brand Awareness, and Satisfied Customers Is Bullshit

Price is only a purchase motivator if you have not established a perceived value/cost differential that is superior to your competitors. This is not even an issue of price, but rather one of customer benefit differentiation. Focus on price erodes your value/cost equation. Although decreasing price may temporarily increase market share, this only occurs until your competitor responds. Discounting prices dramatically erodes margins and, therefore, long-term competitiveness, which eventually leads to disaster. Price is not among the top three reasons people select one item over another when the consumer benefit of a product or service is clearly defined with respect to a competitor. Only when there is no clearly perceived advantage of one product over another is price the likely determinant.

When evaluating products, 92 percent of consumers—and a similar percentage of business buyers—see like products as interchangeable. It is extremely unusual that there is not another product that is either similar to yours or can do a similar job in today's competitive environment. Even if your offering is unique, it is only a matter of time before someone makes a copy. Therefore, the brand that does the best job of understanding customers' needs and selling the solution to their problem will get the business. Forget the product; it is simply a tool. If you are a retailer selling hundreds—even thousands—of products that a myriad of other stores are also selling, how does it build your business to focus on selling products? You must focus on what *differentiates* your business from your competitors, and it certainly is not the products you sell.

With the average consumer recalling only two advertisements they saw yesterday . . . a mere 24 hours later . . . the other 2,998 ads they also saw were also trying to get brand awareness, but obviously failed dismally. What is the likelihood that your message will be one of the two recalled? Even if it is, what are the odds that it has made an impression, sufficient and positive enough to have the potential customer buy your product or switch brands? That is a different, more challenging, and even less likely scenario.

Dot-coms are the perfect example of this. Some years ago, they spent literally billions of dollars on brand awareness. In fact, 17 of them spent $3 million each on 30-second spots in the 1990 Super Bowl, which was broadcast to over a billion people. Though many of these dot-coms had great brand awareness, this simply did not translate into sales. In fact, 12 of the 17 Super Bowl dot-com advertisers were out of business within three months.

> It's time for us all to face a harsh reality: Brand awareness nowadays is bullshit.

A study of 2,000 consumers at the University of Iowa showed no correlation between the messages to which they were exposed and the purchases they ended up making. In fact, none of the studies I have seen in the past 10 years have been able to show *any* correlation between brand awareness and sales.

Advertising for supermarket brands is a good example of advertising waste. Depending on the product, consumer decisions at point of purchase vary from 40 percent up to 90 percent. If, for example, 74 percent of purchase decisions in a particular category are made at point of purchase, then why wouldn't brands spend most of their marketing dollars in stores, where people are focused on buying? Why spend money on TV ads the night before, a time during which people channel surf or go to the bathroom? Even if consumers did accidentally *happen* to watch your advertisement—and did not confuse it with that of your competitor—the chances of it inspiring them to recall your product among all the clutter they will experience before they next walk into a store is almost zilch.

Research done by Harvard Graduate School—and a number of similar studies conducted across a wide range of product categories—has shown that companies with a balanced marketing strategy attain up to 80 percent sales from either repeat business or word of mouth. Only one out of five, or 20 percent of sales are generated by advertising. Despite this fact, I have found that the overwhelming majority of businesses have a significant advertising budget (which is primarily directed at acquiring new customers), but little to no budget allocated to their *existing* customers.

A budget for existing customers is absolutely necessary in order to attain (in a relatively inexpensive way) higher-profit-margin repeat business and drive word-of-mouth (viral) marketing. Yet this lack of existing customer budget (and attention) occurs despite the fact that word of mouth is much more effective than advertising. Gallup shows that some 91 percent of people trust recommendations from friends and family, yet only 13 percent trust what corporations tell them.

Whose Fault Is This?

The blame lies fairly and squarely with marketing and advertising people. Commoditization has made business nowadays more and more price driven, and a price-driven, commoditized industry very quickly becomes dominated by a few huge players with the most purchasing power. It also opens companies up to very serious attacks from price-advantaged web businesses. The result of this trend is that few organizations will survive in the long term.

> In order to grow your business and increase your ROI, you must first differentiate yourself and change the way you do business.

Marketers have allowed this commoditization to happen by failing to clearly differentiate their companies from the competition. Of course, it is easy to blame globalization, the highly competitive environment, the increasingly price-conscious consumer, and so on; after all, marketers need to blame *someone*. To see the real culprit, we actually need to look in the mirror.

The tragedy of all this is that there is a greater opportunity for great marketers now than at any other time. We have extraordinary diagnostic and communication tools to assist us nowadays.

There are three reasons for this trend. First, changes that have occurred in the media environment over the past 10 years, including:

◆ Media proliferation and increased segmentation.
◆ More one-on-one communication.
◆ Media creep (audience overlap due to media proliferation, particularly new media).
◆ An increased amount of content.
◆ A time-challenged public and consumer cynicism.
◆ The consumer's increased ability to access information.

Second and equally important is the consumer's capacity enhancement. For example, look at the TV screen for financial and business news giant Bloomberg; watch a 14-year-old make a call, watch TV, listen to music, send instant messages, and surf the Internet simultaneously on their cutting-edge smart phone. Scenarios like these show us quite clearly that our involvement with the potential customer needs to be challenging, interactive, and multichanneled.

Third, the changes in media vehicles enable marketers to attain:

◆ Immediacy of performance.
◆ Increased response from consumers.
◆ Infallible media metrics.
◆ Enhanced data-mining opportunities.
◆ Opportunities for more dialogue and less monologue.
◆ Dramatically lower cost of new-technology communication—such as SMS, e-mail, and social media.

Therefore, it is obvious that there is a need for a paradigm shift in the approach to marketing. The past 55 years have provided concentrated, focused, and predictable traditional media. Although marketers have been trying to find their feet over the past 10 years or so of new or digital media, these advancements have also changed consumers' behaviors. The combination of transformations on a variety of levels makes all forms of communication—internally, with strategic partners, customers, and potential customers—that much more important.

There are essentially two ways to get your message across:

1. Throw around sheer weight, which leads to price driven business and short-term results.
2. Communicate with the audience, which builds rapport, identifies with customers, and entertains them.

Developing this communication, becoming part of customers' lives, and sharing their interests is the only way to succeed. We must build long-term loyalty through equity.

The Five Drivers of All Business

Marketing has a fairly simple goal: to make the potential client feel better about you and your product or service than they do about your competitor, and to give them an emotional reason to buy from you. Think about the real reason you bought any product or service—from the mundane to the exciting, from the pleasant to the unpleasant. Wasn't it because it made you feel better in some way? Wasn't it the satisfaction of getting a better shine on the kitchen floor or knowing that you sent your mother-in-law off to the big old-people's home in the sky in a manner befitting her?

Success is about building brand equity by developing exceptional customer relationships, providing superior information, adding value at every level of customer interaction, implementing an equitable risk reversal policy, and delivering above-expected levels of service. Whether in the so-called new economy or the old economy, in e-commerce or traditional business, it is essential to remember that there are only five drivers of business:

1. Product/technology/service
2. Funding
3. Business strategy
4. Customer need
5. Marketing strategy

At a time when traditional business was paying more attention to and getting increasingly in touch and in tune with their customers, along came the new generation of business. It began with a technology product, focused on that product, and tried to drive sales through brand awareness, that is, advertising. The result was poor sales, a high burn rate, loss of consumer and investor confidence, and, often, utter failure.

Brand awareness might have been more effective in a supply economy with less clutter and less competition; however, it certainly is not worth much in this new demand environment.

Advertising expenditure across a myriad of ever-growing communication vehicles continues to increase. Yet the number of people contacting my office—who represent corporations large and small, all nature of events, and some individuals—complaining that their traditional advertising is not working is mounting exponentially as well.

The most common complaint is that the marketing and advertising strategies, which just a few years ago kept a steady flow of new customers coming in the door of their businesses, are not generating anywhere near the same response today. Two points emerge upon reviewing their strategies. The first is that the overwhelming majority of these businesses focus on the product's features, which will never drive sales. Second, few have a marketing strategy; most conduct poorly targeted, often shotgun advertising. Advertising is not marketing; it is only a small element of marketing.

In my view, the primary reason for the lack of success is extremely simple: We have forgotten how to plan a marketing strategy, and we have forgotten how to communicate. We have forgotten that marketing is logical, common sense, and simple. We have become carried away with complexity. We have forgotten that the customer has not changed.

> Customers want to deal with someone who shares their values—the same as they always have.

Too many of us have overlooked (or never learned in the first place) how to communicate with our customers, our spouses, our kids, our neighbors, our fellow workers, dissimilar governments, people who are different or have different values than we do, and so on. The pace of change is unnervingly rapid, but that is not the root cause of today's business bankruptcies, teen suicides, and family breakups. Rather, our inability to communicate is to blame.

The majority of traditional advertising is monologue; that is, the advertiser talking *at* the potential client. However, today's sophisticated consumer is seeking to have a dialogue with the advertiser. This requires that any company representative have the information necessary to address questions regarding a client's particular circumstance. Consumers today also have an increasing number of choices from which to obtain the product or service they are seeking. At the same time, many seek to be reassured that they are doing the right thing in making the purchase as a result of the trepidation they may feel.

Isn't that what marketing *is?* Offering quality products, great service, customer care, added value, and reduced (or eliminated) risk? It is a simple communication of your brand equity. What is so difficult to understand about that?

I recently gave a presentation in Barcelona to 1,000 clients of one of the world's leading software companies. After emphasizing that brand equity counts and brand awareness does not, one of the directors—a fixture in today's business magazines—told me that what I said made a heap of sense and that he had never heard of brand equity. He told me that their board meetings are dominated by brand awareness discussions. This is a multi-billion-dollar company—how scary is that?!

I am not saying that communicating our message today is not more difficult; it is. However, *everything* is more competitive today. It is also a lot harder to drive on the freeway or win a gold medal at the Olympics.

Retail is extremely competitive in the United States. Research shows that 60 percent of all retail outlets could close down without affecting the total number of products sold. However, this makes it all the more critical for brands today to differentiate themselves from their competitors and communicate with potential customers in a distinctive, more effective manner in order to succeed.

Marketing Is Logical, Not Rocket Science

No matter what one's industry, product, or service is, the ability to increase sales comes down to two sets of fundamentals; there are only two ways to get more customers. The first is to increase the size of the market; the second is to obtain customers from your competitors.

Once you have the customers, there are four ways to grow your business. The first is to grow the frequency of purchase; second, increase the amount of each purchase; third, increase the profit per sale; and finally, reduce your costs.

A small—say, 10 percent—increase (or decrease, where appropriate) in each of these categories, based on an initial margin of 20 percent, will boost profit by over 300 percent, whereas a 20 percent change in each will boost profit 550 percent.

Some Interesting Facts:

◆ Mintel Research studied 7,000 U.S. consumers and found that 67 percent bought due to word of mouth; only 26 percent bought due to advertising. Our practical experience across a range of business has found the percentage of those buying due to word of mouth to be between 64 and 90 percent, depending on the industry. This appears to be entirely dependent on the level of customer service and added value provided.

◆ The University of Iowa studied 2,000 consumers over two years and found no correlation between the messages to which they were exposed to and the purchases they made.

◆ Our research shows that only 13 percent of people buy because of price. 87 percent believe customer service and other factors to be more important considerations in the United States.

◆ As mentioned earlier, Harvard Business School research shows that 62 percent of consumers who are totally satisfied with the product or service at the time of purchase don't repurchase from the business where they made the initial purchase.

Though knowledge may be king in the new networked economy, knock-their-socks-off service, a strong value proposition, and word of mouth comprise the crown. This alone will drive a minimum of three out of four sales—frequently more—in most businesses. Brand equity creates loyal customers and the power of the loyal customer is awesome. For example:

◆ 5 percent of people buy 85 percent of Levi's.
◆ 8 percent of people buy 84 percent of Diet Coke.
◆ 15 percent of people make 67 percent of credit-card purchases.

This is a very simple equation, and one that must serve as the foundation of your considerations when planning a marketing strategy. When you take into account the power of online communication and the networking involved in social media, the power of brand equity is extraordinary. The challenge comes in figuring out how to create the strategy to achieve these objectives in the new business environment in which we find ourselves.

The New Fundamentals of Marketing

The essential changes to the way we must do business today result from our exit from the industrial age and entrance into the information age. Knowledge is king today, at every step along the chain, from the consumer to the service provider to retail and the manufacturer. Note the reverse order here—that is, consumer to provider—in contrast to the more traditional or legacy supply-chain business.

> Today, we have a demand chain economy in which the customer is *all that counts.*

However, knowledge is not enough. Knowledge does not drive innovation or success. These trends are propelled by ideas. Knowledge is only a benefit if it is stretched, bent, twisted, and hammered into the shape of a great idea.

The fundamentals of marketing used to be the five Ps: product, price, positioning, people, and process, with the emphasis usually being on product and price. However, in today's knowledge era, the marketing cycle begins and ends with the customer. We have evolved from the five Ps to the seven I's*: ideas, imagination, intuition, interruption, initiative, ingratiation, and interaction. Let's take a look at each one in detail.

♦ **Ideas:** As I established earlier, success is not about mere knowledge, but rather the ideas that *come from* knowledge. Ideas are what build brands and businesses. Most companies spend considerable time,

---

*The 7 I's are derived from Ken Hudson, original thinking company.

manpower, and money obtaining information, yet they do not encourage effort toward producing (or provide the time to create) ideas. Management and staff should be persuaded to contribute those ridiculous, off the wall, zany notions, because ideas like these are what generate competitive advantage.

♦ **Imagination:** Imagination activates changes and ideas. At the time it was invented, nearly everything we utilize today appeared to be a crazy idea. All it took was a little imagination. Unfortunately, most businesses are structured to stifle imagination. The Chartered Institute of Marketing cites that 62 percent of corporate CEOs believe their companies' corporate cultures restrict innovation.

♦ **Intuition:** This is the total of all our experiences, observations, and emotions. People buy with emotion, then rationalize with logic. Therefore, one of the most important attributes any marketing person can have in today's commercial environment is intuition. This emotional experience driver is a powerful tool.

♦ **Interruptions:** 99 percent of all our thoughts every day are the same as the ones we had the day before. We need to disrupt this traditional way of thinking, and to begin from a different jumping-off point. To maximize your creativity, make an effort to continually disrupt your current practices, processes, and mindsets.

♦ **Interactions:** Most businesses have various employees in various positions. There are people who create marketing, others who work in administration, others who provide service, and so on. Usually, members of these divisions are totally segregated from each other. It's no wonder most companies are so disjointed! Encouraging and maximizing interaction allows creativity, ideas, and new solutions to emerge. In addition, every interaction with customers must be transparently recorded for all departments involved with customers to see, refer to, update, and act upon.

♦ **Initiative:** It is essential to seize the initiative. If you don't, someone else will, and the world will not wait for you to catch up.

♦ **Ingratiate:** Business today depends to a large degree on the quality of relationships. We truly have to look for the individual in every customer, rather than the customer in every individual. You must ingratiate yourself to your customers and workmates. Don't forget, three out of four sales come from word of mouth, and people need to like you before they will talk about you.

Many advertising agencies acknowledge the changes inherent in these seven I's, and are reorganizing and refocusing the way they do business accordingly. Former CEO of Australia's J. Walter Thompson, Anthony Armstrong, told me that their agency was getting "out of the advertising business and into the communication business" in order to address today's consumer's changing needs. The reason that the majority of advertising does not work is not due to the vehicles we're using; in fact, each is very effective when used correctly. The problem lies with the nature of the messages we're conveying.

One of the reasons the Internet has altered the way consumers relate to and buy products and services is due to consumers' ability to obtain extensive information, ask questions, and get detailed specifics relating to their particular issue from the corporation offering the goods or service. Additionally, they can do it without the aggravation of the often poor and could-not-careless attitudes of many sales personnel. The Internet also enables consumers to obtain information without feeling intimidated. Even more important, potential customers can readily interact online with one (or even thousands of) other individuals who may have used the product or service, and thereby get genuine, firsthand feedback in a matter of minutes.

The social websites can also alert potential users to possible issues. For example, the extremely powerful "United Breaks Guitars" video segment by David Carroll on the social networks changed United Airline's cargo-handling methods and reportedly cost the airline $180 million. This video has been viewed more than 10 million times, creating a PR nightmare for United. What is less well known is that Greg Gianforte, the founder and CEO of RightNow, a customer-service software company, organized a customer-service conference in New York and secured David Carroll to speak. Well, guess what? Carroll flew United to the conference and according to the *New York Times* . . . they lost his bag!

It is unlikely that the Internet will gather a significant percentage of retail sales in the foreseeable future. In 2009, the web captured 6.5 percent of the potential retail sales for products/services that could be sold on the web. Unless a company has developed significant brand equity as a result of excellent service, quality information, expertise, and reliability, most consumers will obtain all the relevant information from the Internet and simply target any local supplier to purchase precisely what they have researched, a trend that will further exacerbate commoditization. An oversupply of retail outlets could cause a dramatic rationalization that only customer-centric retailers will survive.

The Internet has the potential to change the way we all do business. Companies that have seized on online presence can gain significant incremental income. However, only 1 percent of companies that conduct online transactions have any level of traffic.

The Internet provides savvy corporations with an exceptional opportunity to build a pervasive brand culture—something they can achieve by providing information to consumers in their home or office, any time of the day or night, at the consumers' choosing. This will become increasingly important as product expertise becomes ever scarcer, due, in part, to an increasing reliance on part-time staff, geared to high trading periods to reduce wage costs.

The 24/7 focused information on the web is a powerful contrast to today's highly cluttered, fragmented, increasingly expensive media advertising options and gradually more cynical and time-starved consumer. It is extremely difficult for new companies using advertising nowadays to build a brand culture without huge financial resources. The companies who have established brands over the past 20–30 years (when it was relatively easy to do so) have a decided marketing advantage today if they reinforce and leverage their brand positioning wisely. Internet companies will continue to experience high failure rates—that is, until they focus on developing customer relationships and not trying to buy brand awareness through advertising.

E-Commerce Marketing Budgets Escalate

Traditional companies' marketing budgets are customarily set somewhere between 2 and 10 percent of sales. However, e-commerce pioneers dramatically changed that equation as they struggled to rapidly alter ingrained buying patterns and build brands in a continuously cluttered marketplace. E-commerce companies that survived this unique time in history are the ones that realized that it is not brand, product, or price, but rather *brand equity* that is critical to profits and longevity. Companies such as *Amazon.com,* which is totally focused on the customer and provides extraordinary service, advice, and rapid follow-up, built equity but at a high cost. It is not unusual for many failed Internet businesses to have spent 250–1,000 percent of their income on marketing, with the majority in traditional media.

Internet-based businesses that have developed the kind of brand equity that Amazon.com has have mastered the Internet. However, it took them six years of losses before reporting their first-ever profit, a modest $5.09 million on sales of $1.1 billion in the fourth quarter of 2001. Even with this, Amazon still incurred a loss of $567 million for the year. Nearly 10 years later, Amazon is recording quarterly profits on the order of $175 million, but it has taken 16 years to get to this point. The business-to-consumer market online is a competitive one, and the overwhelming majority of consumers, despite their protests, like going to the store, want to see what they are buying, and want to be able to return or swap purchases readily.

No matter how much our method of doing business changes, one thing that does not change is communication principles. The high-risk, high-cost business-development strategy of Internet companies simply makes it vital that the marketing strategy be completely researched, highly creative, and fully tested. It must maximize effectiveness and be measurable at every step along the way.

Retail Faces a New Set of Challenges

Retailers face ever-increasing competition in a rapidly changing world—including:

The Internet. Over four million people a week begin using the Internet, a rate that's growing at 30 percent each year. The range of products being purchased is also mounting; people are buying books, music, cars, tailor-made clothes, and even daily items like groceries. There has also been a massive growth in the number of vehicles that allow consumer-consumer purchases from all corners of the globe—a trend that will continue to impact retail.

Home Shopping. People are banking and paying bills either by phone or the Internet more and more frequently. Television shopping networks are turning over billions of dollars and undercutting retail prices, selling to the public when customers are most relaxed. TV shopping networks provide information, highly personable demonstrations, and a friendly approach. Thirty-minute television infomercials are now a common staple in the television diet.

Automatic Vending. Food and beverages, videos, books, prepaid phones, and an ever-growing range of products are available from increasingly sophisticated kiosks 24 hours a day.

Mobile Vendors. Fast food, prepared meals, groceries, videos, cleaning, gardening, ironing, and even car washing and hairdressing are available from vendors who will come to home or office to meet the consumer's time constraints.

Telemarketing. This increasingly popular sales method is available on TV, radio, and in print. Techniques using information and powerful emotive imagery urge consumers to "buy this product now and get a bonus" (such as a free CD or a set of steak knives) or "get two for the price of one," simply by using their telephone.

Consumers' priorities are changing significantly. For example, people are spending more of their disposable dollars on paying down mortgages and reducing debt or on entertainment, gambling, and holidays, rather than material goods. This further magnifies the pressure on companies who sell via traditional means.

> Most companies' quest to relentlessly seek new market share by high-cost means, such as advertising, is a trend I find quite remarkable and idiotic.

One of the major budgeting characteristics of the clients who come through our organization's doors is that they have a substantial budget for marketing their products and services to new customers but little to no budget to maintain or grow their current client base. There is no focus on ascertaining and meeting the customers' changing needs or motivating them to repurchase—despite the facts that (1) word of mouth is both the least expensive and most effective way to build a business, and (2) it is 7 to 15 times more expensive to get a new client than retain an existing one. Obviously the cost of recapturing the 60 of every 100 satisfied clients that might get away is significantly less than generating 60 new ones, a notion that seems lost on many marketers.

Most Businesses Are Inept at Cutting through the Clutter

Although the numbers vary a little, depending on which research study you are reading, it is accepted that, in addition to the up to 3,000 advertising messages we are exposed to each day, we also see up to 14,000 brand names emblazoned on every moving or stationary object with which we come in contact in any given 24-hour period, from our Polo jockettes to the Manhattan Grill matches we find in our pockets.

> The extraordinary fact is that, when asked to describe the advertising messages to which we were exposed yesterday, the average consumer can only name and describe two.

Sure, most people will guess a Coca-Cola, McDonald's, or Ford; however, they cannot provide any descriptions of the ads.

Two out of *three thousand!* What other industry could get away with that level of failure rate? Would you go to a brain surgeon who only got two out of the last 3,000 operations right? What about a food company that recalled 3,198 of its last 3,200 products? Imagine the world today if condoms only worked twice for every 3,000 uses. The only people that would be smiling would be the testing team.

The average business executive today receives 37 pieces of advertising-based mail each week and retains just two. Just to add a little more insult to injury, these two pieces are usually filed away because it is unlikely that the recipient will be impacted at the very moment they are looking for the goods or services described in the mailer. Once the individual is ready to investigate the goods or services, they get the mailer from the filing cabinet. Unfortunately for the advertisers, they have usually filed all the competitors' brochures or mailers in the same file. Therefore, unless your product particularly stands out, it's going to endure a highly pragmatic evaluation against your competitors—one that is (even worse!) based only on the limited information contained in the mailer. Unsurprisingly, this drastically reduces your chances of being selected as the supplier. Another illustration of many marketers' lack of understanding of today's consumers' diminished brand loyalty is the number of ads you see for companies who tell their potential customers to "look us up in the Yellow Pages" or some other reference directory. It's absolute stupidity; all their competitors are listed there! Why don't they just e-mail, fax, or post a list of their competitors' names and contact numbers to their prospect? It would have the same effect.

Over 85 percent of people reading print ads only read the headlines, and fewer still read newspapers and magazines each year. Less than 2 percent of radio listeners can recall three of the advertisements they heard only one hour after hearing them. Television is the medium of choice, and for the big guys, with huge budgets and mass-market products, it certainly works, but at what level of effectiveness?

The reason ads are not rated in the same way that programs are is not because it cannot be done; it is because the results are too horrific to contemplate. The average viewer uses the commercial break time to accomplish a plethora of chores, with the occasional exception being the sports couch potato who may be lazy enough to sit through it. However, the majority of this audience is actually more likely to add to the slippage by channel surfing during breaks. As a consequence, research has shown the third advertisement in a break can attract less than 10 percent of the viewers who are watching the program in which the ad is contained.

Research also cites the fact that in over 50 percent of television ad breaks, no one is watching. This research, conducted by Dr. Allen of Oklahoma State University, also showed that, of the 50 percent that were watching, 65 percent were severely distracted. Despite this evidence, television stations still calculate the advertising rate on the basis of the program viewing audience. In short, these advertisers may be paying up to 10 times the cost per impression they thought they were.

Banner ads on the Internet are also rapidly losing popularity as a result of the overwhelming evidence that they are hopelessly ineffective. Just five years ago, these ads enjoyed click-through of 15–20 percent. Yet by 2009, they had fallen to 0.2 percent.

The Internet Is Just the Tip of the New Technology Iceberg

Although there is a proliferation of new technologies, I will mention just a few simple examples. . . .

First, integrated SMS and radio broadcasts. Tying SMS response into radio advertising and station loyalty clubs allows advertisers to data mine potential customers and interact with them one on one to buy a pizza, attend an event, or even enhance the radio audience at a specific time. The radio station can SMS its database and let them know that, in five minutes, there will be an advertisement for Pizza Hut—and if they can win a prize, they tune in. Once they do so, they are asked to SMS if they would like a special Pizza Hut pizza for dinner. When they SMS, they get a call center calling back immediately confirming the order and up-selling. This kind of cross-communication marketing is achieving amazing responses depending on the promotion, and it is both measurable and immediate.

A second example is up-selling chat. Chat technology enables real-time, immediate postpurchase online messaging and voice chat that allows retailers to up-sell a customer who has just purchased online. This is not only permission-based marketing; it also enables the sales person to talk to the client about something in which they are interested, making the process much more effective.

A third example is behavior-triggered e-mailing. This software analyzes both real time and historical data, thereby enabling immediate, automated opt-in campaigns based on in-store, catalog, online purchases, biographical data, events, dates, or customer behavior, which greatly enhance sales performance.

Fourth is commercial skipping technology. Products like TiVo and DVR (digital video recorders) have produced a new type of commercial that really engages DVR users. Brands like Coca-Cola, GE, and KFC have produced ads that contain hidden messages, secret codes, and scrambled entertainment. For example, KFC's buffalo snacker sandwich ads contained a subliminal message and secret code that could only be cracked if played back slowly, frame by frame, with a digital video recorder. Viewers then enter the code on KFC's website to win a sandwich. There were 75,000 winners for this particular contest.

Marketers today must keep one step ahead or at least not too far behind the technology. Don King, a group director at The Coca-Cola Company North America, said recently that "There hasn't been a technology invented that can't be leveraged as a marketing tool."

> These new technologies render the traditional advertising response rates no longer acceptable.

Many direct marketers are getting response rates in excess of 20 percent; 40 percent rates are no longer unachievable. Direct comparisons between an identical campaign using traditional methods and variable data and other new technology methods occasionally show increased performance of up to 2,000 percent, so we need to be more analytical when choosing communication channels.

Axe Leverages Viral Marketing at Its Best

London's wonderfully creative Dare Digital Agency has produced a host of results-achieving and award-winning campaigns. My favorite is the e-mail campaign for Unilever's AXE range of men's toiletries. Unilever had e-mailed 30,000 clients a graphic of a sexy girl in red lingerie lying on a bed, with an invitation to use the cursor, which turned into a white feather when activated to tickle her. Participants could use the virtual feather to tickle various parts of her body to get her to sneeze, giggle, or writhe. The site is such fun that many recipients e-mailed it on to their friends, resulting in over 50 million people, overwhelmingly male (the intended target) having interacted with the site.

The most important point here is that the average time spent interacting with the site is in excess of nine minutes. Compare this with a television commercial that would be infinitely more expensive to produce, lasts 30 seconds (compared to nine minutes), attracts a fraction of the audience, is not interactive, is expensive to air, and does not allow online purchasing or identification of the viewer.

This is cutting edge. This is the future of communication.

It Is Extremely Difficult to Succeed

Today's competitive business climate and the costs associated with developing a market niche for a new product are clearly demonstrated by the figures released by Marketing Intelligence Services' product scan. They show that 25,261 new supermarket products were introduced into the United States market last year. The challenging part is that only 1 in every 671 of these new products met its sales target in year one, which is a *one-tenth of 1 percent* success rate! Additionally, *Polaroid Creativity* and Innovation Laboratory figures show that of every 3,200 concepts that are patented, only four go into development, two actually get produced, and only one is released into the market.

This information makes it quite apparent that it's significantly difficult to successfully market a product or service nowadays.

> Unless you have a clear, concise, highly targeted marketing plan that creates a connection with the potential customer, failure is likely a foregone conclusion!

A study by Professor Paul Williams shows that, today, 89.7 percent of all small businesses (those with up to 100 employees) fail within five years. Of those that made the five-year milestone, 80 percent disappeared within 10 years, producing an overall failure rate of 97 percent of businesses within a decade. However, 98 percent of the businesses that had some marketing training were still in business 10 years later. Equally disheartening is the fact that some 99.6 percent of online businesses had failed by the end of 2009. Though this performance is improving, it is estimated to still be in excess of 90 percent failure rate (although accurate figures are difficult to obtain).

A business is not a success if it lasts 10 years, or if growth is a steady 15 percent a year. Today's opportunities are endless; a successful business should be aiming for a minimum 25 percent annual growth.

The customers' decision-making process plays a significant role.

In order to create a strategy to market a product, marketers must realize exactly how a potential customer makes a purchase decision. The inclination to purchase a product first arises when the decision is considered by the (totally emotional) preconscious mind before entering the (much more pragmatic) conscious mind. If any business or product within the category you are considering has made a strong emotional connection with you, via an association with either your behavior, belief system, or through a trust and respect valuation, then it is highly likely that you will purchase from that company without seriously considering the available alternatives.

This is exactly why it is so important to comprehensively understand your potential customers and to build brand equity through use of customized emotional benefits, a powerful consumer purchasing benefit (CPB), great service, added value, and advocate testimonials to develop this first-recall brand awareness in your customer's mind. When you fail to develop this emotional connection with a potential client, the decision-making process passes from the subconscious to the conscious mind. Potential customers then use the conscious mind to analyze their requirements and consider all the available options that might satisfy these requirements. This is when the prospective customer considers reputation, quality, service, competitive products, ease of access, price, and countless other elements that make it a lot more challenging to get the sale. These considerations are far less important in the subconscious mind.

The Fifteen Commandments

So how do we get our message heard above the competitors' and overall clutter? We need to follow a set of simple rules to develop relationships with our customers, to have affinity and empathy with them, and to build dialogue.

> Forget market share. We must build *heart* share.

To achieve this, businesses must be customer centric. The customer today holds the power, they are no longer someone to track down, catch, and close. We must build our companies one absolutely delighted customer at a time. If we build heart share on a one-on-one basis, we create advocates, and market share will follow.

More importantly, building heart share will develop brand equity. It moves our potential customers' decision-making processes to the pre-conscious mind, where the emotional heart share impact is extraordinarily powerful. Since 92 percent of people see the majority of products/services in a category as interchangeable, a failure to establish heart share guarantees that they will make a decision using their pragmatic, conscious mind, where they will inevitably rationalize the purchase. As a result, you will simply get a share of the market relative to the number of competitive players. If this is the case with your product or service, you have not effectively differentiated your product from your competitors. You have not gained heart share.

Heart share also transforms business from the traditional supply chain to the demand chain, a dramatic restructuring that is critical for success of any product in the new commercial environment. At Marketforce One, Inc., we have developed 15 keys that we have demonstrated, time and again, that powerfully address the demands set forth by today's tough market place. We utilize these keys every day for our clients, irrespective of their location, size, the nature of their business, or the size of their budget. These elements have been instrumental in helping literally hundreds of businesses, large and small, beat the failure odds.

As you read through these 15 keys, you will notice that none of them directly relates to making money. We cannot make money the focus in order to achieve success. The Stanford University Graduate School of Business study of the most successful businesses in the world—as detailed in James Collins and Jerry Porras' landmark book *Built to Last*—strongly highlights this point. In this exhaustive six-year comparison of the characteristics of the most successful businesses against their less successful competitors, the authors conclusively found that companies that focused on maximizing share-holder wealth or profit were inevitably less fruitful. However, 94.4 percent of the successful companies focused primarily on their staff and the customer, with profits as their fourth priority (on average).

The study also found that companies that focused on profits and share-holder wealth stifled a sense of experimentation and giving new ideas a try. They did not give their employees the room they needed to do things differently, and they failed to realize that, although the majority of initiatives may fail, the winners could be the very thing that made that critical difference between them and their competitors. The less successful companies also spent more time in meetings, instead of going out and pushing the envelope. They were also protective of their products to the point that they were reluctant to share information—even in favor of relinquishing the chance to develop strategic partnerships with third parties, a critical factor in growing more successful companies. They also exhibited a top-down autocratic approach to their business, and the structure that focused on profits led these organizations to have weaker customer relationships. By comparison, the successful companies encouraged a less constrained, all-encompassing employee environment that fostered empowerment, innovation, and a more fluid, dynamic response to changing market forces.

Remember: If you love what you do, it is a pleasure to learn all you can and discover the best path to take to achieve your goals. Your enjoyment creates passion and this passion produces commitment from those around you and leads to transference of your energy to others. This builds heart share. So love what you do; success and money will naturally follow.

Chapter 2

Keep Learning, Predict, and Embrace Change

The most important factor in attaining (and maintaining) success is continuing to gain knowledge—about your industry, your customer, your customer's business, your competitors, and the world around you.

Change is occurring at an ever-increasing pace, socially, commercially, and technologically. It took 22 years for one million people to get television sets, yet only four months for a million people to get on the Internet—and two months to sell one million iPhones. The new Casio watch has more computer power than the Apollo spaceship that took man to the moon just four decades ago. In 1943, IBM President Thomas Watson made the statement, "The world would only ever require five computers." By 1970, there were 50,000 computers in the world. Chairman of Digital Equipment Ken Olson reflected the popular belief of the time when he said in 1977, "There is no reason for anyone to need a computer in his or her home."

Over 100,000 computers are sold daily in the United States. In 2000, at the height of the boom, 47 percent of financial growth in America was produced in the tiny high-tech center of Silicon Valley, which produced 67 new millionaires each day. It took General Electric 40 years—from 1896 to 1936—to be valued at $1 billion. Online auction site eBay.com achieved this in one day.

Technology has the ability to change our lives in unpredictable ways. I can still recall a time when people believed computers and robots were going to replace human jobs and cause massive unemployment. Yet 300,000 new jobs were produced each month in the United States during the technology boom from 1995–2000, as applications increased exponentially. When introduced, the VCR was predicted to destroy the movie industry, and the advent of computers was supposed to make it possible for everyone to work from home. In hindsight, it's easy to see how off base these predictions truly were.

Business-to-business trade on the Internet reached $3.3 trillion in 2007. In 2009, an estimated 49 percent of small businesses were online; yet only 38 percent of companies with less than five employees had a home page. In 2009, 37 percent of companies were using e-mail to solicit business, and they reported a 32 percent increase in business over traditional mail or phone approaches.

A number of analysts estimate that from 15–25 percent of the world's economic activity will be conducted on the web within 20 years. How much e-commerce will be business to business and how much will be consumer purchases? Experience to date shows it is business to business that provides the largest savings, the most efficiencies, and the largest scope for growth. American domination of this technology could lead to the United States comprising in excess of 30 percent of the world's economy throughout the twenty-first century.

Whereas most businesses, particularly retail, traditionally operated on 12–16-week cycles, new technology has enabled this period to be reduced to one to two weeks. These new distribution cycles are transforming retail, manufacturing, and stock movements, as well as enabling more efficient production and distribution with less warehousing, thereby significantly reducing costs. Many companies simply link their customers' sales to stock distribution systems so that stock replacement is initiated when a purchase is made.

We know that the sell-through rate of traditional retail can be dramatically influenced by a variety of factors: the number of mirrors in a store, the colors used to decorate, the music that's playing while people shop, and even tricks like making aisles wide enough to ensure that customers do not have to come in contact with each other. These factors increase impulse buying. The loss leaders (heavily advertised popular products sold at a substantial discount or even a loss to attract customers to a store) are at the back of the store so customers have to pass hundreds of high margin impulse buy items on their way in and out.

The tendency to pay attention to these details is what makes one retailer more successful than another. However, e-commerce differs greatly from the basic retail store. It comprises inventory that purchasers cannot touch or test. There are often barriers to browsing, and an ever-present cash register. How motivating is that? Not very, which is reflected in the sell-through rates ranging from 0.25 to 2 percent.

Web retailers are addressing this experience factor. Many sites nowadays vary from a pure display of products and services to 3D clothing products that customers can view on digital images of themselves in surroundings that give the brands their suitable images, thereby replicating the impulse buying factors of a retail store. For example, menswear brand Hugo Boss has customers wearing suits around a sports car or hip-hop clothes in a street scene.

A recent study looked at 50 consumers who visited leading retailers' websites and found that over 50 percent of the attempts to make a purchase *failed*. These malfunctions were due to a combination of poorly developed sites and the inability of some too complex sites to run effectively on home computers.

Though consumers have been feted with free online information and services, providers have still been failing badly. Poor performance has made online advertising revenue difficult for many sites to obtain.

> It is highly likely that consumers will very soon have to pay for the content they currently obtain for free. In the majority of instances, they will not.

For example, Yahoo! introduced a monthly fee for its previously free real-time stock-quote service. Many newspapers and magazines are currently establishing such fees for news and articles from their publications. The problem is that only 4–6 percent of consumers say they are prepared to pay for this kind of information online. When Yahoo! began charging for its auction services, listings dropped by 80 percent. In my opinion, the likely end result will be that many online services will simply become divisions of traditional businesses delivering a niche market.

Business Has Become Focused and Global

Companies that had continued to expand their business interests and product ranges for years have, over the past decade, sold off business divisions and either sold or eliminated brands as they refocused on their core, most profitable business sectors. Marketing and sales thrusts are more focused, efficient, and energized, and they are expanding geographically.

Even in times when economies around the world enjoy unprecedented growth and robustness, thereby creating opportunity for the vast majority of companies, it is still a very tough world out there. Inevitable downturns only make it tougher for the majority of businesses. A couple of decades ago, most businesses' competition were simply similar organizations in the same suburb or city. However, technology has made it so that we are rapidly approaching a time when competitors can be anyone in the world who is in the same business as you are. This will clearly elicit a dramatic increase in competition across a variety of industries.

There are considerable financial benefits in becoming a truly global business. News Corporation, for example, reaches 75 percent of the world's population and pays less than 6 percent in income tax, whereas competitors such as Disney, Viacom, and AOL-Time Warner, all essentially U.S. corporations, pay between 20–30 percent tax. This gives News Corporation a powerful commercial advantage.

One example of globalization is the once-common practice of United States doctors taking verbal notes using Dictaphones, and then having someone transcribe those notes for future reference. Until recently, a high school graduate with zero knowledge of medical processes and not much more knowledge of medical terminology did this transcription, which gave the error rate the potential to be quite significant. Nowadays, physicians send the audio files over the net to India, where qualified medical doctors transcribe the notes and return them via the net the next day. The error rate is greatly reduced, and the process is both less expensive and more efficient.

Knowledge and Ideas Rule

We have officially exited the industrial age for the technological age in which knowledge and its resultant ideas are king. Easy to sell, uneducated customers are an increasingly endangered species. Today's consumer is seeking product information. They need solutions and want to know what benefits differentiate your product from your competition. Providing the education and solutions they seek gives you credibility. It shows that you care for your customer and want to assist them in addressing their needs, thereby building heart share and creating a powerful chain reaction.

> Heart share increases brand loyalty, moves the decision-making process to the preconscious mind, and diminishes your competitor's influence.

It helps you develop a brand culture, which further advances market share. More importantly, it greatly reduces price as a factor in the purchase and diminishes customers' purchase resistance. Heart share is critical in altering the focus from supply to demand chain and ensuring success— which eventually leads to increased profitability and increased brand equity.

Anticipate the Future

In order to educate our clients, we must first educate ourselves about our product or service, our competition, community changes, and market trends. It is not enough to adapt to change; to achieve real success, you must anticipate it. Companies today should have an entirely customer-focused team of two or three people whose job is to continually attempt to predict three years into the future. This team can be made of internal employees, or comprised of a combination of internal and external experts. Even simple changes can mean big savings or big losses.

The book-retailing industry is an excellent illustration of how some companies have successfully anticipated changes in their potential consumer with exceptional success. For example, nationwide bookseller Barnes & Noble increased sales from $154 million in 1991 to $4.6 billion in 2009 by introducing a new style of bookstore. Instead of operating under the previous philosophy— discouraging customers from reading books in the store, and running the risk that they might not purchase them—Barnes & Noble established coffee shops, lounge chairs, and magazine areas where customers were *encouraged* to browse and read. They introduced regular book readings and signings by authors, and even musical entertainment. Many parents go to Barnes & Noble to read to their kids, and others with like interests use it as a meeting place. Students take their laptops and spend hours studying. It is a great place to have a coffee, a muffin, sit in a comfortable lounge, and read.

A completely different model is the one utilized by online bookstore *Amazon.com*, which has sold over 7.5 million unique titles. Users can search and readily find any book on any subject, or all of books on a particular subject. They can read excerpts and order their book of choice, all from the comfort of their homes or offices. Amazon's growth has been extraordinary; sales climbed to over $25 billion in 2009, and the site is offering an ever-increasing range of products. Amazon has also acquired several other Internet companies, which is the next step toward their goal of becoming an online total consumer buying resource. They introduced the Kindle, an electronic reading tool that can hold up to 1500 titles, can download a book from the Amazon library in 60 seconds, and sells for less than $200. With over three million sold in three years, it is clear that this item will change the future of books and libraries. Barnes & Noble countered quickly with their online service and the added advantage of having retail outlets.

Both Barnes & Noble and Amazon have been very innovative in anticipating the shifting consumer attitudes, leaving all competition in their wake. Another competitor in the space, Borders bookstores, invented a way to print and bind books to fulfill a customer's orders in 15 minutes. The company claims, "Making a book is no more difficult than making a caffe latte." A customer simply finds the book on the computer and the work is downloaded; one printer prints the text while the other prints the cover, and the book is then bound. This innovation is yet another attempt to compete with the Internet booksellers who have gained a large share of the hard-to-get and specialist books segments. It is an excellent idea for small book shops with little space. Borders have an arrangement with the book publishers to ensure that copyright is observed and that the appropriate royalties are paid.

Many companies who have established retail outlets or catalog busi-nesses are hesitant to set up online sites with lower priced products because they fear they will be competing against themselves. However, the Internet is unlikely to produce price savings in most product categories. If it did, there is no question that these companies would be better off cannibalizing *them-selves* rather than waiting for a competitor to do it.

Levi's is the largest brand apparel company in the world. Yet, as the youth market changed in the 1990s, Levi's did not. The brand's marketing was not imaginative, and it did not connect in ways that matter to young consumers. In 1996, Levi's reported sales of $657.1 million, which had shrunk to $458 million by the end of 1998. The company was caught flat-footed by the loose-jeans look that suddenly swept the market. The primary key to the baggy pants phenomena was rap music; the world's youth related to it en masse, and baggy pants took off. Levi's Chief Marketing Officer Gordon Shank admitted, "We were in denial. We had been cool for decades." However, the brand's market share fell from 31 percent to 14 percent in just two years. The new look rendered previously sacrosanct Levi's criteria, such as fabrication weights and five pockets, no longer relevant. Like Nike, Levi's became part of the establish-ment and, therefore, uncool to the new generation of consumers. To counter the trend, Levi's changed their marketing focus from traditional advertising, of which youth are skeptical, to sponsoring musicians, bands, and concerts.

> Achieving dominance will likely depend on which business in a category predicts the next consumer shift first . . . and *accurately*.

Most Societal Changes Are Predictable

It is usually quite evident how many of society's basic changes —some of which I outline in the following paragraphs—will affect the way that almost every industry does business. Once businesses become aware of these general changes, they must anticipate potential variations that are specific to their industries.

> Additionally, increase in available information in electronic form is raising consumer's expectations and decreasing brand loyalty.

This trend will force corporations to increase quality, service, choice, information, and the ease with which consumers can do business with them. Continued globalization will lead to greater ethnic diversity in most markets, along with changed consumer attitudes due to exposure to diverse cultures and ways of doing things. Technology will add to this less homogenous society as consumers are exposed to more options.

Strong demographic shifts are taking place, and although there is a significant increase in the number of people over 50 in the so-called Western world, these individuals have a lower *perceived* age, a much younger outlook, and are much more active than older people in generations past. Understanding these shifts provides a company with many keys to the products and services required in the future—from basic needs to school enrollments, to health care, child care, and so on.

Tomorrow's consumer will be much more self-reliant, largely due to a loss of confidence that governments and corporations will take responsibility for looking after their well-being. Tomorrow's consumers are likely to have less debt and use their money more responsibly. Another interesting trend: Women will continue to change not only the make-up of the work force, but also the way we communicate and the services and facilities businesses provide.

Consider this issue further. Men have had far more influence on every aspect of our lives than we initially realize; for example, nearly all photographers in history have been men. To that end, all the images in magazines, newspapers, television, and movies that have shaped the way we think have all come from a male perspective. How different might our perception be if women had been the principal photographers?

Women will continue to become a significant percentage of the workforce, as countries like Australia introduce six-month parental leave on full pay for all employees, paid from government revenue, not the employers. Consumers will travel more extensively and will seek an escalating range of innovative experiences. They will have much less time, and will seek practical, secure, and timesaving solutions. All consumers will be more educated, although the gap between rich and poor, haves and have-nots, and discrepancies in education levels will continue to widen. Tomorrow's consumer will demand value rather than price, more choice, more information, more service, easier purchasing, fewer problems, and more extensive guarantees.

Predict and Segment by Lifestyle and Attitude, Not by Demographics

It is not enough to just look at demographics nowadays; we need to understand attitudes as well. Psychographics explain behavior; they highlight what people *want*, not what they need. Ten couples with the same education who are earning the same income and living in the same suburb will have different home designs, plant different trees, drive different cars, and watch different TV programs. They cannot be lumped together as a target consumer based on demographics. Therefore, marketers need to focus on psychographic profiles for market segmentation. Psychographic profiles reflect common activities, interests, and opinions as well as attitudes and values of the group.

> Biological age is of *far less consequence* for brands than perceived age.

For example, someone whose biological age is 60 may behave and think like a 40-year-old—and vice versa.

When predicting community changes, biological age seems to be more important. Baby boomers (born 1946–1964) have had a large impact on business change, from baby food and diapers in the 1950s, to fast food in the 1960s, to appliances to reduce work and shopping malls in the 1970s, healthier products and travel in the 1980s, skin care in the 1990s, financial investments in the 2000s.

The following primary factors will affect every consumer.

Economy. The state of the economy affects businesses' and individuals' ability to access finance. This, in turn, impacts confidence, employment rates, consumer spending, and the amount of money people borrow. An economic slowdown also decreases the rate of technological development, and the rate at which new concepts are embraced.

Technology. This trend affects how companies and consumers go about their daily business. It influences use of time as well as access to and amount of information obtained. This, then, influences what consumers purchase and how. Technology has considerable power over product costs and sales price.

Globalization increases the diversity and number of choices of products available, as well as influencing attitudes and tastes.

Government affects companies and consumers by way of legislation, levels of taxation, and incentives and benefits provided.

Environment. Environmental consciousness of both individuals and corporations affects corporate actions, development, and consumer-buying patterns.

Psychographics. Life cycle stages, sociodemographic changes, family structures, and pressure groups bear upon consumer values, attitudes, and lifestyles, which, in turn, shape the nature of business, entertainment, travel, and consumer purchases.

Health. There is an increasing trend toward healthier eating, getting more exercise, and people's tendency to use preventative and alternative medicines. Medical advances are also enabling people to lead longer, more fruitful lives.

Retailing. Retailing is undergoing substantial transformations that are providing an increasing amount of lifestyle, interactivity and entertainment opportunities. Retail trends reflect and affect what, where, and when consumers buy, and businesses provide what consumers are seeking to purchase. Monitoring shifts in these areas via research, reading, and listening allows you to predict future buying patterns for your product or service. Combined with constant monitoring of your potential customer's needs, your company can begin to anticipate its future marketplace.

How the IT Generation Revolutionized Established Businesses

The generation of the 1970s, 1980s, and 1990s followed the old adage, "If it isn't broken, don't fiddle with it." Today, we must constantly embrace change and a new mantra for business: If it isn't broken, break it before your competitor does!

Today's generation grew up with computers; they have traveled widely, convey a different attitude about employees and customers, and have global perspective. Many of today's family businesses display a clear example of the gap between the attitudes of various generations in terms of how to best run the company.

For example, at Katz Photography, a generations-old professional studio for producing catalogs, David met great resistance from his father before he replaced traditional equipment with digital cameras and computers as a substantial investment. The result? Revenues up 60 percent, costs down 50 percent. After 75 years in Pittsburgh, Lance Reid moved the entire American Textile operation to El Salvador after his father's heart attack. The result was tripled revenue. Jared Shultz took his parents card shop, Blue Mountain, online for fun. The result? Four years later, Excite@Home, a search engine/Internet portal company specializing in high speed Internet, bought the site for $780 million. Excite@Home ultimately failed, but it yielded a great result for Schultz through the buyout, which would not have occurred if Blue Mountain had remained a bricks and mortar card shop. Instead of relying on a local audience, the company could reach across the globe, exponentially increasing its audience and its value.

The other saying I always had thrown up at me as a child was, "Don't just stand there; do something!"

In today's Ideas Age, we need to spend a lot more time working on our businesses versus working in them. We must enhance knowledge of our industries, customers, staff, and overall business operations. It is hard to think on these levels when you are up to your armpits working on the company's mundane daily details. So, instead, the applicable slogan is:

> *"Don't do something, just stand there."*

In other words—today, we need to step back and think.

Retailing Becomes Edutainment

As consumers seek much-needed respite from business pressures, they are looking to retail to provide them with more entertainment and involvement to attract them and eventually compel them to purchase. Consumers' require more and more information in order to make better choices, and the more successful retailers are providing not only highly trained staff but employees who share purchasers' unique passions.

So how are brands today doing this? Outdoor and sporting equipment supply, and apparel retailer Recreational Equipment Inc. (REI) created an 80,000-square-foot store, which includes a 65-foot climbing pinnacle, a rain room for testing parkas and other rain gear, 475 feet of mountain-bike test track, a severe hiking trail, and a 100-seat healthy cafe in which to relax and talk to the store staff, all avid outdoors people. Bass Pro Shops Outdoor World, which attracted over 2 million customers in its first year, incorporated trout, catfish, and duck ponds; pheasant nests; and a snake pit. Shoppers at the 170,000-square-foot store learn about conservation at the on-site wildlife museum or at the 64,000-gallon aquarium, hone their skills at the indoor rifle and cross-bow ranges, relax in a full-size log cabin, or simply enjoy the working water wheel or the four-story waterfall.

Although the majority of music stores frown on musicians playing with instruments in the store, Mark Begelman's 35,000-square-foot MARS Music and Recording Superstores encouraged them to jam on the in-store stage in the fully functional recording studio, or take part in the in-store music clinics. Oshmans Sporting Goods stores were refurbished with indoor basketball courts, and many Sneaker Stadium stores have indoor running tracks to test shoes.

In keeping with the sports theme, Randy Zanatta's Gold Galaxy interactive superstores offer computerized golf simulations of many of the world's great courses. They also have 400 square feet of Astroturf putting greens edged with palm trees, as well as in-house golf lessons with video cameras and computers that analyze techniques. Huge TV monitors offer the Golf Channel while shoppers browse through books, videos, golf bags, travel brochures, and a range of other golf merchandise. The result? Many golfers spend two or three hours in the store, contributing to gross sales that are well in excess of the average golf retailer.

Business—and life in general—are in danger of becoming more impersonal. Thanks to the Internet, however, people with like interests will interact more readily and frequently. This tendency will create a consumer-driven society segment that will comprise powerful brand communities of consumers with like interests who are readily able to communicate with each other through the Internet or through whatever newly developed consumer-friendly technology replaces it. This has the potential to create a serious problem for the majority of companies who are still producing and selling what they believe the consumer *needs*, not what they want to buy.

> To succeed tomorrow, companies need to *anticipate* their clients' needs and aspirations.

They must act before sweeping community changes negatively impact their business, reduce their competitive edge, and allow opponents to secure consumers' hearts and minds. If businesses wait until they are negatively impacted before they change, their competitors will be *miles* ahead. This kind of environment allows small companies to compete with large companies based on heart share.

Once businesses have a firm grasp on customers' needs and desires, they can then lead (maneuver, manipulate) them into a purchase.

In the Future, Made to Order Will Be the Norm

Because most companies are still selling what *they* want the consumer to buy, they are usually structured accordingly, which prevents the essential rapid response to questions and development of new products per consumer demands. The future market will be segmented to a much higher degree, and technology will allow a growing amount of one-on-one product tailoring for consumers.

We are now operating in an era in which mass customization is not only possible—it is becoming an expectation. With more flexible systems arising and the Internet linking supply chains in real time, made to order has an entirely new dimension. Instead of manufacturing product and having a percentage of it sit on shelves or in warehouses, only to be heavily discounted in order to move it, a mounting percentage of products can be manufactured specifically to meet customer's needs. Carmaker Nissan, for example, estimates that making cars to order—with a 7–14 day turnaround—could reduce the cost of a vehicle by up to $4000. Dell Computers became the world's biggest PC maker by offering customized units, and because of their system's level of sophistication, each tailored computer is assembled in less than five minutes.

Motorcycle maker Harley Davidson allows consumers to build their own cycle from options on the interactive video screen. Although this feature costs extra, a significant percentage of consumers today will pay to have exactly what they want. At the other end of the demographic scale, www.barbie.com gives children the opportunity to design their own doll. Kids can personalize their Barbie dolls in their imagination, give them names and personalities, and actually create them to reflect their imaginations.

> To maximize efficiency and profits, the goal must be to sell today, manufacture tomorrow, and deliver the day after.

Continue to Update Your Knowledge

The companies that succeed tomorrow will be those that anticipate and are ahead of the change curve today. So how can the average company anticipate and leverage these modifications?

The first step is to take advantage of every learning opportunity. The business/marketing sections of bookstores are full of works by business leaders, as well as catalogs full of excellent CD's and audiotapes. U.S. business publisher Soundview Publishing produces eight-page summaries of the best business, management, and marketing books in the world every month. The past five years have seen an explosion of business magazines that feature case studies and articles on almost every conceivable element of the past, present, and future of business. Although all this amounts to a substantial quantity of knowledge to guide your future business, the downside is that it involves a considerable amount of reading and listening. However, I am unaware of any shortcut, and isn't it worthwhile putting in a couple of hours a day to secure your success and the success of your organization's future?

There are many side effects of the marketplace's current changes that indirectly benefit smaller companies. The existing economic environment has encouraged a host of megamergers. Not a day seems to pass without another two giants announcing they need to combine operations in order to compete. By following the changes in their industry, small businesses can gain considerable benefit. Far from making it difficult for these organizations, these mergers create a potential bonanza for them. The result of most mega mergers is that talented people are laid off as responsibilities are duplicated, which produces a pool of experienced individuals in your field that you can engage to assist your business.

Furthermore, megamergers usually involve business rationalizations that open up a host of new professional opportunities in niche markets. An efficient small company is usually more flexible and better able to listen and respond more quickly to their customers. They are more apt to work with customers to develop new products; provide better, more personalized service; and build strong relationships in local areas.

The Best Communicators Will Enjoy the Most Success

Businesses of the future will be built on internal and external relationships that are developed through communication. Unfortunately, most of us are terrible communicators. We do not understand body language, we fail to listen when people speak, and we do not understand neurolinguistic programming (NLP). (NLP is recognizing patterns of behavior that can be predicted by understanding what we say, how we say it, and how we act. This enables the tailoring of a message and the calibration of your "target's" unconscious body language to achieve more success. I have a section on NLP later in this book.)

Learning how to communicate better will be crucial to success. Small companies can improve their commerce with these learned communication skills; they enhance an organization's ability to have a closer client/executive decision-maker relationship than is possible with the giant corporations. Large companies tend to have much more rigid structures in place and, as a consequence, often lack the kind of employee dedication and commitment that smaller firms enjoy. Additionally, these bigger companies have a much more difficult time with employee training and corporate culture development; as a result, teamwork breaks down, often leading to higher-ups' tendency to make decisions without consulting employees.

> To be successful in the future, a corporation must focus on education, value adding, service, and support.

The first consideration cannot be profit or sales. My colleagues and I always spent an hour a day—from 8 A.M. until 9 A.M., no exceptions or interruptions—listening to and/or watching CDs and DVDs, and discussing book summaries by the most successful business people of our time. The one-hour session is broken into three phases. During the first 20 minutes, we watch the CD or DVD or review a book summary; then the second 20 minutes is devoted to a discussion about what this information means to our business and how we can apply it to each of our clients. We utilize the final 20 minutes to create or modify business plans to address either our own or our client's objectives. The material we review varies in topic—from leadership to motivation, from NLP to added value, from advanced sales techniques to likely future trends—but it is always relevant, and always involves all members of the team, irrespective of their role in the company. The information we all glean during these sessions is invaluable when we are dealing with clients and managing our own business; it is often even applicable to our personal lives. After several sessions, there was a marked improvement in the research we did on clients prior to a meeting and the way we adapted our presentations and our body language for each client. Our closure rate increased from 64 percent to 89 percent within a month, primarily due to the application of NLP techniques.

No Time? Successful People *Make* Time

Research shows that the typical Fortune 500 CEO reads an average of 22 business books a year, receives five trade or business publications a week, and frequently listens to CDs in his or her car. I ask the attendees in all the seminars I present around the world how many of them read business books and watch or listen to CDs and DVDs. In the majority of instances, less than 5 percent of attendees indicate that they do. When I ask why they don't, the answer is nearly always the same. "I'm working 15 hours a day, I have commitments at home; I simply don't have time."

My organization has worked with some very prominent people over the years. The global marketing directors of the Coca-Cola Company and General

Motors are both extremely busy people with huge portfolios and very difficult, stressful jobs, yet they both find time to read business books. Might this explain the huge discrepancy between the business success and salary level achieved by the Fortune 500 CEO who is continuously learning, and the average businessperson who is too busy to read?

I have addressed a number of motor manufacturers and dealership groups over the years. I frequently discuss the performance discrepancy between the average salesman (who sells 10 to 30 vehicles a month) and a salesman named Mark McGever, who sold over 1,000 vehicles a year. The difference is that Mark continued to learn about sales techniques and time management; he applied his knowledge of NLP and has an exceptional relationship database program. In short, he continued to learn all there is about his craft, and he realized that he is not merely a car salesman. He is an excellent communicator and an exceptional negotiator. He honed his management skills as a businessman and developed heart share with prospective clients. These are all attributes of every successful businessperson, irrespective of his or her profession, and they are all skills that one acquires and finesses through learning. Unfortunately, very few people realize this and are consequently relegated to the lower end of the business spectrum as this knowledge (technology and ideas) ages.

Study Your Competition

Another point that never ceases to amaze me is how few business people today bother to learn about their competition. As already discussed in Chapter 1, there are only four ways to make more money in business: Grow the market, increase your market share, increase your level of profit, or cut costs. In order to increase market share, you need to take some from your competition. Even football players learned a long time ago that you need to study your opponent if you want to win a game.

> Only once you know how your opposition plays, individually and collectively, are you in a position to plan a strategy to beat them.

Continuing to adjust this strategy to offset new competition, or changes in your opponent's strategy, allows teams to continue to win.

I will never forget when three-time World Heavyweight Champion Evander Holyfield came to my home in California for the first time back in 1989 (when he was the number-five contender in the world). I learned an extremely valuable lesson during that visit's few hours. At the time, Mike Tyson had demolished every contender within a round or two, many lasting no longer than a minute. However, Evander was extremely confident that he could beat him. Because the reason for the visit was that I was trying to convince Evander to hire our company to develop his corporate relationships (which he subsequently did), I was not about to disagree with him. Actually, the reason he *knew* he would win against Tyson made very sound business sense. Evander told me that he had a videotape of every one of Tyson's fights, from his amateur days through his professional career. He had studied every move and reaction Tyson employed. He learned how he would respond in any circumstance; so accordingly, he could create a strategy to counter any move and to exploit any weaknesses. Evander said to me, "When I step into the ring with Tyson, it will be like I have been there one hundred times before. When he steps into the ring with me, it will be the first time."

It is Evander who put Tyson down and earned a place in the record books—simply by studying his competition. The business world is no different. Unless you totally understand your competition, exploit their weaknesses, and create a powerful point of differentiation, your chances of success will be severely diminished.

The first thing you should do when you wake up in the morning is review your competitor's web site. Most companies cannot wait to boast about the initiatives, the training sessions they are conducting at their next sales conference, and so on. Occasionally, they might accidentally put up information that they certainly do not want *you* to know. All this incredibly beneficial information will help you to anticipate their moves and gain market share at their expense, which can be invaluable.

Only through continued education can you anticipate changes in the factors that will affect your business: the economy, technology, globalization, government policies, environmental concerns, demographics, health trends, consumer psychographics, and the way products are offered.

Remember: When you're not learning, a competitor somewhere else is— and if they know more than you do when the two of you meet, they will win.

Chapter 3

Moment of Truth

The Business and Marketing Audit

The most critical elements for any organization to develop are the business model, the business plan, the marketing strategy, and the resultant marketing implementation designed to achieve established goals. A brand can have fantastic offerings; however, unless it can precisely identify its potential clients, differentiate from its competitors, clearly target the correct message as cost effectively as possible, and then motivate a purchase, it will not achieve its true objectives.

It is essential for all professionals to realize that merely having an office, plant, equipment, stock, and staff does not make a business. A real company exists only when customers buy your product or service, and your net income exceeds your gross expenses.

There are only five drivers in any business. These are:

1. Product/service/technology
2. Business strategy
3. Funding
4. Customer need
5. Marketing strategy

All businesses have some kind of product/service/technology. Some have a proven business model, and some have a business strategy. Few differentiate themselves clearly from their competitors, and most usually have some level of funding. Yet none of these elements is sufficient to make a business.

> In far too many instances, it is the two elements that really *make* the business—understanding the customer's need and developing a quality marketing strategy—that is lacking.

This is why the majority of traditional and web companies fail. It has nothing to do with the idea, product, service, or price. Countless professionals complain that lack of funding is the reason for their failure. This did not seem to affect Hewlett and Packard, who worked from their garage with $635.00, or Gates, Bulmer, and Wojack, who were forced to share a motel room in Albuquerque due to lack of funds. These are clear examples of how a business model, marketing strategy, and resultant plan are far more important than a company's financial plan or production schedule. It is clearly the size of the idea that counts, not the size of the budget.

Marketing requires that companies create solutions (in the form of products or services) that address customer's needs, provide them in the form to which the customer most readily relates, offer them at the most convenient purchase point, and make them available at a price whose perceived value is greater than purchase price. Marketing needs to occur at every interaction between a company and a customer—by phone, via the web, in the reception area or the store, and during every delivery, repair, customer service call, finance and delivery transaction, and so on. Unless every one of those touch points provides customer sentiment of "WOW," your business will ultimately not achieve its potential—and will likely fail.

It is equally critical for professionals to realize that marketing and sales are totally different disciplines. Too often, the two are regarded as interchangeable. The marketing strategy can only be developed after obtaining a thorough understanding of the total market environment in which you are operating or plan to operate. Sales are but one element of the marketing plan's implementation that has been developed from the marketing strategy.

So . . . what *is* marketing?

To understand the difference between marketing and the disciplines that comprise it, let's use the analogy of a building. The marketing strategy is the architectural design. The walls, doors, windows, and such are elements within the design, akin to the elements inside the marketing framework such as advertising, public relations, social networking, sales, sales promotion (both consumer & trade), cause tie-ins, direct marketing, direct response, merchandising, strategic business relationships, sponsorship, hospitality, sampling, customer service, and added value.

The following provides a brief description of each of these marketing disciplines.

Advertising is the placement of a message to reach the target market. This can be print, broadcast, signage, online or offline.

Public Relations are generally third-party stories, articles, or segments that favorably mention the product/service in order to positively influence potential customers.

Social Networking/Media is the use of social interaction sites on the Internet for research, marketing, promotion, education, sales, customer support, and developing customer relationships to highly targeted market segments.

Sales are the act of motivating potential clients to purchase the product or service. Usually, irrespective of the technique used to communicate the information, the sale is closed (completed) by personal communication of some type.

Sales Promotion uses a promotion, often tied into an event that is meant to compel either the trade (distributor or retailer) or the customer to buy.

Cause Tie-ins connect the business or product with a cause or charity to demonstrate to a potential client that the company shares their values in order to solicit goodwill and ultimately secure a sale.

Direct Marketing entails delivering the sales message directly to the potential customer by e-mail, post, telephone, magazine subscription, tapping into a database of targeted users, and other tactics.

Direct Responses are advertisements that use proven techniques, such as added value, risk reversal, limited offers, or price reductions, to motivate potential buyers to respond immediately by phone, Internet, or mail.

Merchandising is the use of branded merchandise to drive brand awareness or equity, depending on the application, through provision with the product (with or without charge) or as a stand-alone item.

Strategic Relationships are associations with companies that target a similar market segment to maximize customer benefit, increase reach and frequency, or minimize communication costs.

Sponsorships involve underwriting the cost (either in cash or kind) of an activity in return for visible association with the activity, and provide the opportunity to use any one or combination of marketing techniques to impact the activity's supporters. Sponsorships create the impression that the company and supporters share values.

Hospitality requires providing business customers or consumers with the opportunity to attend events as the company's guest. This creates goodwill with the guest, quality face time, and a subconscious obligation to reciprocate with a purchase.

Sampling is providing a free gift of the product to encourage use and/or repurchase.

Customer Service entails providing the customer with the absolute utmost in assistance, advice, respect, courtesy, and rapidly addressing issues at every point of interaction with the company.

Added Value enhances the customer experience at every interaction in various forms: training, information, assistance, gifts, and so on.

Each of these elements is a discipline unto itself, but each can also be a critical element of the overall marketing strategy. This strategy usually contains a combination of these disciplines, designed in a balance to obtain optimum results. The specific disciplines a company selects to utilize within a strategy, and the weight each one is given, depends on the objectives you are seeking, the type of product or service, the target market, and relative costs of execution.

Supply and Demand versus Demand and Supply

Most products have traditionally been created as a result of a producer's idea rather than customer needs or requirements. As a result, we have spent decades having products pushed upon us, down the supply chain from manufacturer to shelf, being forced to rely on mass advertising and strong sales personnel to sell it.

However, the past 20 years have seen a fragmentation of the market place due to an explosion in the number of communication vehicles, customer demand for dialogue instead of monologue, clutter, globalization, and increased competition. At the same time, consumers' attention spans have shortened significantly. Consumers have become increasingly cynical, are faced with more choices than ever before, and are more informed. As a consequence, we have entered a demand–and-supply economy.

> Customers, whether business or consumer, require solutions specifically designed to address their particular requirements.

An increasing number of companies anticipate this customer demand and supply it. This trend is evidenced by the rapid increase in customized products—everything from the choice of ingredients at the noodle bar to customizing a Toyota vehicle on the assembly line. The ability for organizations to anticipate customer needs requires them to develop a thorough understanding of the complete market place and its underlying trends.

The Marketing Audit: Vision, Market Analysis, SWOT

It is absolutely vital to business's success to conduct a financial audit, and, though fewer companies do so, it is equally important to conduct a marketing audit. The latter entails a thorough evaluation of how you are performing with respect to your customers, the marketplace, and your competitors. It, therefore, requires that you analyze the complete market environment and consider the following elements.

THE BUSINESS VISION

What is your company's or your particular product's vision? For example:

- ◆ Do you aspire to be local, statewide, national, or international? If international, which markets do you want to target? Once you determine the answers here, you must conduct a complete audit for each market.
- ◆ Do you aim to achieve this growth organically or through acquisitions/mergers?

This vision can incorporate positioning, sales, profitability, customer service, market penetration, and products. Developing a clear vision enables management to design proactive operational plans and allows for the filtering of opportunities based on an agreed strategic direction.

Additionally, you will want to decide upon a time frame for these objectives' achievement. This is usually established as short and long term (12 and 36 months, respectively). These principles must be shared with and understood by everyone involved in the business. They will then become the yardstick by which you measure company progress and performance going forward.

MARKET AND ENVIRONMENTAL ANALYSIS

This is an evaluation of the external factors and trends likely to impact the business in the foreseeable future, including:

- **Economic:** What effect will the economy have on the product or service?
- **Sociodemographic:** What impact will the social, behavioral, and demographic trends have on the product or service?
- **Technology:** How will technology affect the business?
- **Politics and Legislation:** Are there political or legislative influences that may determine the company's path?
- **Physical/geographic:** Do either of these elements have an influence on potential market expansion, perhaps in terms of distribution, for example?
- **Industry trends:** What are the overall industry tendencies, both in the local market and internationally? Will international trends influence the local market at all?
- **Competitors:** Who are the competitors? What is their market share? How does their business operation differ? How are they marketing their products? What distribution channels do they use? What are their price points? How are they likely to react to your business initiatives?
- **Customers:** Who is the customer? What and where are the customer segments? Consumer behavior is driven by significant social paradigms such as perceptual age versus biological age, wealth creation, lifestyle quality, timesaving preferences, working dynamics, and countless others. It is essential to understand as much as possible about the customer's behavior and motivations.
- **Changes:** What changes are currently taking place or likely to take place in the industry? What steps are you taking to address these coming changes?

The marketing audit will provide valuable, up-to-date information on customer needs and purchase motivators; explain how, where, and when consumers purchase; identify the primary and secondary benefits they are seeking; and highlight your competitors' positioning and strategies.

> As a result of this marketing audit, your challenge will be to create a distinct point of difference from your competitors, which impacts directly the potential customers' hot buttons.

You must give these prospective buyers a clear reason to purchase your product rather than that of your competitors.

You should regularly conduct a marketing audit to stay ahead of the changing and evolving marketplace and remain aware of the initiatives your competitors are undertaking.

SWOT ANALYSIS (STRENGTHS, WEAKNESSES, OPPORTUNITIES, AND THREATS)

A SWOT analysis is an honest appraisal of your business's strengths and weaknesses, and a clear analysis of the opportunities and threats that you face. You must consider all areas of your business, including:

- Company image and position
- Management and staff
- Corporate culture
- Financial resources
- Products/services
- Market situation and trends
- Physical resources
- Government policies

Strengths and weaknesses are generally elements that are internal to the business, and are things you can directly control. Opportunities and threats are generally external to the business and are those elements over which you have little to no control. The SWOT analysis is highly objective and involves a critical look at the capacity of your business, product, marketing, and personnel in terms of key strengths and weaknesses.

Depending on your requirements, you can analyze each element of your business separately or as one. For example:

Strengths: These may include exceptional personnel, a strong financial position, a good performance record, efficient organizational structure, flexibility, high-quality product, brand equity, quality of research, and expertise of consultants.

Weaknesses: These may be current performance; personnel qualifications, experience, or attitude; lack of brand awareness or competitive advantage; high manufacturing cost, low return on capital; poor market intelligence; strength of competitors; lack of direction; or poor management culture.

Opportunities: These can encompass company stability, financial strengths, competition in disarray, trends, strategic alliances, global knowledge, cost containment, or technological advances.

Threats: These might be market trends, competitor performance, experience, market-segment retraction, decline in demand, potential acquisition, and product affordability.

When evaluating your personnel, in general or a specific team, for example, the marketing team, considerations are somewhat similar:

Strengths: Qualifications, experience, enthusiasm, contacts.

Weaknesses: Lack of experience and knowledge, lack of planning, poor communication skills, responsibilities exceed resource capabilities, lack of performance-measuring program, lack of empowerment.

Opportunities: Leadership, develop communication strategy, training.

Threats: Lack of strategy and leadership, lack of success culture and team relationships.

Corporations usually prepare a SWOT analysis in a freewheeling brainstorming session with the whole team; it is often very laborious, lively, and tense. Most people do not like to have their own weaknesses or those of the organization for which they are responsible or a part of exposed, discussed, and analyzed. However, an honest SWOT can really provide a clear picture of the current organization and the priority of the steps that you need to take moving forward.

Often, developing the SWOT completely will require substantial research and critical, objective analysis by an independent organization. We have seen countless instances in which an internal SWOT is carried out, resulting in a few entries in each column. Unsurprisingly, there are usually more strengths and opportunities than threats and weaknesses. However, when our marketing team completes the task for the client, there are often a couple of dozen entries in each column.

Business and Marketing Audits Are Critical for Start-Ups

When launching a business, it is essential to ensure that you have covered all the bases by thoroughly thinking through every aspect of the business model and strategy. This will be particularly helpful when you are seeking finance.

Basic Rules for Start-Ups

1. You must be *absolutely passionate* about the business, but not *so much* in love with it that you cannot be *completely objective*. You must listen to others, seek advice, vigorously evaluate competitive options, and, above all, be realistic about the value of the business.

2. Make sure that your *business model is the correct one.* There are usually many options, so evaluate them all and be careful to select the one that works best for your organization. For example, there are two obvious business models if you make printers. One is to sell the printers and ink at cost price plus your regular margin, and the other is to sell the printers at a highly discounted price and make a very large margin on the ink (a recurring purchase). Think about how much we complain about the price of gas—then consider that it would cost you nearly $30,000 to fill your tank with printing ink.

3. If your company is distributing product, one model is to establish your own sales offices, warehouses, distributors, and so on. Other options are to develop strategic relationships with large companies who already have a sales force and distribution. Or, perhaps your product/service is best suited to a licensing model.

4. Use your executive summary to *tell your company's current and future story*. Executive summary is a term used in business for a short document that summarizes a longer report or proposal in such a way that readers can rapidly become acquainted with a large body

of material without having to read it all. Make sure it is easy to read and understand; omit any technical or trade language. Write it in a simple, logical, and straightforward manner.

5. Build a *detailed business plan* that reflects the way you believe the business needs to move forward, the marketing strategy to get there, the competitive analysis, the real costs involved, the personnel who will deliver the promise in the business plan, and, also important, the exit strategy. Detail how you are going to protect your intellectual property, safeguard it from legal action by a competitor who simply wants to take you out of the game or someone who infringes on your patent or trademark.

6. Make sure that the *marketing strategy and marketing plans* you create are *realistic*. Too often, people who have never been out of Mississippi, or Redfern, or Boxted, create great plans about how they will market globally. These are nearly always crap. Make sure you understand a market before you determine how you are going to penetrate it.

7. Do not forget that success is about *sales*—as is your ability to attract investment, strategic partners, staff, good management, and directors. Your plan must lead to sales either in the immediate term or in the future.

8. Once you have completed your plan, it is likely that you will need funds to be able to achieve the plan. At this point, you need to *modify your business plan to become an investment document.* The first thing to remember is that you and your product/service are not important here; what is important is the investor. When seeking financing, remember that investors focus on three main areas of the business plan: The *executive summary*, from which they determine whether the project is viable; the *board and management,* from which they determine if this team can deliver the promise; and then the *exit strategy*, to ensure they can get out and recoup their investment (along with a profit) in a realistic amount of time. Without a solid exit strategy, it is difficult to attract investment. If you pass these three hurdles, then real due diligence on your whole offer is likely to take place.

9. Be prepared to *step aside to allow excellent proven performers* to take the roles that are vital to your company's success. Remember that being a great inventor does not make you a good CEO or

financial controller or production manager. Know your limitations, and do not let ego get in the way of profits.

10. Remember that *only one to two start-ups or new businesses out of every 100 actually get funding;* only one in 3,600 patents are financially successful; and less than 5 percent of new companies ever become profitable. Most of these cases began with a good project but failed due to lack of funding or—more likely—poor management. The underlying lesson is that you must be absolutely realistic about the difficulty of market entry and penetration, the length of time it will take to achieve goals, and the amount of money it will take. Rule of thumb is that it will be 10 times harder than you anticipate, take at least twice as long, and cost three times more than you expect. The other lesson is that entrepreneurs usually make lousy CEOs. You need a CEO that has considerable experience, and if you plan to launch internationally you need someone experienced in international business.

11. You should begin by approaching *friends or family to raise initial funds* and get your business as far as possible. Once you have exhausted these sources, you can contact financial planners and accountants or list with one of the *online angel investment companies*. The majority of the responses you receive will be from consultants or business advisors. Some will be genuine; most will be unreliable, even fraudulent. Many will require up-front fees. There is nothing wrong with that, and you should expect it. After all, you pay a plumber, electrician, lawyer, accountant—all of whom provide you with a service but diminish your assets. A good business consultant will take you from being broke to perhaps a multimillionaire if you have a good product. So really, this should be someone you are willing to pay. However, you must be sure they are reputable and have a track record, so do your due diligence in checking them out.

12. One of the keys to driving your business is to have *good management and a good board of advisors*. If you have a high-quality concept, you will attract high-quality people; however, good people come at a price. You will have to commit to both money and shares or options in the business, both of which should be tied to key performance indicators (KPIs). This is worth the investment for three reasons: First, you will receive invaluable advice. Second,

these people will bring credibility when raising money. Third, they will help you make contacts. It is no coincidence that well-qualified directors also usually know a lot of potential investors.

13. Realize that procuring *investment is only one way* to build your business. Another option is to form a strategic relationship with someone who has the market muscle, reach, reputation, and financial grunt to get your product into the market. This option also allows you to retain more equity.

14. You need to *give part of your business to any investors* you obtain. It is usually a pretty straight commercial relationship. If your business is worth $2 million and you need $1 million, you will likely give away 50 percent. Most entrepreneurs usually believe investors are too greedy; however, you have to be realistic and look at the situation from the investor's perspective. Their decision to invest in your start up is a major risk. Remember that the percentage of the business that you own does not matter as much as what that percentage is worth, and 100 percent of nothing is nothing. A good business consultant can usually increase a business's perceived value, thereby minimizing the amount of equity you give up.

15. Always *go for the big picture first*. Establish the end goal for the business and secure the funds you need to get there. If you receive funding in small increments, you usually end up giving away too much.

16. *Do not try to grow organically.* In most cases, someone else will beat you to the market, or a big guy will reverse engineer your product and take you on, patent or no patent. Either way, you will lose.

A Few Other Pieces of Advice:

If it is a *really difficult challenge, do not take it on*. It will prove to be too expensive with too much likelihood of failure.

Any situation in which *you need to educate the market* will also be too expensive and *more apt to fail*. Very seldom is the first company into the market with a new product successful. It is usually the second or third market entrant that reaps the benefit.

Most entrepreneurs *do not spend enough time researching* or developing their businesses and marketing strategies.

Only hire people who *share your passion*.

Minimize your costs; do not waste a single dollar!

Reward your employees generously, particularly those who are with you in the tough days!

Five Basic Tips for Potential Investors

When entrepreneurs present business plans for investment, it is very easy to get caught up in their enthusiasm and passion, along with the information they are presenting. I have never seen a business plan or met an entrepreneur who gets even close to achieving their projections in the early years. When someone who is about to start a company claims that they are "the only people in the world working on this solution," they usually have just done a quick Google search. Again, I have never seen a business plan in which there has not been substantial competition when you really go looking. Therefore, it is critical for a potential investor to be detached from the emotion, question the assumptions, check with experts, and do their homework before writing a check. The following are some basic tips:

1. Although, initially, you may not totally understand the technology or the product, make sure the *executive summary is well thought out,* logical, shows that the company leaders know what they are talking about, and have great future prospects. Remember, change is rapid; you do not want to be investing in a project that is obsolete before it begins.

2. If you believe the executive summary makes good sense, *ensure that the board and the management have the core competencies* to make it a commercial success. Make sure they can deliver not only a good product but excellent management and market performance. If the product has global potential, ensure that someone with global experience is on the board.

3. Ensure there is a *logical and feasible exit strategy.* When you put your money in, make sure you can readily get it out at a multiple.

4. Be sure that *you can get along with the entrepreneur.* Make certain that they listen to reason and are not totally enamoured with their product to the point that they are not realistic about it.

5. Ensure *you have a board position* so that you are present for every decision and have real-time access to all financials.

6. Ensure that the organization's leaders *specify their five-year goal.* If they claim they will be a billion dollar company and have their photo on the front cover of *Time* magazine, dump them quickly; they will always be a pain and cause you immense amounts of grief.

Be Thorough; Do Your Basic Due Diligence

When creating a business plan or a document to present to a potential investor, you must address the following elements. Potential investors should also consider these same fundamentals when reviewing the entrepreneur's proposal.

Company Details, Including:
◆ Company name
◆ Address
◆ Key contact person/people
◆ Management resumes
◆ Board officers' addresses, phone details, company fax, e-mail
◆ Website, www
◆ Description of the company's business, services, and products
◆ Key milestones achieved
◆ Jurisdiction where business is incorporated, corporate structure, and the regions in which the business is currently operating, company registration, and tax information
◆ Share holding of the company
◆ Examples of current customers or target market
◆ Funds used in running the company over the past three months
◆ Contact information for attorneys, accountants and consultants
◆ Company banker and contact details
◆ Founder's history with the company

Funding and Resource Requirements
◆ Funding stage, type of funding received to date, expectation for any other funding to be closed
◆ Amount of funding sought
◆ Funding purpose
◆ Detailed explanation of fund use
◆ Are the funds sought sufficient to achieve the established goals?

Management Team and Employees

- Biographies of key personnel
- Board of directors' or advisory board CVs
- Employee headcount and whether key positions are filled
- Any stock option grants to personnel

Market and Competitor Analysis

- Description of target market and customers, market dynamics, characteristics of the market environment, market size, historical and projected growth of target market
- Analysis of competitors and comparables
- Key competitive advantage and barriers to entry

Products and Services

- Description of each product and service offered, stage of development, examples of the product/service use

Technology and Intellectual Property

- Ownership of intellectual property (IP) or technology
- IP protection in place, licenses or trademarks owned by the company
- Product or service differentiation
- Achievements to date that indicate that the product or technology is superior to what is currently available

Financial Model and Business Economics

- Assumptions supporting revenue sources
- Gross profit margins versus competitive norms
- Staffing plan
- Monthly expense budgets

Revenue and Sales Cycle

- Source of key revenue streams
- Forecast revenue (best- and worst-case scenarios for the next three years)
- Estimated gross margins achievable and how these are achieved
- Length of sales cycle
- Reference customers

Go-to Market Strategy
◆ Strategic relationships, distribution channels available
◆ Ability to scale

Detailed Marketing Strategy
◆ Precise details of how the product/service will be marketed
◆ Channels employed and related explanation
◆ Return on investment (ROI) of each channel

Risk Assessment
◆ Major risks to the successful execution of your business plan
◆ Risk mitigation strategies

Exit Strategy
◆ Identified exit strategy

General Questions to be Answered
◆ What experience do the board and management team have in relation to running high growth/high risk businesses using other people's money?
◆ Describe the complete use of funds in the next twelve months.
◆ Define the milestones to be achieved over the next twelve months with the funding.
◆ What are the current and proposed salaries and benefits of the company officers?
◆ Any legal actions being brought against the company or its officers that may be in process or are expected?
◆ Define the customer base.
◆ Define the marketing strategy.

Conclusion

A highly thought out business and marketing strategy is the key to developing any successful enterprise. A good product or service at an acceptable price—along with a first-rate business plan—will get you nowhere if it does not fulfill a potential customer need, offer a strong value proposition and is presented in a cost-efficient way that motivates a purchase.

The key to creating a good marketing strategy is to conduct a probing, entirely honest investigation of your company and the market in which you operate. You must analyze all of the potential factors that can influence your business, competitors, internal team, and potential customers.

We have a great deal of success with the think tanks we organize for corporations. We assemble a group comprised of usually 10–12 leaders in various fields of endeavor, along with two or three experts in the area in which the client is involved. A few days prior to the session, all attendees receive a detailed brief. Depending on the product or service, the group will contain experts in various forms of advertising and promotion, marketing, finance, media, web, corporate structure, taxation, and so on.

What follows is a 10-hour, no-holds-barred, completely thorough session. At the end of it all, we create a business model, marketing strategy, and plan. More often than not, the end result is significantly different than the views that many members initially took into the meeting. It takes an honest, no-restrictions debate to ensure that a business is on the right track. Once you have completed this audit, you are in a position to begin to develop the marketing strategy.

Remember:

"If I had eight hours to cut down a tree, I would spend six hours sharpening the axe."

—Abraham Lincoln

"Skate to where the puck is going to be, not where it is."

—Wayne Gretzky

Chapter 4

Formulate a Clear Business Vision

In all the presentations I have given throughout the world—to CEOs and senior executives of both small and medium businesses—I am constantly astounded by one thing: At least 50 percent of them *do not* have a clear, concise vision of their business that they can readily articulate. Most do not even have an up-to-date business plan. Less than 10 percent have a separate marketing strategy, and only 1–2 percent set daily, weekly, or monthly goals.

I am fairly sure that these same people would certainly not attempt to build a home without a firm vision of what they wanted or a detailed set of plans they had agonized over. Nor would they build it without a timetable (goals). Yet when it concerns something as important as their life's work—on which their family, health, and happiness will depend—they have no plan whatsoever.

If I was standing in the middle of a sports arena with the world's greatest sprinter (this is a big "if," as I cannot run to save my life), and I knew where the finish line was and had a plan to get there but my opponent did not, I would win, no matter how good he was. Earlier I discussed how Evander Holyfield prepared so studiously before he fought Mike Tyson. Evander knew precisely what he had to achieve, and he planned accordingly. Business is exactly the same. You need to know what you want to achieve, and you must develop a plan to get yourself there.

A study of the Yale University class of 1973 showed that only 3 percent of the graduates set daily goals. The study revisited the class of 1973 in 1993, and found that the 3 percent who had set daily goals had a greater income than the other 97 percent of graduates combined.

The Parallels between Business and Life

To be successful in business, as well as in your personal life, you need several things: a vision, a mission, a set of values, specific goals, a strategy for achieving them, and a system for measuring them.

Let's use another sports analogy. Successful athletes visualize the result they want to achieve over and over again. They visualize the golf ball dropping in the hole or the backhand going over the net. They focus on very specific objectives that are ambitious yet achievable.

You can do the very same with your own goals. Memorizing your objectives means that you will commit them to your subconscious mind, which cannot differentiate between reality and imagination. Meanwhile, the clear, concise focus will prevent you from being distracted and going off on tangents. Setting short- and long-term objectives, with constant reviews, maintains your forward momentum.

You can adjust your long terms goals as you move forward and obtain more information. Reviewing your goals regularly enables you to overcome the inevitable setbacks and keep them in perspective.

> A great strategy poorly executed will likely fail. On the other hand, modest plans that are executed well can produce great results.

The reasons come down to passion and commitment. You must be prepared to do the hard yards and not use an escape hatch.

When John Kennedy announced his vision to put a man on the moon within a decade in 1961, he did not know how it could be achieved. It had not previously been a priority for the country. However, the president's vision and passion led others to expend tremendous energy on this goal. People across the nation in a variety of industries now had a defined purpose toward which to work. From that point, their awareness, energy, effort, and execution simply made it happen.

Business success is exactly the same. Most of us are so busy doing the daily tasks and grunt work required to "get there" that we lose sight of our dreams. Goals are simply dreams with a timetable. If we lose our direction, we lose our clarity; after all, it's impossible for us to get where we want to go if we don't know where that is. To achieve success, we must inspire our employees, our customers, and suppliers.

> Great vision creates passion; passion in turn inspires and generates commitment.

You must make every decision on the basis of whether it will enable you to achieve your vision. Once you begin operating with clear vision, your strategic business planning will suddenly take shape and you will be able to clearly articulate your objectives. Without it, however, you will struggle aimlessly.

I have been fortunate to work on the speaking circuit with legendary English coach and motivator, Frank Dick, who writes the following passage in his great book *Winning*:

> *The skills required to think for yourself, for your teammates and for the collective pursuit of the team objective do not just automatically follow because a group of people is referred to as a team. They must be constantly coached and serviced to make the whole greater than the sum of the parts; to make the performance of the team more and more effective; to make the performance of the team more and more outstanding. You do this by establishing each person's value in the team context, and by cultivating the culture of team-work as something that is not just a topic of conversation but a way of life.*

What Dick has said, in an incredibly eloquent way, is that the most effective companies are those where the corporate culture is a way of *life*, not simply a way of doing business. It is most effective when the company and the business units within are tight knit and of manageable size. In my view, this group should ideally be fewer than 12 people.

The quality of your people is equally vital. An old Chinese proverb says, "If you want one year of prosperity, you plant grain; if you want 10 years of prosperity, grow trees; but if you want 100 years of prosperity, grow people." The problem today is that most businesses are too busy growing grain.

A Strong Corporate Culture Results in a Strong Brand

A clear vision results in a strong corporate culture that in turn serves as the foundation for building strong brand equity. Brands begin in the hearts of the company's management and employees, as well as the user. They are most powerful when they reflect the belief system of the company and involve the consumer. To that end, a strong brand positioning produces:

◆ High customer commitment
◆ High quality sales
◆ A strong sense of loyalty
◆ Word of mouth promotion
◆ Supplementary sales
◆ Increased profits and future earnings
◆ Increased accrued equity

Customers *buy* products and services with strong brand positioning and equity. However, offerings with poor brand positioning must be *sold*. For example, Mercedes are bought; Daewoo vehicles must be sold.

Word of mouth is the most powerful sales tool there is. Research by Professor Ehrenberg of Britain's South Bank University found little correlation between what people bought and the advertising to which they were exposed; however, there was a high purchase correlation with third- party recommendation.

> Studies have shown that the degree of trust people have for various sources of information varies dramatically, with almost 10 times more people trusting family members and friends than trust either corporations or governments.

Organizations that operate based on a powerful guiding vision, one that shares the target community's values and shines through in the brand, have much more powerful marketability through the resonation of family and friends than through media or advertising by the companies themselves. Once corporations achieve this, they can then amplify the product and shared values through all forms of community involvement and reinforcement. Rather than employing a hard sell, these firms can use public relations and other forms of communication to simply re-acquaint or reinforce the company's vision and values.

The advantage of building this vision and values-based brand culture is that the passion for the product results in the transfer of energy to others, which itself produces a subsequent chain reaction. Opening up dialogue with potential customers, reflecting the brand through management and staff, providing information, and letting potential consumers in on the product development are all part of the community's process of embracing the brand. All this aids in developing the brand's core community-support base.

Marriott Hotels is an example of a corporation that has a global reputation for exceptional customer care; it is one that they have achieved by developing a corporate culture that permeates every aspect of the organization. Marriott listens carefully to their employees' business and personal problems, ideas and solutions; they pay attention to detail on every aspect of a guest's stay at their hotels. You frequently hear stories of Marriott hotel staff lending money to guests out of their own pocket, baby-sitting, or lending clothes or jewelry in an emergency.

A wonderful example of Marriott's culture involves a bride-to-be who booked her honeymoon at a Caribbean Marriott. A few months after she initially booked, she phoned to let the hotel know that her fiancé had a brain tumor, and that they would be moving their wedding date forward. Despite the fact that the change occurred during a blackout period, the hotel arranged the couple's travel and accommodation at no cost. Before he died, the husband confessed to the hotel that this time had been absolutely precious to him.

Marriott believes that a combination of caring for employees and developing systems based on customer needs and expectations bring order, efficiency, and consistent product delivery and service. This approach consistently creates loyal and happy customers. As with most successful companies, there is a strong core of brand advocates and loyal users.

> This small core of frequent users creates most of the company's wealth; they cost less to attract and maintain, they reduce the influence of price in the buying decision, and they consequently increase profitability.

One of the most critical keys to creating a successful product or service is the ability to differentiate your offering from your competitors'. Additionally, the ability to reflect your customers' values and determine what makes them different from your competitor's clients adds to this distinction. Building brand equity involves vision, business planning, human resources, customer service, marketing communication, and product development. It is really a simple chain reaction. Companies must create a clear vision that their customers share. This commitment develops passion, the consumers create a powerful brand, and the marketers manage them.

The e-commerce revolution brings a new vision challenge to traditional businesses. The Internet and other new technologies are not just an adjunct to the traditional ways of doing business; they must be a fully integrated part of the entire process. It is a critical channel that must be connected with production, fulfillment, information provision, and customer interaction. This requires that your organization totally rethink the relationships with staff members, distributors, resellers, systems, and perhaps even products. Restructuring the connection with the traditional sales channel is one problem that entails a quantum leap in thinking. The web net, as we at Marketforce One have termed it, enables all the influences in a transaction to come together at a particular point in time, a process that greatly increases efficiencies for companies, consumers, or business-to-business transactions alike.

When formulating your business vision, you need to look at the company in its entirety and every element in detail. Every aspect must be in sync. For a company to succeed, no detail can be overlooked. The company must be offline, online, and in line. The traditional company vision will need to be revolutionized to integrate the "e" into the business or the corporate culture and the business will likely fail.

Remember: A clear vision unifies, motivates, and inspires—the essential elements of success.

Chapter 5

Research Is the Foundation of Success

The 15 principles that have proven to be so successful for us in business are interrelated, and all necessitate extensive dialogue with potential customers. This is the case whether the process involves creating an appropriate name and image for your business, determining what business you are truly in, creating your customer purchasing benefit (CPB), adding value, determining the motivating benefits, communicating your message, creating a risk reversal, or thinking creatively in order to stand out from your competitors.

The CPB is the demand and supply equivalent of the unique selling proposition (USP) that was applicable in the times of supply and demand. The difference is that the CPB puts the benefit emphasis on the customer, whereas the USP is all about the seller, who is now essentially irrelevant in the current demand/supply economy.

The level of effectiveness achieved in each of these critical communication areas depends on the quality of information you can obtain from your potential customer; essentially, your success rides on how well you do your homework. Supply in almost every category of product or service exceeds demand nowadays, making it so that every potential customer has multiple choices—no matter the product or service they desire. It is, therefore, essential to understand your current clients', your competitor's clients', and potential future clients' needs, expectations, and perceptions. The companies that best understand the customer will always enjoy a substantial advantage.

Research does not have to be a convoluted, highly complicated exercise that produces a mass of information created mainly to justify research companies' exorbitant fees. In over 30 years of addressing marketing challenges, finding out why something works or does not (or what will make it work), our organization has simply asked logical, straightforward questions. In my view, these are the kinds of inquiries that provide simple answers and make for simple applications and effective communication.

The Common-Sense Approach

Before you can successfully launch a product or service or maximize an existing product's sales, it is absolutely essential to understand what the potential customer is looking for, what they want it to do, how they want it packaged, what their hot buttons are, what the attributes/disadvantages of competitive products are from the customers perspective, and what the perceived value is. Of course, the only way to get the answers to these questions is to actually ask the customer or potential customer, or preferably, to work with the potential customer on developing the offering they are seeking. This is the final step to take before you are in a position to begin designing a marketing strategy for your business or product.

Studies by McKinsey Group suggest the key measures of business growth preparedness are the customer satisfaction index, performance gaps, and competitive position. The following performance scores are indicative of your customer's loyalty:

79 percent: Highly regarded as "different and better" than competitors

74–78 percent: Customer retention, but little word of mouth

69–73 percent: Problems, prime target for competitors

<69 percent: Customers actively seeking an alternative

The customer satisfaction index reviews every aspect of the company from four perspectives by asking the following questions:

1. **Financial:** What do the *shareholders* think of the company?
2. **Customer:** How do *customers* view the company?
3. **Internal:** How well does the company manage the *internal processes?*
4. **Innovation/Learning:** Is the company *improving and creating value?* Is there a learning culture?

There are multiple evaluations in each of these aspects. In total, in excess of 100 areas of the company's operation are considered and receive a value. Therefore, a company needs to measure and understand the implications of its performance as it relates to customers. Ongoing customer intelligence allows management to monitor and proactively rectify any deficiencies as they crop up.

Why is it that 62 percent of all satisfied customers do not repurchase from the supplier with whom they were satisfied? Because customers who purchase a product or service are *entitled* to be satisfied! Giving your customer something they have the right to receive should not elicit an endorsement of your business.

Remember that, depending on the category and difference between the level of customer service provided by you versus your competitors, between 65 percent and 90 percent of all purchases *must* be due to word of mouth. If not, you will fail, because your cost per sale will be far too high.

> You cannot get word of mouth by merely satisfying customers. You only get word of mouth by knocking their socks off and converting satisfied customers into advocates for your business.

And you can only achieve this by obtaining a thorough understanding of your customer and potential customer. As I have stated several times before—and I cannot emphasize it enough—the only way to accurately determine what your own, you competitor's, and your potential customers think is to *ask them* in face-to-face interviews. Of course, you need to specifically design your questions and hone them for each particular business or product. It is also preferable to use an independent organization to ask the questions, because they can usually elicit more honest answers. In the following example, XYZ is the researching company, and ABC is the competitor.

Basic Questions to Your Customer May Be:
◆ How long have you been purchasing XYZ product or service?
◆ What product did you buy prior to this?
◆ What was the reason for the change?

- How well does the product perform? (Excellent/Good/Adequate/Poor)
- How could the product be improved?
- How would you describe XYZ customer service? (Excellent/Good/Adequate/Poor)
- How could XYZ improve it?
- Is XYZ's after-sales service excellent/good/adequate/poor?
- How could it be improved?
- What is the advantage of XYZ over competitive products?
- What advantage does the competitive product have over XYZ?
- What would cause you to switch to the competitive product?
- Projecting into the future, will XYZ be sufficient for your needs in five years, or do you see industry changes that will require product modification?

Basic Questions to a Competitor's Customer Might Be:
- How long have you been purchasing ABC product?
- What did you buy prior to this?
- What was the reason for the change?
- How well does the product perform? (Excellent/Good/Adequate/Poor)
- Have you considered purchasing XYZ product? Yes/No
- Why haven't you? What are the advantages of buying ABC over XYZ?
- What could XYZ do to cause you to switch over to their product?
- Projecting into the future, will ABC be sufficient for your needs in five years, or do you see industry changes that will require product modification?

Questions to Current Nonusers of Either Your Product or Your Competitor's Products:
- Do you use XYZ or ABC in your business?
- Are products such as XYZ and ABC applicable to your business?
- If so, why don't you use them? Do you have a better alternative, or is there another reason?
- Has XYZ or ABC ever approached you?
- What was it about their approach that did not convince you to buy?
- Of the various products in their category, if you were to begin using them, which would you prefer and why?
- What could XYZ do to get you to buy their product?

Nowadays, everyone in your business must be customer centric. All information gleaned from any source should be fed back to the marketing department. This is excellent customer intelligence.

> Research shows that, providing the price differential is 13 percent or less, price is *very seldom* a contributing factor in a customer's purchasing decision (if all else appears to be equal).

Of course, if all else appears equal, they *will* buy based on price. That is why the objective in marketing is to have sufficient knowledge to be able to create a powerful differentiation from your competitor. Accordingly, we never mention price in any research discussion with our customer's clients or potential clients. If it is an issue, the customer will raise it.

There Is a Good Reason We Have Two Ears and One Mouth

I learned early in my career how important listening was. In a particular global sports series for which I was marketing director, we found that the most important advice we received came from the potential spectators, despite the multimillion dollars we were paying our advertising agency to create the campaigns.

Make no mistake—the agency would make a terrific presentation when they introduced new campaigns. They would give the reasons behind the theme, display the ads on huge multiscreens with quadraphonic sound, and exhibit unbelievable graphics. I always responded to the first viewing of any new campaign with a sense of, "Wow"! However, it was what we did after the initial presentation that mattered. We would get into our T-shirts and shorts, drive out to the suburbs, sit in a bar, and show the campaign to the patrons. There were plumbers, truck drivers, electricians, and accountants, people from all walks of life.

> It is amazing how many times the ideas that looked so great at the agency presentation did not work with the only people who really count: the potential customers.

After these trips, we would often return to the agency with major changes recommended by people who had no marketing training at all. They just knew what appealed to them about attending a sporting event. After achieving record attendances every season, we came to the conclusion that the spectators always knew what they were looking for—and that often, we did not.

The Customer Frequently Identifies Critical Points the Company Misses

On another occasion we helped a corporation develop an automatic ticket and merchandise kiosk to be placed in high traffic locations, such as malls and supermarkets. We had extensively tested each screen's effectiveness, the way the on-screen graphics interacted, the colors, and the typefaces to ensure the program's maximum value to each demographic, which we determined by likely purchase. Most importantly, we ensured that the program was people friendly.

When we thought we had gotten it right, we invited 50 people across all demographics to use the kiosk. To our amazement (and disappointment!) we found that *only seven* could use it. After the months we had spent developing this highly sophisticated program, the problem came down to just one word. In the opening sentence that both the audio and screen display delivered, the customer was asked to push the button to continue. Forty-three of 50 people searched the kiosk for the button. Though we thought it was obvious and logical that the rectangular area shaped like a ticket on the screen was the button being referred to, it was not obvious to the public. Had we not bothered to test out the program before launching it, that one word could have caused the $100 million program to fail. That last bit of homework, at a cost of just several hundred dollars, likely meant the difference between success and failure.

It is obviously much easier to sell to someone if you know exactly what they want to buy. This is the reason there is a rapidly increasing trend for companies to produce new products in very close collaboration with their customers. The usual practice in the past was for companies to make items they *thought* the marketplace wanted, making decisions based on information supplied by the sales force to their managers. However, sales people were often not skilled at soliciting comprehensive information, and they often had a vested interest in providing certain feedback. For example, if you are unable to close a sale with a particular company, it would be far easier to tell your boss that your product is "not quite what they were looking for," rather than credit a competitor's superior sales skills or persistence.

History is littered with products whose designs were based on less-than-accurate information. Companies often become so totally engrossed in a particular industry or project that they are easily sucked into its hyperbole, and their efforts and involvement reflect this. This prevents companies from obtaining an objective view of the real position. To use an old phrase—many people get so close to what they are doing that they *"can't see the forest for the trees."* This inability to see the true picture of what the customer really wants is often compounded by the isolated, often elitist views of academics or industry experts. These experts often offer theoretical perspectives in seminars and articles in trade publications upon which members of a particular industry rely for guidance.

Listen to the Marketers, Not to the Accountants

However, there is frequently a giant chasm between this kind of theory and your customers' reality. Without constant feedback from the people who are actually going to purchase your product—which you must obtain through deliberate dialogue and not from gut feelings—it is extremely easy for both big and small companies to lose the customer pulse.

Online service firm Prodigy was a perfect example of this. As a pioneer in consumer online services, Prodigy grew rapidly in the early 1990s. With IBM and Sears investing over $1.2 billion, Prodigy began with extraordinary vision and ambition. Soon after its launch, the company was adding over 100,000 new users a month. The computer industry was booming and corporations and individuals the world over were getting into e-mail and the World Wide Web. Yet despite the online boom, Prodigy was reported to be losing $12 million a month by mid-1995.

Just one year later, in early 1996, Prodigy was sold to International Wireless for $200 million. In under a decade, this company went from being the industry leader—bankrolled for $1.2 billion in an industry that was booming—to being worth only a fraction of this investment.

What went wrong? Here was a company at the forefront of the biggest communication boom in history. According to the experts who have studied the company, the problem occurred because Prodigy stopped relating to their customers and made no attempt to understand what they wanted. Business was so good, the company tried to tell the consumers what they needed.

Unfortunately, consumers wanted something different than what they were being given. When e-mail on the system boomed, Prodigy introduced fees for this and other services. This move infuriated their customers.

Meanwhile, Prodigy's rivals responded with fee cuts and provided the new products the consumer was seeking. Prodigy did not anticipate the various ways in which the online market could evolve, but their competitors did. While other online services embraced Microsoft Windows because of its extraordinary consumer acceptance, Prodigy did not. Their competitors also continued to listen to the consumer. They were in tune with the rapidly changing online user's requirements. Because of this, they flourished; Prodigy did not listen and, therefore, failed.

There is a vital lesson to be learned in Prodigy's story for those online and traditional providers who are looking to introduce fees for products that were previously free, or who do not give clients what they want when their competitors will. History is often a great teacher.

A Small Investment in Research Can Return Millions

We at Marketforce One insist on conducting research for all clients before we undertake their projects. Clients will frequently assure us that they have "been in the industry for many years, know everything there is to know," and claim that the research we want to conduct "is unnecessary."

> More often than not, it turns out that although most business owners know a lot about their industry, they know very little about their customers, potential customers, or competitors.

Therefore, the research we conduct usually turns up simple reasons they have not been as successful as they would like—simple reasons that have been right under their noses for awhile.

Case in point: We were hired by one of the world's largest corporate travel companies, with a multibillion-dollar turnover. Although their inbound business into the United States was excellent and highly profitable, their outbound business was losing well over a million dollars a month. They had tried several different managers, advertising agencies, and public relations companies, and they had slashed their prices, but nothing had worked; and all the while, the financial hemorrhaging continued.

We spent two days in their office looking at how they operated, and we met with their staff on a confidential basis. We conducted a SWOT analysis to ascertain their senior management's perspective on the marketplace. We spoke to 20 clients they had lost as well as 20 of their current clients to determine the company's attributes and deficiencies and their competitors' positive and negative attributes.

We also met with 20 of their competitor's customers to ascertain why they used their current travel agent instead of our client. We then contacted our client and their competitors via a third party and made inquiries for travel as if we were a potential new customer, a process that enabled us to directly compare our client's service to their competitors. We took careful note of how each agency communicated with us, the information they sent, and their follow-up processes.

We then purchased travel packages anonymously from our client and from other agencies that we deemed to be the 10 best competitors. We compared the staff members' attitude, service, speed, helpfulness, as well as how the tickets were delivered, the letter (or in most cases, no letter) that accompanied the tickets, follow-up calls after the trip, and so on, in order to ensure that the campaign we created for our client was superior to the competition. In today's competitive marketplace, that is what it takes! Only after we had undertaken all this homework were we able to objectively review our client's (and their competitors') performances through the eyes of the only person who is truly important: the customer. This enabled us to review their past and current marketing campaigns in the context of the consumer's perspective.

Although our report to the client, as well as the subsequent marketing strategy and campaign we created, included a number of dramatic changes from their previous programs, many of these alterations were very simple. First, our client had installed a multiprompt voice mail system to cut costs. Although research has proven that public tolerance diminishes rapidly after two prompts, our client was not aware of this research and had multiple prompts in their system. Travel is a highly personal service industry—something that all our client's competitors realized, since they still had real, very friendly voices answering the phone. Despite the efficiencies our client gained from voice mail, they lost their personal touch—and, consequently, many clients.

We also uncovered a top-down management system that adversely affected staff morale. In short, everyone felt out of the loop. Each time there was a management change, the staff became nervous about their jobs, further diminishing morale and reducing loyalty to the company.

> The 70 or so staff went to their cubicles in the morning, did what they had to do and did not feel as though they were part of the bigger picture at all. This kind of environment certainly did not encourage anyone to go the extra mile.

A serious consequence was that, although the staff had received a number of complaints about the voice mail and other problems, they were not relaying these messages to management, because of this low morale and top-heavy company structure. To the majority of the staff, this was just a job. They felt disenfranchised, as though nothing they could say or do would be listened to.

When we reviewed the material our client sent to potential customers, their brochures and collateral material fell into the same trap as do so many others. Although crammed with features and pretty pictures, there was no focus on the emotional benefits of using our client's services. Sure, there were some positive features buried in all the jargon, but few people have time to read pages of material to find this information in today's business environment. In contrast, a competitor—tiny in size by comparison to our client but much more successful in the local market—clearly articulated their benefits on the cover page of their simple brochure.

> Our client's materials were not customer friendly, whereas their competitors' materials were. Hence, the competitors got the business.

Our client also wisely articulated their services in both English and their native language so they could effectively tap into the vast U.S. marketplace as well as attract business from ex-patriots. However, the English contact listed in their advertising and promotional materials had a name that was foreign and extremely difficult to pronounce to most Americans. Our research demonstrated conclusively that the overwhelming majority of people were embarrassed to phone and ask for someone whose name they could not pronounce; rather than fumble, they simply would not phone. Therefore, we strongly recommended that our client list a name like Helen or Mary for the English contact, even if the same person took the calls.

Of course, we understood that people are proud of their names and heritage and that the person handling this role may have been reluctant to change her name merely to answer the phone. However, when each call potentially represented a gross sale of several thousand dollars—and the name used during each may be responsible for a substantial reduction in the number of calls received, then it is a logical commercial decision. After a lot of persuasion, our client embraced this change.

We greatly improved customer follow-up, for both before the purchase and after the trip was concluded, and we even sent a gift of a client branded power adapter to overseas travelers. We know from experience that having your electrical equipment not work in another country is extremely annoying. This was a very valuable and appreciated, yet very inexpensive, gift. After implementing many of Marketforce One's recommendations, the firm's sales increased 157 percent over the previous year's figures for the same period.

This simple case study illustrates the importance of doing your homework and analyzing your business practices and performance. Our client had a sales problem for many years. Although it was simple to rectify—and although they knew all there was to know about the travel industry—they clearly knew very little about their potential customers. The majority of problems we identified were little things, but they made a big difference to the bottom line.

It is also critical to remember that people are only motivated to buy by *benefits*, not features. In short, they do not care about what your product merely *does*; they care about what it does *for them*. Customers initially make all decisions emotionally and then justify them pragmatically. Too little marketing is directed at the heart, where the initial decision is made.

Listen to Your Customers

In *any* business or industry, customer feedback is critical to achieving success.

We need to listen to both our internal and external customers.

Every company must have a structure in place that makes it easier to communicate both internally among your team, and externally with your customers. Internal customers can have ideas that improve communication, efficiency, and customer service. Many employees have contact with a client or potential client to provide information or other services after the initial contact has been made. The feedback those employees can provide the company about this customer can be highly beneficial to developing relationships, which can lead not only to repeat sales, but also to information about products or services that may be required in the future.

With today's technology, every customer interaction can be recorded in a transparent system that can be accessed by all of the company's personnel. A firewall with various levels of security access can be added to protect sensitive information.

It Is Extraordinary How Often Little Things Mean a Lot

A couple of years ago, Marketforce One worked with a major sports team. Our goal was to build their attendance and streamline their ticketing, membership, and season's ticket systems. As is the case with many sports, a significant part of this team's ticket sales came from recreational groups associated with major corporations. Every Tuesday for more than 20 years, these companies' social secretaries would come to the team office and pick up their tickets. This meant a constant stream of people coming to the office throughout the day.

Most of the social secretaries would stay around for some time and chat with people. Though sometimes inconvenient, this was not really disruptive. However, team management demanded that we institute a new procedure that would have the tickets delivered by courier to the corporations to save them the trouble of coming to the sports team office. They saw this as a time-saver for the purchaser and a way to stop people disrupting the flow of work at the organization.

As is our policy, we decided to do our homework before we instituted any changes. We spoke to the relevant people at the sports organization and at the corporations to ascertain what effect the new ticket delivery policy would have. A junior clerk in the sports office told us that many of the people that came into the office only did so to get a glimpse of—or maybe even meet—the players. He had told management of his concerns about the new policy, but he had been ignored.

Our discussions with the social secretaries made it quickly apparent that this change would have a profoundly negative effect on ticket sales. We reported our findings to the event management committee, but they insisted on going ahead with the change. Within two weeks, group ticket sales had fallen by over 40 percent. We were not surprised, but the team management was.

Our research found the young clerk was spot on. Many of the social secretaries promoted group ticket sales just so they could go to the team office and hopefully meet one of the star players, a real highlight for them. Once they lost this privilege, they lost their interest in pursuing group ticket sales for the team. It took nearly two months for management to reverse their decision; however, group ticket sales had slowed to a trickle by this time. What had been a regular flood of ticket sales was now just a drip. It took the team a couple of seasons to return to their previous level of support.

For literally a few hundred dollars invested in homework, we had been able to predict these losses. Yet the sports organization believed we were overstating the potential losses and that their popularity was sufficient to overcome the problem. They ignored our advice and lost several million dollars. This example emphasizes quite clearly that research will not only prevent losses; it can also help increase margins.

We were also hired by a cosmetics company that had, among its many product lines, a wrinkle conditioner that guaranteed to diminish wrinkles around the eyes. Despite being an excellent product, its sales were slow. In order to promote sales, the company had reduced the price and had offered purchase incentives with other products in their range.

Our research showed that people doubted the product's quality, not because of the product or the packaging, but because it was *too inexpensive*. It rapidly became obvious that price relates to quality in the consumer's mind when it comes to health and beauty products. We asked potential customers what they would expect to pay for such a product. As a result, we had a simple recommendation to the company: *Triple the price*. They followed our advice, and within weeks, sales outstripped supply. The fact that the product was even being back ordered—an unusual situation for our client—also assisted to fuel demand.

The bottom line is that research and consumer/staff feedback is critical to success, to the extent that we do not do anything for a client without doing our homework first. It is really amazing what you can find out with a series of simple, well-thought-out questions.

> Research usually represents a small cost in relation to the overall investment in time and money involved in marketing most businesses, products, or services. More often than not, it represents a very significant difference to the ROI.

It Is Vital to Research Not Only Potential Customers, but Competitors as Well

Although many large companies spend considerable funds hiring consultants to gather information on their competitors, few smaller companies have the resources to do this. However, smaller companies can often use the Internet to determine a wealth of competitive information. Online research offers free access to company websites that contain product and pricing information, catalogs, details of new products, and so on. Many websites have an interactive capacity that enables the asking of specific questions about these products. The Internet also provides free access to online chat groups that debate companies' products, images, and problems—sources that can provide authentic and valuable insight into the customers' real attitudes about products or services.

With the rapid change in the business environment and consumer attitudes, it is important to not only conduct initial research but to do so on an ongoing basis to keep abreast of consumer trends. If you are in the retail arena, it can be extremely constructive and very revealing to call your competitors' stores and have phantom shoppers call your own. It is also advantageous to visit stores that *do not* compete with you to see what they may be doing that you may emulate or improve. For example, you can determine how long it takes for someone to ask if they can assist you and how products and prices are displayed. Can the staff answer you correctly if you ask them a question? If you ask about a product, do they point to the aisle and move on or do they take you there to ensure you get the product and information needed to make a sale? The U.S. mystery shopping company TrendSource said in *Business Review Weekly* that changes made after a recent six-week mystery-shopping blitz for a fast food chain boosted revenues by 17 percent.

In every aspect of your business, you need to outshine your competitors in providing what the potential customer wants. To achieve this, you need to know what customers want and what your competitors provide.

Always Analyze Data Thoroughly; the Obvious Often Is Not

The ABCD of marketing is to Always Be Collecting Data.

There is no such thing as an average customer.

Think about it: If you stand with one foot in a bucket of ice and the other in boiling water, do you feel comfortable, on average?

The same notion applies to today's market place, and there are some interesting statistics at play. For example, airline frequent-flier programs show that 4.1 percent of customers make 70.4 percent of trips. Once the airlines discovered this situation, they developed subniches. United Airlines introduced the 1K, executive, and premier status categories. They realized how vital it is to focus on heavy users; however, you must not ignore the less frequent users. Because there are so many more of them, they represent a great deal of potential.

Although I fly United Airlines frequently—as do my management and colleagues—they appear to be part of the old school that believes in the weight of expensive, ineffective traditional media rather than appreciating the importance of testimonials and the power of word of mouth. I have flown many million miles with United, and because I featured them in my presentations to major corporations, raving about their great customer service, a senior manager obtained the elite Global Services rank for me. For someone who travels as much as I do, it was a huge advantage.

However, several years later, United canceled my Global Services status because I was "not spending enough money on tickets." They ignored the fact that my clients usually bought and paid for my tickets and I always specified United. They also ignored the fact that I promoted and personally endorsed United in over 1,500 presentations to senior executives in over 1,000 companies, 91 of which are Fortune 500s. Needless to say, I have stopped promoting the company in presentations, not out of spite or any petty reason, but because I thought their actions represented very poor customer service. Now, I also fly lots of other airlines. What was an unfailing loyalty to United and 300,000 + air miles a year has now become simply flying sufficient miles to maintain my 1K status.

The 62 percent of people who stop doing business with you because they feel you do not care? I'm one of them!

Companies in every industry make simple mistakes and fail to anticipate the future. A decade or so ago, Ford and General Motors ignored small-car buyers in the United States while the Japanese did not. The result? The Japanese own the small-car category.

A dedication to continued learning is the only way to understand market trends. The marketplace, as well as the customer's needs and wants, are changing quickly. As a result, products can rapidly become more or less relevant to the marketplace. For example, disposable diapers were initially introduced as a convenience product that now dramatically outsells the cloth alternative. Skim milk used to be sold only in powder form. However, the major health trend in the community led to liquid skim milk and a huge niche market.

It is also very easy to look at nationwide trends and make incorrect determinations, whereas detailed research can provide totally different results. In the United States, the percentage of small-car sales on the east and west coasts are double and often triple the sales in central states, where trucks, vans, and SUVs are the dominant sales segment. It is important to realize that different psychographic groups often have different price sensitivities. Accordingly, psychographic segmentation of the customer's real values, including performance, reliability, fashion, aesthetic, and financial considerations must be evaluated.

Different psychographic groups may react in distinct ways to various promotions and incentives. You must ascertain what kinds of promotions are cost effective, depending on what segment of your customer base you are targeting.

One of the other critical pieces of marketing information is to determine who is making the *purchasing decision* for your product. The approach taken to marketing the product to different market segments may vary dramatically.

One of the examples I use in my workshops with to sales and marketing executives concerns the Chevrolet Geo. There were literally thousands of these compact fuel-efficient vehicles on every U.S. college campus that were driven primarily by young female students. I ask my audiences to create a concept for a promotion or advertising campaign aimed at the primary target audience. In the majority of cases, they create a program for teenage girls without asking another question. However, this is the wrong target market! Although the female students drove the cars, the purchasing decision was being made overwhelmingly by their fathers. Their considerations of safety, reliability, and economy were likely different than the considerations of the young driver.

Research Is the Key to Retaining Customers, Motivating a Switch, or Securing First-Time Use

There are three potential markets in any business:

1. Consumers targeted perfectly to your product
2. People using another product or service in your category
3. People who do not buy from you or your competitors, but could have the need for the product if adequately convinced

The only way to determine the hot buttons, the risk reversal, and/or added-value policies required to attract or maintain any of the segments listed is through research. The only way to determine consumer trends or anticipate emerging markets—and what it is these new markets want—is to conduct thorough research.

Research Shows You How to Differentiate Your Products

There are six primary areas in which you can differentiate your products from your competition, an essential element if you want to be a market leader and not just a me-too product. These six areas are product, customer service, distribution, communication, information, and price. Only by comprehensively understanding your company's and your competitors' operations—as well as the advantages and disadvantages of each from the customer's perspective—can you create a marketing strategy that focuses on product differentiation. This differentiation is what will motivate the potential customer to buy *your* product instead of the competitors', and this applies equally to business to business as it does to retail.

1. **Product.** This is clearly not new. Henry Ford told his customers they could have their cars in any color they wanted as long as it was black; then General Motors offered their cars in several colors and nearly put Ford out of business. Uniform products will be less and less appealing to consumers in the future. Look at sports shoes; they are individually developed for all sports now. The large environmentally safe detergent company Simple Green changed their marketing strategy from the one all-purpose product to specific packaging addressing windows, tiles, cars, tires, kitchens, bathrooms, and so on. Consumers are looking for answers to their specific needs, and believe a designated product will do the job better.

2. **Customer Service.** Supermarkets now take your packages to the car; city apartments offer every conceivable service from day care and babysitting to valet parking and shopping services; and sports stadiums provide banking and shopping facilities, child minding, and so on. Superior customer service is an essential element in differentiating your product or service.

3. **Distribution.** Companies are now making their products and services much more accessible to potential customers. Supermarkets

deliver to your home; you can have your car serviced in a parking lot while you have a manicure or a haircut in your office upstairs. Customers nowadays demand convenience; so the more convenient you are, the more business you will attract.

4. **Communication.** We need to segment our messages very carefully and specifically. For example: people in the U.S. drink Lipton iced tea from a can; in England, it is served hot in fine china; and people (mostly men) in the Middle East consume it predominantly from small cups. Similar variations may also exist for many products within a seemingly homogeneous market.

5. **Information.** Today's consumer is seeking simple-to-understand, nonjargon-filled information that specifically lets them know how to resolve their individual issues. The company that can best articulate that information—and make themselves clearly seen as the one company that relates to the customer—is more likely to differentiate themselves from competitors.

6. **Price.** This should be considered only as an *absolute last resort*, because price is never an influencing reason for purchase for more than 80 percent of the population. It only becomes a factor if consumers perceive all else to be equal—a scenario that will only come to pass if you have not used your research information wisely. In this case, you likely have not differentiated your business or given your potential customers a compelling reason to buy from you. After all, any idiot can cut prices and get a fleeting market *share gain— until* their competitor cuts prices as well. All this does is lead to decreased profits and competitiveness. If you have to discount to get business, either your price is too high or your quality and service standard is too low.

The only way to identify which of the aforementioned elements (or which combination thereof) to use to differentiate yourself from your competition is to conduct thorough, careful research.

Remember: You cannot control what you cannot measure, and you cannot measure what you cannot control.

Chapter 6

Know What Business You Are In

There are a number of elements involved in creating a successful campaign that enable you to differentiate yourself from your competitors, be heard above the clutter, create first-recall brand awareness, and generate success. However, none is more important than knowing what business you are *in*!

> After all—if you don't know what business you are in, your customer certainly will not. And if you don't know, how can you effectively communicate with the customer? You can't!

Whether it is during a business consultancy or via a presentation, one of the first questions I ask people is, "What business are you in?" It is unbelievably disturbing to me that, in this day and age, probably 499 out of 500 people answer by citing the category of their trade or profession. People who work in a computer company or store enthusiastically volunteer "computers"; insurance people say "insurance"; and so on. If that is the case, then Home Depot in America, Australia's Bunnings, and B & Q Hardware in Europe are in the hardware business. After all, that is what they sell. Well, perhaps—but it is certainly not what people are buying. No one, at least no one in his or her right mind, wakes up in the morning and has a burning desire to buy a hammer. You buy a hammer because your spouse threatens to hire a handyman if you don't fix the door, and visualizing the cost of such help sends you scurrying to the hardware store to buy a hammer.

You go to a hardware store to solve a problem, not because you must have a hammer. A few years ago, we ran a campaign for a well-known chain of hardware stores that had fallen on tough times. Their traditional advertising campaign was based on having "the biggest range of saws, drills, screws, etc. in the nation!" Reality check—no one cared. Our approach was to forget about the hardware business, and have them emphasize the fact that they were in the problem-solving business—an entirely different industry. We recommended that they advertise in the following way: "If you have a problem around the home, we have an expert to provide the advice (and) to show you how to repair the problem, inexpensively and professionally."

The result was exceptional. Within two months, sales were up over 235 percent. The difference? They now knew that they were in the problem-solving business—a different one than hardware, and one that needs to be marketed in an entirely different way.

A few years ago, the major household window blind manufacturer, Luxaflex, found itself in a financial downturn. Their whole advertising campaign focused on the huge range of blinds they stocked. They had wooden blinds, plastic blinds, aluminum blinds, thin ones, wide ones, vertical, horizontal, yellow, pink; essentially, they had a blind for everyone, and they proudly let the world know that they were in the blind business. Unfortunately, they were also losing money, because no one cared about blinds. That was merely the *product.*

When potential customers were asked why they were considering buying blinds, almost everyone responded, "To keep the house cooler." Of course, once they decided to keep the house cooler, they wanted to do it decoratively; that is where the pink, wide, vertical, and so on came in. However, people did not respond to a blind commercial. When the ad changed to "Keep your home 15 degrees cooler in summer," the phones rang off the wall. Luxaflex thought they were in the blinds business, but they were actually in a totally different business—climate control.

We had a client who sold window frames whose advertising showed a lovely wooden frame with a nicely shaded area to depict glass. There was immediate customer-product disconnect. Their potential customers were not buying window frames; they were buying *views*, a totally different product. A little research showed that many customers were installing windows to better watch their children around the swimming pool. For that reason, when we showed the view of a pool and children in the window frame instead of simulated glass, with the heading "Watch your children 24/7," inquiries increased by over 1,100 percent. An advertisement for window frames that shows a wonderful landscape or a clear picture of a backyard pool where kids are playing will convincingly outperform an advertisement that solely focuses on a window frame.

So—what business are you in?

The World's Biggest Sports Revolution Worked for One Reason

In 1977, the global cricket revolution took place when billionaire Kerry Packer hijacked the world's most popular summer sport, which is fanatically supported by more than 2.5 billion people. Packer's PBL Marketing organization changed the rules of the game and the players' apparel. He secretly signed the top 120 players in the world to agreements to play for a private organization instead of their national teams, thereby causing an upheaval in the over-150-year-old sport. After the High Court challenges, a barrage of accusations, and airing of much dirty linen, the game never looked back. Cricket now generates record crowds, television audiences, and merchandise sales.

How did the new regime dramatically increase support for the game? For many years before "World Series Cricket," as the new order was named, the controlling bodies of the sport in each country promoted and advertised upcoming international series by highlighting the skills of the game on television, radio, and print ads. The result of this focus on the product was quarter-full stadiums, at best.

I was fortunate to be marketing director of "World Series Cricket," a wonderful period of my career where I spent a lot of time traveling and learning about different marketing approaches in a number of countries with very different customs and heritages. Yet the advertising focus was the same in each country: We had to concentrate on the real business the public were interested in . . . providing entertainment, and having fun! One of the other challenges facing cricket was the 90:10 male: female spectator imbalance. Because we realized that the most popular entertainment forms in the future would be those enjoyed by both sexes, we began to feature women in our advertising, both in same-sex groups and enjoying the experience with men. Instead of focusing on players doing great things (i.e., the skills of the game, therefore, the product) in our advertising, we featured people having fun. We also introduced and created players' personalities, instead of merely emphasizing their playing skills.

> Why were we so successful? We focused on elements to which people could emotionally relate. Emotional connections create a commitment.

Anyone selling a product or service, irrespective of what it is, must create that emotional bond with the consumer to develop loyal returning customers.

Another of our initiatives was to extend the business of fun by providing a wide variety of entertainment, competitions, and attractions at the games. We scheduled these to occur during the breaks in play, thereby providing continuous entertainment for the spectator. Today, added attractions are commonplace in major sports. In the late 1970s when the World Series Cricket revolution took place, it was unusual and it upset many of the sports traditionalists.

The result of developing this emotional connection between the fun of attending a game and the consumers' desires resulted in attendances of 40,000–100,000 people. The establishment had previously attracted 7,000–20,000 spectators. The major difference was that we realized that this was not so much a competitive sports event but an entertainment spectacle providing fun and excitement for the fans. We knew we were in the fun business; we were not in the cricket business or even in the sports business.

The other element that we heavily promoted in a fun way was the nationalistic fervor generated by international competition. Again, it is a highly emotional driver that has little to do with the actual event. Witness the 4 million people—almost 20 percent of the country's population—that stayed up all night in Australia to watch that country win the America's Cup. At any other time, most people didn't give a hoot about sailing!

Sometimes You Need to Dig a Little Deeper

When we were marketing a series of health clubs, we assumed (probably reasonably) that people joined to get fit. Yet research rapidly highlighted that while this was true for some, the majority of people joined to meet people. Attending a gym or getting fit was simply the means by which they opted to do it.

We identified that the major appeal of the health club was the ease of communication it allowed. When people from totally different walks of life meet in a normal social setting, there is a tremendous hurdle to overcome to find a common ground in conversation. However, if you have just completed an aerobics workout, you immediately have a common interest with others who have done the same.

We realized that if we had marketed the health clubs as fitness centers, we would have had considerable difficulty in getting sales, because we would have been competing head to head with literally dozens of competitors that were focusing on this same fitness-and-health angle. We began to appreciate that health clubs were not in the fitness business at all; they were really in the meeting-people business. Because we concentrated our marketing on social interaction and attractions, membership sales boomed.

These are actually fairly straightforward examples; it is not always that cut and dried. Often, determining what you are selling can take considerable research.

It has been demonstrated consistently that an insurance salesman who is selling insurance, irrespective of how big the marketing budget is, will not perform anywhere nearly as well as the insurance representative that is selling peace of mind. A building company selling a home will outperform one selling houses.

The one thing that all the examples given above have in common is that they are all emotionally driven. Solving problems, keeping comfortable, having fun, peace of mind, lovely views are all quite different from the product actually being sold.

What Business Are You In?

It is obvious from each of these examples that the people who can best determine what business you are in are your clients or potential customers. The public determined that the hardware chain is in the problem-solving business, that Luxaflex is in the climate-control business, and that Cricket is not a game—it is really entertainment and fun.

The first step in determining what business you are actually in is to ask current or potential customers exactly what they are seeking when they buy your product or service. You should analyze the answers into demographic and lifestyle segments, since different groups buy for different reasons. If you obtain a pragmatic answer such as, "*I hired the painter because my home needed a bit of a clean-up*," then dig a little deeper to determine the emotional reason behind the decision, because only emotional benefits sell! In this case, it may be to re-establish pride in the appearance of the home. Pride is a very powerful emotional trigger.

One thing is for certain: If you don't know what business you are in, you certainly cannot determine the hooks that are essential to sell your product or service.

Remember: Don't judge a book by its cover.

Chapter 7

Your Name and Image Are Critical Success Tools

It is critical in an extremely competitive market, in which an increasing number of companies offer similar products or services, that a potential client thinks of your company first when they consider your category.

There has been a proliferation of communication vehicles, clutter, 10-, 15-, and 30-second advertisements, advertorials, social and digital media, escalating communication costs, increasingly segmented audiences, diminished attention spans, and increased consumer cynicism over the past decade.

> Research shows that 92 percent of all consumers believe that the majority of products or services within any category are *interchangeable.*

It is, therefore, essential that you seize and maximize every opportunity to communicate who you are, what you do, and why consumers should select your product or service instead of a competitor's. That single extra opportunity can be the difference between success and failure in this highly aggressive market.

Given all of this clutter, you must provide your potential customer with a simple but powerful recall ability in order to think of you first. It will create an additional barrier to recall if your company or product name does not readily convey precisely what it is that you do, or it is difficult to spell or remember. The customer must first commit the relationship between your name and what you do to memory before considering the benefits of your product. This becomes a three-step process instead of quick, simple recollection. If your name clearly explains what you do, then it is only a two-step process to consider your brand's benefits, making it significantly easier to create first recall brand awareness.

What's in a Name?

One of the most underutilized communication vehicles available to every business, large or small, any product or service, is their name and logo. When a company name clearly states what the business does and positions it correctly to the potential consumer, that one element alone will give you a head start over the vast majority of your competitors, simply because over 78 percent of companies do not do it. A quick check of business registers highlights very plainly that it is almost impossible to tell what a large percentage of companies actually do from their name alone. Take a look at some of the ads for plumbers and gynecologists; same size, same type, same copy . . . go figure!

Frequently, when people come across a business name, they do not derive any information about what the business does. Unless the name conveys the correct message, it fails to reinforce the product or service. We know from research that the two most important elements of differentiating yourself and getting your business or message recalled positively are the frequency of impacts of your name and your customer purchasing benefit (CPB).

It is true that a number of major corporations have names that mean nothing or are not related to their product or service. However, these companies have a luxury that is not available to most small businesses: huge marketing budgets.

You Must Get into Customers' Subconscious Minds and Trigger First Recall

Your mind files information in the same way that a computer does. If you see a sign, letterhead, advertisement, or any other mention of John Smith Plumbing, for example, your mind will file the name under "plumber" along with all the other plumbers you have heard of. When you are looking for a plumber, your mind will go to the plumber's file and automatically pull out the one that has made the most impact on you.

However, let's say that John Smith called his company Mr. Fix It for example. Although it may be a cute name, your mind does not know where to file it and it will not be readily recalled when you are looking for a plumber.

Even if it gets filed in the plumber file, a competitor with a more powerful emotional trigger will win out.

In addition to including what you do, it is important that the name has appeal to your target market. For example, offering you a Bronx Ice Cream would have much less appeal than Haagen Dazs. Why? It is not only the sound of the words but also the connotation of the image. *Bronx* conveys "tough," whereas *Haagen Dazs* conveys "Scandinavian," "clean," and "refreshing"—a much more appropriate image for smooth, creamy ice cream.

A Change of Name Can Reposition Your Product

One of my favorite examples of appropriate product naming is that of Dorman's cheese in the United States. The product—an ordinary low-cost brand competing with big names like Kraft and Bordens—was getting badly outperformed by its rivals, so much so that supermarkets were taking it off shelves at an ever-increasing rate.

Dorman's faced one of three options: Kill the brand; slash prices and, therefore, profitability and competitiveness; or change the name, image, and reposition the brand. They wisely chose repositioning, and Deli Singles was born. This provision of cheese in precut single slices provided a strong point of difference from their competitors. Rather than cut the price of the product below that of its competitors to drive sales, Dorman's actually *increased* the price by 50 cents. The result? The same low-quality cheese, but with increased retail facings instead of deletions. Deli Singles became a best seller.

This example illustrates not only the importance of name and image, but also the sales power of product differentiation. It also highlights dramatically the fact that sales are only price driven if all else is equal. If you are selling based on price, look in the mirror, because that is where you will find the problem!

For that reason, a marketer's primary job is to ensure that their product is *not* seen as equal (and, therefore, interchangeable) but, rather, perceived to have a distinct advantage over competitors.

It Is Not Just the Name but the Overall Image

You must design your name and logo so that the typeface, shape, and color reflect the image you are trying to convey. For example, the color blue denotes peace, calm, and stability; green suggests money; and purple suggests modern or cutting edge. The same type of situation exists with the logo design. A fluid modern art or abstract design suggests dynamism, daring, and adventure, whereas a mountain denotes stability. Therefore, a purple and orange abstract logo is hardly appropriate for an investment or banking institution that wants to convey responsibility, stability, and even a bit of caution. On the other hand, a blue mountain with a gold monogram stamped on it is hardly relevant to a punk rock music shop.

The combination of typeface and style, graphic, use of color, and the inclusion of an excellent CPB can often tell the potential customer a lot about your business without utilizing valuable advertising or communication space.

You can then use this space to differentiate your product and motivate a response. This is a gigantic benefit when you are in a highly competitive marketplace where communication is a major expense.

Just the Image Alone Can Create the Picture for the Consumer

According to a study I recently saw, the majority of women (some 89 percent) believed, based on the product name, that the popular skin care line Clinique is French. Because France is one of the beauty capitals of the world, the product instantly conjures up beauty, style, and quality. The brand develops this imaging further through their highly sophisticated packaging. In reality, the product is made in the United States and, as the most obese nation in the world, the images people conjure up are not always of beauty, style, and quality. If Clinique replaced that attractive packaging with an image of the Midwestern factories where the products are made, my guess is that it would impact sales considerably and not favorably.

Yet despite the influence that a name can have on a product and business's success, many people create names that do not relate to either. The most popular example of this is coming up with an idiotic combination of their children's names, or including a reference to some weird place or happening that has personal meaning for them. These people will tell you that the name and image is not important; it's just a name, and, after all, it is the product that really counts.

They are wrong.

In a day and age in which fierce competition exists in almost every field of endeavor, any small advantage you can gain over your competitor is absolutely critical. Unless you have a huge amount of money available to build a brand—and to get your obscure name, who you are and what you do recalled—the name you select can have a major effect on your success.

The same is true for your logo. Depending on the design, it can convey excitement, fluidity, dynamism, stability, creativity, or other emotions. However, it is important to realize that although a logo can say volumes about your business, it can seldom do so without combining it with other factors.

Unfortunately, far too many companies rely solely on their logo to convey their image. Yet every research study I have seen on the public's ability to match a number of logos and the appropriate companies show results of less than 5 percent success. If major corporations who have spent millions on brand awareness for their logo cannot get better than single digit percentage awareness for their logo, then what chance does the small business have?

This is precisely why you must ensure that your name, logo, and image always clearly identify what it is that you do. This improves your recall potential and enables you to singularly convey your business message without having to use valuable time or space to also say who you are and what you do. Never leave it to chance or guesswork.

Remember: Perception is reality.

Chapter 8

Customer Purchasing Benefit

The major cause of corporate and product failure, as well as the rapid increase in marketing expenditure required to meet sales targets, is a result of companies' or brands' inability to effectively differentiate themselves from their competitors.

> Without establishing differentiation, there is little to no equity in the brand, and a poor performance is almost guaranteed.

Consumers see the overwhelming majority of brands in any category as being "me too!" Brand loyalty has broken down substantially, a fact that is strongly evidenced by the past three decades' rapid increase in decisions made at point of purchase. In 1975, the percentage of buying decisions made at point of purchase was, on average, 36 percent. Today it averages 74 percent. It is important to note that this percentage varies considerably between product categories. Even 10 years ago, the consumer shopping list specified brands; today the list is products, with the choice of brands being made at point of purchase. Most consumers today are happy to buy any one of three or four brands in the product category.

Strong brand positioning creates high customer commitment and loyalty. It produces compelling word of mouth. Each sale generates another sale, increased profits, and equity. Research shows that 60–75 percent of people try new products because of word of mouth compared to 25–40 percent due to advertising.

> With strong brand positioning and product differentiation, a brand is bought. Without it, the product must be sold.

This represents a huge difference in marketing cost.

Differentiating Your Product Is the Key to Brand Equity and Sales

It is essential to differentiate your product from your competition in today's highly competitive marketplace. It is the only way to develop heart share, build first-recall brand awareness, and secure a purchase decision in customers' subconscious minds. Customers do not buy the difference between products; they buy the most persuasive benefit. As we already know, pragmatic benefits do not motivate a purchase decision as powerfully as emotional benefits do.

Despite all the dramatic technological changes, increased pressure, varied business structures, and new industries, people still have the same emotional needs they did 10, 20, and 50 years ago. The clutter of today's marketplace simply makes an excellent customer purchasing benefit (CPB) all the more critical to success.

For example, once upon a time, all athletes drank either water or soft drinks. Then Gatorade was introduced as a sports drink (a significant point of marketing difference) and rapidly became almost every athlete's beverage of choice. Once a company has built a reputation, this positioning can be used to fringe. For example, Midas became known for mufflers and then used their reputation to branch out into a broader range of motor vehicle repair.

Your CPB is the one message that hits your potential client's hot button, and communicates your corporate philosophy in just a few words. *It is the single line or, preferably, word that differentiates your product from your competitors'*. It is the phrase that impacts the customer's pre-conscious mind and creates first recall of your product.

The Emphasis Has Moved from the Seller to the Buyer

Most marketers are familiar with the unique selling proposition (USP), the decades-old strap line used to deliver sales. The USP suggests that the most important entity in any transaction is the seller. On the contrary, the CPB recognizes that the buyer is the only person that counts and represents the primary benefit to the buyer.

> In the past, corporations used to spell out their corporate philosophy in half a page. In today's fast-paced world, you have 10 seconds.

Despite the ever-shrinking time available to get your message across, this positioning is critical to your success.

Can you convey your company's advantage over your competition in just five or six words? Can you tell me why I should buy from you? If you cannot articulate these reasons to me, how are you going to sell your product or service to prospective clients en masse?

The CPB needs to achieve one, or both, of two objectives:

1. Highlight your primary emotional competitive advantage, for example, "Washes whiter than white" – Blue Omo laundry detergent. (Old, but a favorite.)
2. Highlight **your competitor's** perceived weakness, for example, "Everywhere you want to be" – Visa. This draws attention to the fewer number of establishments that accept American Express.

The majority of the most well known brands have a CPB, yet, astoundingly, some 90 percent of all brands do not utilize this most powerful of marketing tools. Merely having a CPB puts you in a very strong position to generate first-recall brand awareness—a critical quality in an increasingly crowded marketplace.

The Power of a CPB

In the previous chapter, we discussed how the mind files "John Smith Plumber" under "plumbing" with all of the other plumbers you have heard of. If, however, John Smith had included the CPB "No job too big or small, any time of the day or night" with his name, the brain will recall John Smith when it scours the plumber file, because he is most likely the only plumber who has given the consumer a powerful reason to remember him.

There are many examples of great CPBs; however, I think Domino's Pizza company did it especially well.

Domino's Pizza was simply another corner pizza store in a country with literally hundreds of take-out food joints in every city and suburb. In the United States, where over 60 percent of all meals are not prepared in the home (generating a staggering 1.5 billion eat-out or take-out meals every week), food is an extraordinarily competitive business. It is, unlike so many of the other examples we've discussed, also reliant almost entirely on price. The cheaper you can sell reasonable quality food, the more successful you will be.

Domino's Pizza's research of take-out food customers showed that a major concern of people who ordered home delivery was not great food or price—it was speed of delivery. If a customer ordered at 7 P.M., they did not want to be putting up with the blood-curdling screams of a hungry family or starving friends two hours later. People wanted take-out food fast. Domino's Pizza's promise of "Delivery in 30 minutes or it's free" connected with the public's hot button with a direct hit. This was their CPB; it differentiated Domino's Pizza from all the other companies who were promoting their products based on taste, serving size, or price.

Business boomed and the opposition was blitzed. Domino's Pizza is now the largest home delivery food company in the world, and they no longer have to compete solely on price. They achieved this result not by offering a good pizza, a cheap pizza, or even a hot pizza; they did it by providing a pizza for which you didn't have to wait. Price was eliminated as an issue because they impacted people's primary motivation: the time element. Domino's Pizza became resistant to their competitors' price attacks. The Domino's Pizza corner store rapidly expanded throughout the world, dominated the home delivery business, and significantly increased profitability.

Another excellent example is Federal Express. Federal Express is not in the parcels business, it is a world-class information management organization that happens to move parcels to pay for it. In the 1980s, Federal Express used the slogan "We own our own planes" to suggest reliable service and to convey the message that they didn't depend on others for transportation. However, this did not convey a benefit to potential clients. Businesses did not care whether they owned their own planes or not; they only cared about getting their parcels to the appropriate destination on time. So clients did not respond, and Federal Express was on the verge of bankruptcy.

Then they introduced the perfect CPB: "When you absolutely, positively, have to have it overnight." They hit the hot button by capitalizing on the executives' fear of not getting a package on time. This was the CPB they desperately needed. The result was meteoric success!

Every telephone book in the world has dozens of pages of courier companies. At the time, Federal Express was not offering anything that differed significantly from any of their direct competitors. However, once they articulated the primary benefit to the customer better—and did so in just a few words—they managed to become a billion dollar company in just 10 years.

A Great CPB Works for Any Category of Business

In November 1995, a house across the road from Zuma Beach in Malibu, California went on the market. Despite heavy advertising, open houses, and a procession of agents representing the property, it remained unsold for several years. Coldwell Banker agent Carol Bird visited the home and noticed there were thousands of butterflies on the property. She christened the house Butterfly Haven, put a brass nameplate on the gates, and advertised it as Malibu's Butterfly Haven. It sold almost immediately thereafter, for well above the listing price. This is an excellent example of a CPB: The butterflies differentiated the property from all other listings. It is also an example of the effectiveness of name and image as discussed in the previous chapter.

I remember several years ago (before I became conscious of melanoma) that the motivation for me to buy Coppertone suntan lotion was their CPB, "Tan, don't burn." It was an extremely simple but effective promise; it addressed your desires (to get a tan) and took away your fears (sunburn) in just three simple words.

Similarly, the Avis car-rental slogan "We try harder" says it all. Avis was number two to Hertz, and wanted to do everything they could to be better. This simple slogan convinced me, and millions of others like me, to use their vehicles.

> The right CPB can make the difference between success and failure for any business.

The Blue Omo example used earlier emphasizes that the CPB doesn't have to represent fact; it just needs to differentiate powerfully. If you analyze the statement "Washes whiter than white," it doesn't make sense; however, it sure conveys a powerful meaning and resulted in emptied shelves.

The rationalization of the financial services industry and the creation of mega banks have created the impression among consumers that banks have become too big to worry about the small customer. Many worried that banks had become impersonal and uncaring. To that end, Bank of America introduced a CPB that said, "If we don't call you by name, we will give you $5.00." It was great when you walked into the bank to be greeted with, "Hi, Mr. Pritchard! How are you today?" All of a sudden, I felt as though the teller really cared how I was, and, of course, I responded positively. This simple CPB allowed Bank of America to correct the public's negative image of their industry very easily and quickly.

The CPB Can Be the Difference between Full and Empty Stadiums

We have carried out extensive research on the attendance, sponsorship, and merchandise performance of sports teams in Europe, South America, Australia, and the United States. Interestingly, we found that teams whose CPBs related to winning or on-field performance, such as "A winning season," actually performed poorly in comparison with those who emphasized what the spectators really wanted—entertainment. The result for teams who used CPBs like "A great night out" was far superior.

Too many companies *think* they know what the consumer wants. For example, most athletic administrators with whom I have worked believe that a winning season is the most important issue to the fans. In reality, that is superficial. Extensive research in more than a dozen sports has found that winning or even watching the event is not in the top three reasons people support or attend.

This is the same with products. Almost every company that comes to us for assistance is selling something totally different from what the consumer is buying. For example, the CPB we developed for health and fitness company Planet Fitness has been phenomenally successful. The phrase we introduced, "We make fitness fun," challenged the notion held by most people that getting fit was boring, hard work. This serves as yet another reminder that your CPB is an excellent way to change people's perceptions of your product or service.

Creating a CPB Takes Substantial Research

Before you begin to develop your own CPB, I recommend you take note of a few from other companies that convey a powerful message. For example: Mercedes-Benz's "Engineered like no other car," and Blockbuster's "Go home happy" both say it all, don't they? Think about how some other brand's messages differentiate their product from the competition.

Each of the following CPBs say something quite different about their company's product, their competition or the consumer's fears or aspirations.

Avis "We try harder"

BMW "Ultimate driving machine"

Coppertone "Tan, don't burn"

M&M's "Melt in your mouth, not in your hand"

Wheaties "Breakfast of Champions"

British Airlines "Putting people first"

Johnson's Baby Shampoo "No more tears"

Miller Lite Beer "Tastes great, less filling"

Kodak "You push the button, we do the rest"

How to Determine *Your* CPB

So how do you figure out your own brand's CPB? In reality, you don't; your customer does. The CPB's job is to address your client's desires, fears, or frustrations.

> This statement is the simple expression of your competitive advantage or capitalization on your potential competitors' weakness.

It is the solution to your client's desires or concerns expressed in just a few words.

Determining your CPB is one of the most difficult marketing assignments you can undertake. The essential elements required to do so are brainstorming with your team; undertaking an extensive SWOT analysis; and conducting face-to-face interviews with your current and prospective customers. It is ultimately your potential customer who will tell you what will motivate them to buy one product or service over another. You then need to ensure you can meet this requirement and create a few powerful words to communicate it.

Steps to Take Before You Can Create a CPB

◆ Clearly define your *target market(s)*.
◆ List your most important *current clients,* and specify the reasons that make them so critical.
◆ List your most *important* potential customers and specify the reason they are.
◆ Meet with both current and potential customers and ascertain the most important reasons, either pragmatic or emotional, *they buy* either your product or service or a competitor's.
◆ *Conduct a SWOT analysis* on your product or service as well as those of your competitors.
◆ Analyze the *attributes and deficiencies of your competitor's* products.
◆ List **every** *possible reason someone would buy* the product *you offer.* Now list every reason they would *buy your product over your competitors'*. Do this during a brainstorming session with all the staff involved with your product or service; include *administration, creative, and front line* staff members.
◆ Once you have listed every possible reason, *prioritize these in purchase motivation power*.
◆ *Delete every reason* that can also be claimed by your competitor.
◆ Determine the *emotional benefit* behind all of the reasons remaining.

Then ask the following questions for each remaining benefit.
Is it *believable?*
Can you *deliver the promise?*
Is it a *compelling reason?*
Can it be expressed in *six words or less?*
Is the promise *crystal clear?*
Is it *distinguishable* from your competitor's messages?
Test each of the options with both current and potential customers.

A CPB Is Both Persuasive and Pervasive

Disneyland tells guests that it is "The happiest place on earth"—and they make it so. When I first heard that the highest paid casual worker at the theme park is the person who sweeps up the trash, I was surprised. But the job requires a comprehensive training program and it took me a few minutes to work out why. The information booths intimidate many park visitors; people don't like to be embarrassed by having to ask what they fear to be silly questions. So these cleaning attendants provide an easy-to-approach alternative, and hence are a primary source of information.

The staff at Disneyland is always bubbly and happy, extremely polite, and courteous. When you ask someone what he or she thought of Disneyland, what do they say? "I loved it! Everyone is so friendly and it is sparkling clean." Do they tell you about the hour wait to go on the rides? Do they complain about the $69 park admission? No! Disneyland has an emotional, motivating CPB conveyed in every conceivable application, and they do everything possible to live up to it.

The Most Effective CPBs Are Emotional and Appeal to the Senses

The magic you convey to customers will outweigh any inconvenience or cost, and is applicable in almost any situation. For example, let's say that you have a stand at an exhibition. You have less than 10 seconds to catch an attendee's attention; 10 seconds in which you compel them to think, "*Wow*, I need to look further into this." Sure, theatrics, lighting, sound, design, color, food, coffee, bar, and so forth are all important and will capture the initial interest. However, to a prospective client and not just a casual observer, nothing is more important than clearly, boldly, and simply expressing the clear benefit of your product or service over your competitors—your CPB.

So the next time an exhibition planner tells you that only the image counts, fire them! Unless the first image provides a simple, powerful benefit in 10 seconds, the prospect will keep walking. Remember: It's not the size of your stand or your budget, but the power and clarity of your CPB that counts. *And always be sure to appeal to all of the senses; sight, smell, touch, taste, and sound all improve your neurolinguistic programming and emotional connection.*

Many corporations have multiple images and reputations to market. One may be to the financial markets, one to the consumer, one to employees, yet another to the media, and perhaps even to government. The CPB may be different in each of the market segments and be communicated through various vehicles in distinct ways. These diverse strategies must be independently effective but combined so that the overall result is greater than the sum of the parts. The most important thing is to ensure that you are not sending mixed or confused messages. The only way to ascertain this is to test, test, and test with each of your constituencies.

Your CPB Offer Must Be Important, Deliverable, and Unique

One test for your CPB is called the IDU test—a test that measures whether your CPB is important, deliverable, and unique (IDU). In other words, is what you are promising *important* to your customers? Can you deliver what you *promise* to your customers? Is your promise *unique?*

The only people who can answer these questions are your customers—certainly not your corporate personnel. Though the vast majority of companies pass the I and D parts of the test, most fail the U part of the test. As I have stated previously, if you are not unique, you will be a target of price competition.

> You *must not* be just another "me-too" company.

You must be different and competitive. You need to create a service or product differential as well as added value for your customers. You must show potential customers that you are prepared to go the extra mile and then some.

> **Remember:** The world is full of me-too's. There is only one Microsoft, one Edmund Hillary, one Elvis Presley, and one Picasso. Every person is born with his or her own unique DNA. Why would you want to be the same as everyone else?

Chapter 9

Success Is About the Customer, Not the Product?

If you wanted to get my undivided attention with an advertisement, how would you do it? In today's chaotic world of endless information, commercials, infomercials, a barrage of ads every time you log onto the Internet, and cities littered with signage, it is extremely difficult. Unless, of course, your opening line or headline, if in print, was, "This ad is for Bob Pritchard". Were that the case, you can bet that I would move heaven and Earth to get from the shower to the TV or pull up on the busy freeway to turn up the radio or stop in front of the billboard to get the message! Would I have the same reaction or even notice an ad for corn flakes? Absolutely not! Research has shown that the average person's recall of ads is less than one in a thousand.

So what causes the difference in my reaction to the two advertisements? The first advertising message is about me, my interests, my concerns, my aspirations, or my requirements of a product or service. The second is about a product.

> The truth is that every ad should be *about the customer.*

If you sell the same product or service that others offer, what is the point of advertising it? When people want to buy this particular offering, they are more likely to recall the actual product or service, not the brand or the particular store doing the advertising. They totally forget who ran the advertisement and begin to shop around for the best price. I cited earlier the fact that people have changed from listing brands to primarily listing categories on their shopping lists, and the brands on the list are those that have made an emotional connection with the customer.

You must set your product apart to attract customers and build your business. If you just advertise what you have to offer, a percentage of potential customers *may* buy from you if you have the best price. However, this assumes that one of your competitors hasn't given them a compelling reason to buy from them by providing a promise of better service, greater experience, or another personal benefit that is more important than price.

If Customers Are Not Buying the Product, Then What Are They Buying?

In order to develop customer loyalty and grow the critical profit drivers of repeat business, increased margins, positive word of mouth, and brand equity, you must develop a relationship with your customer. You cannot do this by promoting a product that is the same or not significantly different from that of your competitors in the consumer's mind.

> Think about anything you have ever purchased. Didn't you buy it because it made you feel better in some way?

Your marketing must focus on what it is that will benefit the customer emotionally. This will vary by product or service category. It may be the quality of the shopping experience due to store layout, additional attractions, or services offered; it might be speed of service, ease of parking, the training and knowledge of the staff, or after-sales service. It may be a combination of these and many other factors. It is often a difficult notion for many businesses to grasp, but the product is the item the customer has wrapped and carries out to the car. In the majority of cases, it is not what the customer actually *buys*. If they do buy the product based solely on price, it is because you failed to provide or convey what they are really after. The result is most likely a one-time sale—an extremely ineffective way to build a business and one that requires constant expensive advertising to drive it.

For example, a motor dealer can look at a new customer in one of two ways. Firstly, here is a customer for your terrific new $20,000 release or, second, they can be a $300,000 lifetime customer making the first of many transactions with you. Which is more important, the customer or the product?

> To develop a successful business, your advertising, marketing, and promotion must be about the *customer*, not the product.

Yet if you look at the advertising and communication materials your company has produced, the ads in today's paper, and the billboards on your drive to work, chances are you will find that the overwhelming majority focus on the product. We are all out there selling something that is the same or similar to what all our competitors are offering, yet few of our potential customers are primarily interested in merely the product. They know *where* they can buy the product or service; what they want to know is where the *best* place to buy it is—and why. We need to sell something in which they are all extremely interested—themselves. You must offer something that makes them feel better, something no one else is providing. And that something is not the product.

I am astounded by companies that use their expensive advertising space to focus entirely on the products they offer. Unless these products or services are unique to that business, or they are selling solely on price, all these businesses are doing is driving general advertising for the products that can be bought anywhere, without providing a compelling reason for people to buy from them. How does that bring customers to your business?

Price is seldom the major motivating factor in achieving a sale. Research clearly demonstrates that less than 20 percent of customers, both consumer and business to business, buy solely on price. This figure varies from country to country, even region to region, but, in all the research I have seen, it is always less than 20 percent. For example, in the United States the nationwide average is on the order of 13 percent, in Australia it is 17 percent. The remainder weighs a number of other considerations.

> The important point is not that some 20 percent of people buy based on price; it is that 80 percent do not!

If you have the best price, you probably have the smallest margin. You will, therefore, make less profit, become less competitive and, in the overwhelming number of instances, eventually go out of business. That is certainly not a good business strategy.

The majority of businesses that come to Marketforce One for advice believe their companies are totally price sensitive. It does not matter whether it is real estate, motor vehicles, or widgets for lawn mowers. Clients almost always begin our briefings with them by claiming that their business is in some way unique and a cent or two makes all the difference to their sales performance. The reality is that we have yet to find a business, product, or service that is actually as price sensitive as the management believes it to be. In fact, the overwhelming majority of cases show us that once we establish a strategy to differentiate the business from its competitors, create a Customer Purchasing Benefit that hits the potential customer's emotional hot button, and design an added value and risk reversal policy, we are able to significantly increase profit margins. This should be the goal of every single company.

For example, a local camera store called Noble's uses the same equipment as all its competition. As a point of difference, they introduced a double weight paper and put white borders around the photographs. This makes the photographs not only a better quality but also gives them a natural frame. Their price for 24 prints is $19.69 against a multitude of competitors at $12.99. Noble's grew to 72 employees and $7 million in sales in just three years.

This example highlights the fact that you can get a premium on any product, providing you justify your benefits to the customer. Of course, this is not to suggest that price does not figure at all into the equation; it does. However, there are a number of other factors that today's consumers regard as equally and, often, more important. In fact, research shows that companies that are perceived as service leaders in their category can charge between 9–13 percent more for their product or service than their competitors.

Customers who buy on price alone are not loyal.

Research also shows that the same 20 percent or so that buy based on price also complain more often, return purchases more frequently, are difficult to satisfy, and are more likely to spread negative word of mouth about your brand. So who needs them? They reduce your profit, increase your costs, and then make disparaging remarks about you anyway! Let them go to your competitors, screw up *their* businesses, not yours.

Although price is not the critical factor in most purchase decisions, the consumer must be aware of your true price. In the United States and, likely, in other first-world countries, 71 percent of people think that the leading brands in a category are significantly more expensive than the number two, three, or four brands in the category without any perceived additional benefit. Although this is untrue, more often than not, perceptions are fact in the real world, and part of your marketing strategy needs to reinforce your (real or perceived) quality-to-price ratio. It is not important to most consumers that you are more expensive, but you must position yourself to not only justify this difference, but also to convince the consumer that the additional benefit to them is essential—and that its value exceeds the price differential.

E-Commerce Is No Different

The most successful sites on the web are for companies who engage site visitors through interaction and involvement in the process. Contests and promotions that appeal to the precise mindset of the audience they are trying to reach are extremely popular and make a major contribution to increased sales. The Internet is a combination of information and entertainment; it is all about the customer. Your site must be fun, entertaining, and challenging.

Customer Share Is More Important than Market Share

Marketing used to focus on market share; today, it begins with heart share and then becomes share of customer. We need to ensure that our customers buy from us more regularly, we need to sell each customer more items more frequently, and we need to have these customers sing our praises and create a brand community. We need to get more of our competitor's customers.

In order to achieve all this, we must treat the customer as a loyal, trusted friend. Once you develop that rapport, they will never leave you. But how do you do that? Well, when you are working on selling your product or service to people, you are a consumer just like your customers. So think about how you like to be treated by the suppliers with whom you interact. Take a step back and become one of your own customers.

For example, assume you have been going to the same tailor for several years and they have always been interested in you as a person. They ask after your family and show concern when your kids are ill. They have always been reliable and make you feel special in the clothes they make for you; you always receive lots of compliments when you wear them. Now, let's say that a new tailor shop opens down the street and offers you a 10 percent discount to come and buy from them. Would you try this new place? If you are like the majority of people, you enjoy the fact your regular tailor takes an interest in you. You take comfort in their reliability and you love the fact you always feel good and receive compliments on your clothes. You are not going to risk that, even though the 10 percent discount could represent a saving of $50, or more.

Would advertising the product or even cheaper prices get you to change tailors? Neither of these elements will motivate the majority of consumers if they have an existing good relationship with a vendor they like. It takes something extraordinary, and price is not extraordinary. However, if your current tailor had attracted you on product or price only and had not developed a relationship with you, then there is a good chance you would give the new tailor a try.

How Do You Determine What Your Customer Wants?

How can the new tailor in the preceding example go about attracting the competitor's business? There is no trick here; in my experience, the best way is to simply ask people what they are looking for. Your potential customers will tell you what they want if you engage in dialogue and listen to what they have to say. And don't just listen to the words; actually listen to what they are saying. Often the two can be quite different.

If the current tailor has listened to his customers and is meeting their needs, the chances of a competitor attracting his clientele—or countering the positive word of mouth and brand equity he is building—is very remote. However, if there is a chink in his armor—for example, slow service—then a conversation with potential customers will highlight this. That may be the point of differentiation that the new tailor could use in their marketing to attract customers.

The first tailor's customer dialogue then becomes equally important, as they need to counteract this weakness. They can do this in two ways. The first is to improve the service, although this is not always possible. The second is to turn whatever weakness their competitor has exposed into an advantage. For example, they may emphasize the fact that "buying an outfit from us takes a little longer than with other tailors because every stitch is done by hand, creating a better fitting garment." Though the other tailor may also do every stitch by hand, the customer perception is that the one who promotes it is more meticulous. By telling people they will be a little slower, they turn this weakness into a benefit by convincing the consumer to equate it with a better quality product.

The only person that counts is the customer.

The unfortunate fact is that a very small percentage of businesses consult with their target audience on issues ranging from product design, product packaging, through to marketing strategy. Despite this fact, any company's entire focus must be the customer.

This situation does not apply just to small businesses. In many ways, large companies have even less customer feedback. How else do you explain such expensive failures as the fast-food industry's McDonald's McLean sandwich, KFC's skinless chicken, and Pizza Hut's low-fat pizza? These brands all focus on fun, fast service, and consistently reliable quality. Their regular customers don't go to them to buy the best hamburger, chicken, or pizza in town. Nor do they go to buy healthy food; they know they are eating junk food. So why on Earth would current customers visit these restaurants to buy something even marginally healthier? To that end, it is equally unlikely that health-conscious people will go to a fast-food restaurant to buy marginally more nutritious food than they regularly serve.

The result of these initiatives was very few new customers for these businesses, and little to no consumption of these new products by regulars—despite the fortune spent in advertising, promotion, and other resources. They failed to meet their customer's needs and aspirations. Instead, they focused on the product and lost.

Building Loyalty

Customers' sense of loyalty to most brands is diminishing at a time when its enhancement can have the most profound effect on the bottom line. In their book *Up the Loyalty Ladder,* Murray and Neil Raphel propose the following steps in a customer's evolution:

Prospects –> Shoppers –> Customers –> Clients –> Advocates.

The definition of each is as follows:

> **Prospects**—Most prospects spends 10–15 seconds observing a business's attitudes, atmosphere, and merchandising, and then deciding whether or not to buy. Merely getting more prospects through the door is not the key to success; the objective is getting them to stay once they've entered.
>
> **Shoppers**—If you impress the prospect, they will become a shopper.
>
> **Customers** —Once shoppers buy multiple products from you, they are customers.

Clients–Depending on the added value you provide the customer, they will return regularly and become a client.

Advocates–A highly satisfied client that continues to receive excellent added value will become an advocate—something that's more valuable than any amount of advertising.

Retailing giant Walmart is a hugely successful company that has enjoyed extraordinary success by building giant stores with a very substantial inventory. By cutting out all the frills, minimizing staff, and operating on a very thin margin, they have been able to drastically undercut their competitor's prices. The result has been that, when they build their mega stores in relatively small communities, they literally put dozens of smaller stores out of business. When Walmart decided to open in Decorah, Iowa, the local stores realized that there was no way they could compete on product range or price, since Walmart had 20 times the inventory and was 20–40 percent cheaper on nearly all items. So in order to survive, the small stores had to win the customers' hearts and minds.

The stores formed a local traders' organization and planned a combined strategy. They designed their storefronts to give them all a small-time, friendly, good country-service feel. They trained their staff in old-fashioned friendliness, hospitality, and exceptional customer service. They went overboard to show they cared for the customer. They did everything from park cars, provide coffee and snacks, hand out toys to kids, learn people's names, engage them in conversation; essentially, they showed that they cared. As a result, the town was swamped with shoppers, and the stores' combined sales increased by $30 million in the first year.

These small businesses of Decorah did not run a massive advertising campaign. They did not slash prices or promote products. Instead, they made themselves all about the customer. They concentrated on developing relationships and their businesses, one person's heart at a time.

Remember: The product is what people walk out the door with. It is never what they buy!

Chapter 10

Sell Emotional Benefits, Not Features

This is Marketing 101: Sell benefits, not features! The very first thing we ever learn in marketing is that people *only buy benefits.* They are not motivated to purchase an item or service because of features or attractions; they only do so because these features somehow give them an advantage.

I can hear all of you respond—yes, we all know that, we don't have to be told again. Well, pick up almost any brochure, turn to any display page in the Yellow Pages or a magazine, look at almost all newspaper advertisements or pick practically any direct mail piece. Guess what? They are absolutely full of features, usually about the product. And it only takes one glance to determine why they don't work.

On the way to your office one morning, pay particular attention to the advertisements on the radio.

> On average, less than 20 percent of the ads you will hear will provide a benefit to the listener.

Yet, only those featuring benefits catch people's attention. The others just become the audio version of wallpaper.

To Cut Through the Clutter, You Must Get into the Preconscious Mind

As I have emphasized time and again, it is absolutely vital to differentiate yourself from your competition in this highly competitive and increasingly global and accessible marketplace, to the extent that when anyone thinks of your product or service category, they think of you first. If they don't, then your likelihood of attracting their business is significantly diminished. If they do, then you will at least get an inquiry. Whether you actually convert the sale is up to you, but at least you are in the game.

Therefore, the key is obviously to get into the potential customers' preconscious mind. Because this is a totally emotional region of the brain, it is fair to assume that an emotional trigger will give your product or service recall over that of your competitors.

When you really think about it, isn't every reaction you have in your life emotionally triggered? Why do you cry at the movies, become engrossed in a book, or interact with family and friends? Isn't it true that every decision you have ever made in your life was made because it made you feel emotionally better in some way? Even if it was a decision made in light of a tragedy, the action you took was an emotional response that made you feel better. It was likely one that provided an emotional benefit, albeit perhaps small.

Motivating people to buy a product or service is absolutely no different. The most effective way to impact the consumer—to obtain preconscious-mind recall and to motivate them to purchase *without* a pragmatic evaluation of your product or service against your competitors—is through the selling of emotional benefits.

You need to capture the consumers' hearts, since that is where you want the decisions to be made. Pragmatic benefits aim at the head. This is the one circumstance in which companies actually need to set their sights lower.

Behind Every Pragmatic Benefit Is an Emotional Trigger

When the majority of businesses look at what they can offer their prospective customers, they inevitably come up with a range of pragmatic features or benefits, which may or may not compare with their competitors. The key is to look *behind* this pragmatism and identify the emotional benefit the consumer obtains from the product or service. For example, if you asked a customer why they bought a particular motor lawn mower, they may say that it was because they like the extra horsepower. That is a *feature*. Further discussion may reveal that this additional horsepower means the machine does not stall in long or wet grass. If that is a common complaint among motor lawn mower owners, this emotional benefit is a much more powerful sales motivator than a line that says something along the lines of "New 3 horsepower engine."

Here is a list of the primary selling points on a few mailers that came into our office in just one day:

Headline 1: "Beautiful New Salon, Eight Chairs" Mailer from a hair salon.

This is a feature that represents no benefit to me whatsoever. I have no need for eight chairs; I only have one butt. Perhaps they were trying to convey the fact that there is no waiting at this particular location; however, in a city like Los Angeles that is absolutely teeming with salons that are much bigger (yet still requires you to book weeks and, often, months in advance), this headline is pointless.

However, if they can provide hairstyling on demand, the headline could read: "We will fit your salon appointment around your schedule, not ours."

Headline 2: "G4's with OS 9 starting at $1594!" Mailer from a computer company.

If there hadn't been a graphic of a computer on the postcard I would never have been able to guess what the headline even referred to. I did call the company and ask them who they included in the postcard mailing. The answer? All businesses in the area. This may have worked had it been targeted at computer experts; however, I'm confident that 99 percent of recipients of the postcard would throw it straight in the circular filing cabinet. At the time, the G4 with OS 9 was apparently the fastest desktop ever built, with exceptional graphic and video capabilities. How was I to know that?

A headline that would grab the attention and cause you to read on might be: "You can create award winning graphics and video, more simply and faster than ever."

Headline 3: "Our printing equipment is state of the art, the newest in the country." Mailer from a printer.

Again, this is a feature that offers me absolutely no benefit whatsoever. I need to know things like will the completed job be better or quicker in some way? Will it change the cost? The answers to these questions may be of benefit to me, but maybe not. There is insufficient information for me to even extrapolate into an emotional benefit. However, if, for example, the new equipment really sped up the process, a better headline would be: "The finest quality printing with one day turnaround . . . guaranteed!"

Consumers don't care about you; they care about themselves.

Many business people are so proud of what they have achieved—as well as the trials and tribulations they've faced along the way—that they forget what motivates people to buy. This, of course, is the benefit the customer is going to derive from the purchase. The only exception to this is a story woven around the proprietor that shows extraordinary commitment or sacrifice in order to be able to offer the consumer a product or service that is perceived to be excellent.

On the front page of many brochures, you frequently see a photo of the factory or office, often with an empty parking lot because the photograph was taken on a Sunday morning so the shoot did not disturb anyone. This does not impress the buyer as much as a clear explanation of the benefits they will receive from making the purchase, if it impresses them at all. Our experience with focus groups shows that this kind of building photograph may also trigger other reactions that have a significant potential downside and little upside. If it is a wonderful building, it can convey to some consumers that your product or service is expensive. If the parking lot is empty, it suggests that no one patronizes you; and if the parking lot is full, some people think the service will be slow. On the other hand, it does suggest that you are a solid, reliable company. Yet this can be said just as effectively in a fraction of the space. For example, "Established 1962" or "$10 million in sales" or "Over 10,000 satisfied customers."

> To gain recall, you must sell the emotional benefits your client will obtain from the transaction; you cannot focus on the benefits you will enjoy from obtaining their business.

Look at What the Successful Advertisers Are Doing

The Coca-Cola Company has been advertising their product for over 119 years. Do you ever recall seeing an advertisement that told you it was a brown liquid? First, that is a feature and not a benefit. Second, have you ever seen an ad that tried to explain what Coke tastes like? The Coca-Cola Company has never run one—because, again, that is a feature, not a benefit. When have you seen a Coca-Cola ad focusing on price? Never.

Despite not doing what most advertisers do—that is, basing their message on the offering's features or the price—Coca-Cola has managed to remain one of the top three recognized brands in the world.

So what does Coca-Cola sell? If you are drinking Coca-Cola, you are going to have fun. People want to have fun in this stressed out world. Fun is completely emotional.

Of course, the Coca-Cola Company does have a full, head-to-head competitor, and on the whole, it's been found that Pepsi overwhelmingly wins the taste test war, a fact they actively promote. Yet despite the fact that people prefer Pepsi's taste, Coca-Cola dominates market share on a global basis. Why? Because winning taste tests is not a benefit to the consumer; it doesn't hit their hot button. Neither do slogans such as "Next Generation." But "Fun" does.

Johnson's Baby Powder is a huge worldwide seller that constantly blitzes the competitors. Although the competition focuses on the product and its features, such as absorbency tests that show that their product absorbs an extra volume of liquid, and so on, Johnson's advertising just keeps emphasizing a highly emotional loving mother-child relationship. Mothers are much more attracted to a great relationship with their child than an extra liter of water poured out of a jug!

How Do You Determine the Difference between a Feature and a Benefit?

To distinguish between the two, I simply apply the so-what test. If I can say, "So what?" after the statement, it is a feature; if I can't, then it is a benefit. For example, if a motor vehicle manufacturer advertises that it has developed a new car seat at a cost of $250,000, I then say, "So what?" because they are not giving me a specific benefit. They are suggesting that there is a benefit merely because they spent $250,000. However, because they don't specify what the benefit *is*, the promise is meaningless. However, you would never respond, "So what?" to a statement like, "We spent $250,000 developing a seat that sends out electrical impulses, relaxes your back muscles, and keeps you alert while you are driving." The benefit is clear.

The next step is to ascertain what the major emotional benefit to staying alert is. For example, it may be a concern for the family in case of an accident. The emotional hook used in the marketing of the product may be "Revolutionary new seat protects your children." This is much more powerful to the family market segment than, "A seat that keeps you alert." It is impossible to say, "So what?" to this statement. Therefore, it's a benefit. I, for one, would race out and buy it.

Use Emotional Benefits in All Applications

Any form of communication you design—be it advertisements, brochures, or fliers—must always be consumer friendly. Do not use industry terms that people don't know and do not include loads of information about how wonderful you are. Focus on addressing what will make the customer's life easier; simply doing so makes it easier to convey your product or service's benefits. If you do use measurements or statistics, spell out precisely *how* this information is advantageous to the customer. Focus on clearly and concisely spelling out the emotional benefits the potential client will obtain from becoming your customer. After the initial warm-and-fuzzies in the first sentence of a sales letter to a potential client, eliminate all sentences that do not provide the reader with the pragmatic and resultant emotional benefit. You do not have time in today's fast paced world to write meaningless sentences and the recipient does not have time to read them.

I often have people tell me during my seminars that they understand how selling emotional benefits applies in retail or in a service industry. However, they protest, they sell widgets or heavy equipment business to business. How does this philosophy apply to them?

It applies in exactly the same way. Everyone has an emotional trigger; it is up to the sales or marketing team to determine what that is. The purchasing officer that buys your widget or heavy equipment may be motivated by a number of sentiments: pride in his buying choices, ego gratification by finding a better solution than is currently being used, fear of purchasing a product that might not be totally proven, concern over the financial viability of one of your competitors, a desire to help a cause, an interest in helping minority businesses, and so on. To get the sale, you need to differentiate yourself from your competition by highlighting the emotional benefits that hit his or her hot button, irrespective of the industry or product.

Remember: People are all driven by emotion. To achieve success, focus on emotional benefits, not on meaningless features.

Chapter 11

Positively Outrageous Service Is Great Business

There is only one boss in every business: the customer. They can fire everyone in the company, from the chairman down, simply by spending their money somewhere else. Remember, your employer does not pay your wages; your customers do!

> The customer does not care about you. They care about *them*. Tell them something interesting and treat them the way they expect to be treated, or they will go away.

Back in 1993, founder of clothing manufacturer Espirit, John Bell, said, "Today, service is not an issue; without great service you are out of business." This statement, although relevant then, is even more relevant today. There is an increasing emphasis on providing good service, mainly because today's customers will accept nothing less. But giving good service is like giving value. You will never develop heart share and the resulting critical brand equity and customer loyalty by giving people merely what they deserve. Your customer care must extend over and above their expectations.

Make no mistake: Their expectations are higher than ever. Despite the apparent emphasis on customer service over the past 10 years, the *Harvard Business Review* shows that customer satisfaction rates in the United States are at an all-time low, whereas complaints and boycotts are rapidly rising. Why? Because customer expectations have doubled in the last two years and customers are harder to satisfy. Research suggests that more than 60 percent of service is not only far from awesome; it is actually *below acceptable*.

> Although there are many reasons for this decrease in customer satisfaction, the primary one is that, in most industries, people want to deal with people.

Unfortunately, many companies have made the mistake of taking people out of the entire process. Their use of answering machines, multiple prompts, online generic answers to questions, offshore call centers, and so on are substantially hurting relationships with customers.

A high percentage of customer-relationship management programs (CRM) have been more about reducing staff and increasing contact through-put than about providing what the customer regards as better service. Indeed, one of the primary reasons for the extremely high failure rate in the dot-com industry was the lack of customer service and human interaction.

But wait. Aren't the plethora of CRM programs out there designed to improve customer service?

I was the keynote speaker at the global CRM conference in Paris a couple of years ago and studied the sales pitches at the event for over 40 leading CRM products. All stressed benefits, such as cut staff, save money, or reduce processing time. This does not sound like customer service to me; the customer doesn't even get a mention in most of the material. Most CRM programs are a synonym for "cut heads, increase productivity."

Truly customer-centric, specially tailored CRM programs are the tool that will drive the companies of the future. However, is it likely to make much difference to any but the few rare companies today that have a long-term perspective? Have most companies merely embraced CRM because some nerd on staff has espoused it as the quick-fix, end-to-end solution to improve relationships and reduce costs of staff, turnaround times, and so forth? Unfortunately, this nerd has found dedicated listeners in the finance people who run today's companies and who are, in the main, totally obsessed with this quarter's financials and the resulting stock price.

There is almost a complete disconnect between the members of the finance division and the marketers who keep talking about a variety of topics: long-term relationships, understanding customers, knowing their past and present needs, trying to anticipate their future needs, customization, developing a long-term sustainable advantage. The financial guys can't work out why marketers don't understand that this stuff takes both time and money?

Do the financial people even care about spending more time talking to the customer? What is wrong with pouring buckets of money into totally ineffective but immediately explainable (even if illogical) one-size-fits-all monologue advertising? After all, we have been doing it for years. Do financial people even understand what dialogue *is*? Or do marketers simply not grasp that the financial people need to be persuaded that it is not just cutting heads and acquisitions that drive stock prices?!

> Are CRM programs—once thought to be the ultimate people solutions— being designed and sold by individuals who have no people skills whatsoever?

Isn't CRM just a faster and more efficient way of returning us to the good old days when dialogue was in vogue, when suppliers knew that Mrs. Jones had three kids named Tommy, Billy, and Zachariah who play football and need a dozen Krispy Kreme donuts every Sunday morning from the first of September through January?

If so, why have we screwed up the customer/supplier relationship so badly?

Of course, the other solution to building customer relationships is the notorious *call center*. There has been an explosion in call centers over the past several years; indeed, it is now the fastest growing business in the world. However, if I have a problem with my product in Boise, Idaho, and the guy at the call center, even though he is great, is sitting 7,000 miles away in Karachi, never having been out of Pakistan, the first requirement of good customer service—empathy—is nonexistent.

However, that's another subject. I'll get back to my original point:

> There are four elements that are no longer important in marketing today: the product, price, brand awareness, and satisfied customers, the four pillars upon which the industry has built its very foundation.

Not one of these is worth a damn in today's information-driven, increasingly competitive marketplace, with its proliferation of communication vehicles, increased media clutter, customer skepticism, and overload.

Despite the quality of the product or service, a marketing strategy and its advertising campaign really fly when there is an absolute, direct connection between the emotional message being conveyed (or the closing techniques being employed) and the customer's desire. In order for our communication vehicles to really work, we must focus on company-customer links, while ignoring disconnects that dilute or confuse the message or, in the case of the four traditional pillars, are completely unrelated elements. Indeed, none of these four components are even remotely significant to today's customer; none of them cause a company–potential customer connection. Although each of these elements is a consideration, none is critical. For any of them to be a focus of the message is a recipe for excessive marketing costs, low return on marketing investment, decreased profitability, poor shareholder returns, and an invitation for eventual takeover.

The majority of marketing and advertising materials—whether TV, radio, print, billboards, Internet, or a brochure—almost all focus on one or a combination of these four elements. Honest marketers will admit that they are disappointed with the results they obtain from their campaigns 90 percent of the time. They seldom perform to expectations, except in cases in which the marketer is a seasoned professional who has been broken in by years of poor performance and, therefore, is mentally conditioned for low expectations.

> Fortunately, the marketers behind these unsuccessful campaigns are extremely creative. They are usually able to effectively blame insufficient budgets, the economy, government policy, competitive initiatives . . . in fact, anything that sounds plausible.

God forbid they look in the mirror or take stock of the fact that the world has changed from being supply-and-demand driven to being demand-and-supply driven.

Why Good Service Is Good Business

Evidence from a host of studies has shown conclusively that high customer satisfaction provides enhanced customer loyalty, staff motivation, and satisfaction, along with strong growth and positive financial results. Research at the U.S. Service Intelligence shows that customer service is, on average, four times more important to customers than price. Perceived service leaders grow twice as fast as their competition and improve market share by up to 6 percent per annum compared with a 2 percent loss for poor service performance businesses. They also have a return on sales 12 percent higher than the average.

Companies today cannot underestimate the importance of loyalty. United Kingdom bank First Direct established a 24-hour banking system that focused on precisely what customers want; speed, convenience, great service, and value for money. By doing so, they attained the highest rate of customer satisfaction in the British financial services industry, with 38 percent of new customers being referred by existing ones. It is extremely difficult for competitors to attack First Direct's customer base. Let me tell you about a couple of examples that happened to me recently.

I recently phoned a motor dealership near me to inquire about leasing a new vehicle for a member of our team. I was greeted by a recorded message that informed me, 'Thank you for calling. Currently all our operators are busy, but we appreciate your business. Please hold for a moment; your call is important to us."

No thanks. I called another dealership, which answered immediately, sent a car to pick me up, and introduced me to the key people in the organization. Guess which one got my business?

One of the most competitive industries in the world right now is tele-communications. Our office phones in Los Angeles suddenly went dead one day, so we placed several calls to the carrier and did not receive a call back. We finally got in touch with an operator who grumpily asked us, "How am I supposed to know what your problem is? I'm 1,500 miles away." We were then promptly disconnected. I have since found out that there is quite a bit of pressure on call centers to keep to a certain statistical average time for dealing with inquiries. Consequently, up to 20 percent of calls get transferred to another party and either cut off or transferred back to the end of the line to meet these averages.

There are many companies who fully understand the importance of providing great customer service. For example, Jiffy Lube President Rick Altizer states: "We're not going to build this company by servicing cars, we're going to build it by servicing customers."

Zappos began in 1999 selling shoes online and have continuously expanded their range. In 2010 their turnover exceeded $1 billion. CEO Tony Hsieh has initiated a number of programs and policies that the majority of corporate America regarded as financial suicide. One initiative encourages customers to call the company about absolutely everything. Their domestic call center takes in excess of 5,000 calls a day and employees do not have scripts, quotas, or call-time limits. The longest call to date is in excess of four hours. Zappos views the phone experience as a branding device and speaks to every customer on the phone.

Most companies have very strict controls on call centers, compete on price not service, reign in service costs, and implement call times and upsell rates that their agents must meet.

One of the best examples of what can be achieved by providing extraordinary service is Snap-on tools who, through 4,500 franchises, sell to 1.25 million car and truck mechanics worldwide. In this age of mounting online servicing, *Snap-on* has 6,000 dealers who *personally visit* each one of their 300 customers each and every week. Each van carries $200,000 worth of merchandise, from $1.50 spark plugs to a $40,000 diagnostic system. Most of their mechanic clients spend $30,000 on *Snap-on* tools in their career, which the dealers encourage customers to pay off bit by bit . . . with no plan . . . and no interest!

Snap-on vehicles are 90 percent computerized, and sell half their products with a hardware component. To address their new technology focus, Snap-on put 300 training vehicles on the road to visit customer sites at dealers' request. Dealers check their laptops at each stop to see what products they already have and what they may have asked about at the last visit. Snap-on charges premium prices, 10 percent more than competitors; they never discount; and they have never deviated from their premium brand. They also spend no money on advertising. Their remarkable focus on exceptional customer service allows Snap-on to generate some $2.5 billion a year in sales, maintain a 60 percent market share, and make 10 percent net profit. The company also has an electronic arm, Snap-on online.

How Good Is *Your* Customer Service?

Despite the fact that 92 percent of CEOs believe customer service is critical to differentiate their key products and services, 70 percent report difficulty in aligning their business around customers. To that end, let me ask you a couple of questions:

◆ Have you been delighted, excited, or overwhelmed by a great customer-service experience in the last 12 months?

◆ Has your company given someone else a great customer service experience lately?

Unfortunately, most people answer no to both questions. If you did the same, ask yourself these questions:

◆ Can every person in your company explain how they add value to the customer?
◆ Is your customer focus only applicable to people in the sales and service realms?
◆ Do your internal values match your external values?
◆ Do your employee performance measures encourage great service and development of long-term relationships?
◆ Do you regard your staff as a key source of differentiation from your competitors?

If you did not answer yes to all five questions, well—you have some work to do.

Too many businesses have been slow to realize that it is not their product, brand awareness, advertising, or price that drives sales. Your competitors can offer each of these also. It is the quality of the relationship they have with you that people appreciate, long after they have forgotten the price and the product.

In the United States, 21 percent of customers leave banks because of poor service—nearly double the number that leave because of interest rates. 27 percent of women abandon a hair salon because of poor service, yet only 13 percent leave because of a bad haircut; and while 67 percent of patrons do not return to a restaurant because of bad service, only 18 percent do so because of the poor quality food.

> The driver of four out of every five sales today is not advertising, price, or product—it is word of mouth.

Word of mouth occurs as a result of the equity you have built up with the customer. What percentage of your new customers come to you due to word of mouth? If it is not in the 60–80 percent range, your customer service needs a critical review—urgently.

An Excellent Customer Relationship Management Program Is the Answer

Customer-relationship management (CRM) is hailed as the single tool that will drive the companies of the future. It is the biggest application area of all time, with a global market estimated to be worth $9.6 billion in 2008.

CRM's primary objective is to create a seamless, transparent relationship with customers by understanding their past and present purchasing tendencies, and using that knowledge to anticipate their future needs, thereby enabling customization and developing relationships and customer loyalty.

To date, however, not many companies have grasped the importance of CRM. For example, I just got my 53rd letter from American Express offering me a credit card, which would be great, if I hadn't had one since 1972. American Express should obviously know this; they have certainly sent me enough bills over the years!

Strong customer relationships take time to build. Unfortunately, the overwhelming majority of companies are controlled by financially minded individuals who are primarily concerned with the end-of-quarter bottom line and the stock prices. It appears that many companies jumped on the CRM bandwagon because some financial person has bought the quick-fix end-to-end solution sold by an overzealous, high-pressure software hawker. Other companies simply did not want to miss the boat, and have tried to upgrade former e-commerce tools and disguise them as CRM packages. In fact, Sam Clark, in his role as senior research analyst for Meta Group, was quoted as saying "More vendors will lie about CRM than any other area of enterprise software."

The Standard CRM Line

The majority of sales pitches for CRM claim that this tool will:

◆ Revolutionize business
◆ Cut costs
◆ Cut staff
◆ Make turnaround quicker (product, responses, service, etc.)
◆ Improve customer relationships

At the CRM conference in Paris, I mentioned earlier a plethora of CRM software companies exhibited programs designed to assist businesses develop loyal and returning customers.

Prior to my presentation, I gathered all the marketing and promotional materials and customer service manuals from the exhibitors—a total of 136 pieces in all. I made a list of the stated principal benefits of the CRM products being offered and then counted the total number of references to each of these benefits.

I have listed the stated benefits here in order of frequency of mention, as well as my comments on each of these from the customer's perspective. After all, CRM is supposed to be about the customer.

- ◆ **Simplify scheduling** (373 mentions). This may be a benefit to the company implementing the program, but is it a benefit to their customer? It could possibly lead to increased efficiency. Arguable benefit to the customer.
- ◆ **Reduce overstaffing** (318 mentions). This will reduce the company's cost but it is unlikely to lead to better relationships with their customers. More automation, less people contact. Is this a benefit to the customer? No.
- ◆ **Increase revenue** (313 mentions). This revenue increase is achieved by the company implementing the CRM by slashing costs in managing their customers, not from helping them generate repeat business from the customers. Is this a benefit to the customer? No.
- ◆ **Fast, flexible, and powerful** (246 mentions). Is this a benefit to the customer? Maybe, but it is worded in such a vague manner, how are they to know?
- ◆ **Innovative design** (213 mentions). Is this a benefit to the customer? Maybe, but more likely it refers to ease of implementation by the company.
- ◆ **Easy to implement** (205 mentions). Is this a benefit to the customer? Maybe, as above.
- ◆ **Cost effective** (173 mentions). Is this a benefit to the customer? Unlikely, because client is likely to provide the same customer service at less cost.
- ◆ **Improves customer satisfaction** (108 mentions). *Wow,* one that is actually a specific benefit for the customer!

Of the eight principal benefits promoted, only one can really be described as being of true benefit to the end customer and that was mentioned the least number of times. It quickly became apparent to me that the primary focus for a lot of CRM software developers is really to enable operating efficiency, chop heads, and slash costs.

Is There a Gulf between Finance and Marketing Departments?

The software sales nerd appears to have a dedicated listener in the finance people who is focused on:

◆ Running the company
◆ Maximizing the bottom line for the quarter
◆ Reducing overheads
◆ Seeking acquisitions
◆ Increasing shareholder value
◆ Selling their options (sorry, cheap shot)
◆ Priming the books (sorry, another cheap shot!)

On the other hand, the marketing and sales departments are (or should be) focused on:

◆ Developing long-term relationships
◆ Understanding customers
◆ Knowing customers' past and current needs
◆ Predicting future needs
◆ Increasing sales and revenue per customer
◆ Customization
◆ Developing long-term sustainable advantage

The financial wizards seem to argue that marketers need to understand that all these things cost both time and money. The marketers say that the financial people do not even care about talking to the customer.

Many financial people have never heard of the word *dialogue*.

CRM is nothing new to me. Our organization has always known that treating customers as individuals, showing empathy, solving their challenges and developing products to meet their future needs is great business. In my younger years, every shopkeeper knew your name, was interested in your family's well-being, and anticipated your likely requirements.

So what has caused the recent disconnect? In my view, there are two reasons:

1. Many large companies have operated under the assumption that globalization—and, therefore, marketplace size—would allow them to maintain high churn rates with plenty more customer fodder where they came from.
2. Marketers have failed to properly communicate to management the profit benefits to be gained from the loving-the-customer-to-death side of CRM.

This disconnect cannot continue because:

◆ Dow Jones statistics show that the average corporation loses 50 percent of its customer base every five years.
◆ The arguments for implementing a truly customer-focused CRM program are overwhelming.

In our current demand-and-supply economy—one that focuses on mass customization and uses the new technologies such as interactive TV, Internet, social media, e-mail, and PDAs to build relationships—the flow of information is a two-way street. Companies can gather, store, sort, and maintain highly detailed information on their customers, keep it available to everyone in the company that has any influence on the customer's opinion, and do it in real time. Customers can also obtain masses of information, product comparisons, critiques from satisfied and dissatisfied users, and all manner of advice on companies and their products. Therefore, companies today must understand and relate to their customers—consistently.

> Unfortunately, too many companies still think of customers in terms of numbers and processes.

They still consider themselves and what they do to be the most important part of the exchange. The business, product, and price are their primary focus. They don't realize that customers only care about their own needs.

CRM Is Not Technology

CRM is not about technology, software, or systems; it is about listening, empathizing, relating, and customizing. Eighty percent of CRM is—or should be—about people. It cannot merely focus on investing in database capability and system integration. It must involve a combination of information-based technology, relationship building, and marketing and sales skills to deliver a unique customer experience.

We use technology to store and compare information. We *need* to use it to build unique relationships with customers. We need to source all possible information about an individual, and use it for his or her benefit.

There Are Rifts within Organizations

One major problem occurs when different departments within companies do not understand each other, and operate under totally different philosophies. Many companies only introduce CRM into their sales and marketing divisions. However, the whole organization must be involved and converted to a totally customer-centric company in order for CRM to work. It must be fully embraced and introduced from the top down.

> Companies need to be offline, online, and in line.

Implementing CRM Is Not Easy

CRM must be customized for every business. No two customers or two companies are alike. Because most CRM systems require major changes in business processes throughout the company, many staff members resist this change. This reluctance is exacerbated if the system is technologically complex or if there is lack of staff training.

There is no one-size-fits-all CRM solution, and a great CRM solution is very difficult to achieve. However, it's also necessary.

Why CRM Must Be Customer Centric

It is up to marketers to educate management about how the benefits of excellent service greatly outweigh the benefits of advertising and one-time sales. Here is some great ammunition:

1. In the 2007 PriceWaterhouseCoopers CEO survey of 402 of the fastest growing businesses in the United States, the sources of ROI were:
   • Customer service, 31 percent
   • New products, 16 percent
   • Advertising and promotion, 8 percent
   • IT, 3 percent
       In other words, customer service made *four times* the contribution of advertising to the ROI.
2. For driving company growth, the same survey showed:
   • Customer service, 87 percent
   • Product improvement, 62 percent
   • Advertising and promotion, 58 percent
       Therefore, customer service is 50 percent more powerful in driving growth than advertising and promotion.
3. The Harvard Graduate School study by James Collins and Jerry Porras, cited earlier in this book, showed that the order of priority in 94.4 percent of successful companies was: customers, staff, product, and then profit. Companies whose primary focus was product and profit were less successful financially, had less empowerment of staff, less experimentation, held more meetings, and were less creative.
4. A recent survey by *Harper's Bazaar* magazine showed that in this new age of brand communities, the average person tells 355 people of a good customer experience. A review of the so-called benefits of the CRM products as promoted at the CRM conference in Paris shows a very heavy emphasis on product and profit, which in my view is a major mistake.

Hopefully, companies are beginning to get it.

Online Business Generally Fails the Awesome-Customer-Service Test

The web has created a culture in which, from the moment they log onto a website, customers expect 24-hour, online, quality personalized service. Successful online companies have focused on highly personalized service including "me" mail instead of e-mail, and they have introduced human communication to their sites by engaging traditional call centers. A recent AchieveGlobal study showed that reintroducing people into online communication through call centers increases customer satisfaction by 59 percent and improves customer loyalty by 44 percent.

Why is it so difficult to give good service? The corporations I speak to about this always concur that service is critical to success. Yet when I ask whether they have a budget for staff training in customer service, or whether they have a focused service and added-value strategy, they usually answer no.

I find it ridiculous that so many companies have a substantial budget for expensive advertising that—although frequently credited for attracting new customers—only draws, at best, between 20 and 40 percent of their business. However, they've established little to no budget for service and added value, which is the primary low-cost contributor to 60–80 percent of their business. Go figure!

What Do Customers Want?

The customer service playing field is leveling off in today's highly competitive market. Any customer who does not receive the highest level of quality and service will buy their product or obtain their service elsewhere. Companies today need a proactive dedicated approach to attracting customers.

CRM research conducted by Zeithaml, Berry, and Parasuraman showed that the five most important things to customers are:

1. **Reliability**–Delivery of promises
2. **Responsiveness**–Willingness to help, time on hold, speed of response
3. **Assurance**–Inspiring trust and confidence, technical knowledge, communication skill.
4. **Empathy**–Treating customers as individuals
5. **Tangibles**–Service, price, delivery, etc.

Awesome customer service is not only the key to word of mouth; it is critical to retaining existing clients.

Why Is It So Vital to Keep Existing Customers?

Well, for several reasons:

♦ It costs 5–15 times more to attract a new customer than to retain an existing one, depending on the industry.

◆ Existing customers who use your services or product are quick to inform you of problems or suggest beneficial changes.

◆ Existing customers are easier to attract *back*, satisfy, and are walking advertisements for your business.

◆ Loyal customers will pay higher prices, therefore, producing higher profitability.

◆ Loyal, repeat customers reduce the marketing and solicitation cost per customer.

Excellent Service Is Critical for Online Businesses

Consumers are still experimenting on the Internet to some degree, and recent studies show that up to 30 percent of web buyers are returning to their traditional buying sources. Providing great service will be the key to getting customers coming back. Some of the keys to retaining online customers are:

◆ Provide downloads as fast as possible and immediately highlight benefits, added value, and risk reversal.

◆ Quickly and simply answer customer questions.

◆ Advise customers immediately if a product is out of stock.

◆ Emphasize online transaction security.

◆ Recommend other products that meet the customer's profile or are an adjunct to their purchase.

◆ Provide information on use or caring for the purchase.

Web Sites and Customer Service

Look at your site from the customer's perspective. Determine what the most frequently asked questions are and have a prominent frequently asked questions (FAQ) page. It is critical to make sure you actually *answer* the questions. For example, when someone asks about warranties or guarantees, they are also asking about reliability and performance.

The best way to figure out what questions are most often posed is to extract all the customer information you can from the members of your team that interact with current and potential customers. Remember to always answer the questions in the customer's language, not industry-speak jargon. You must keep information on your web site simple for most users, and make more complex details available for those who want it.

We advise our clients to have two levels of FAQs: one for new customers who are finding out about your products and one for existing customers who are likely to have totally different questions. They should differentiate between the questions and answers by color, size, and font on the web pages. It is also a good idea to use hypertext, which allows a user to click on a word and find out more about that subject, and makes the web page a true educational tool.

> Think about it: A high percentage of online customers are there in the first place because they are not getting a memorable experience at traditional vendors.

You need to give them the experience, level of service, and added value they are seeking. Irrespective of what a business does, whether online or offline, those that really care for their customers are those that will be successful.

How Much Is Your Customer Really Worth?

Too few businesses consider the importance of future-customer value. The amount that the average customer will spend over the next decade in a supermarket is more than $50,000; $120,000 on motor vehicles; $35,000 in restaurants; and $9,000 on clothing. Because each one of your customers will tell up to 10 others about your fantastic service, that customer is worth 10 times the amount they directly spend with you. For example, a customer who spends $30.00 per week at a dry cleaner and is an advocate of the business is worth $15,000 to that company each year.

This realization can influence many of your decisions For example, do you really want to argue with a customer over whether a lost shirt was worth $50 or $100? In the perspective of what they spend weekly, a $50 difference seems significant. However, in comparison with their annual value to your business, it is really insignificant.

How to Develop Great Customer Service

There are two aspects to customer care: One is to provide awesome service, and the second is to add value to every interaction with the customer. We will cover added value further in the following chapter; for now, keep in mind that the key to providing exceptional service lies in the quality of your companies' people management.

> A recent 10-year study by Sheffield University in England demonstrated that people management is three times as important as research and development in improving productivity and profitability, and six times more important than business strategy.

For successful management, a high emotional quotient (a measure of self-awareness, self-control, motivational ability, empathy, and social skills) was more than twice as important as intellectual skills. These are also the skills that are essential to creating a customer-centric culture in a company. For that reason, the first step in developing an excellent customer service culture is to hire the right people.

A Great Service Culture Must Permeate Your Entire Organization

Many businesses believe that the only employees who need great customer service skills are those on the front line. However, you'd be surprised how many members of your team actually deal with customers. Take our business as an example. Our clients don't just speak with me; they also speak with a number of other people in the company throughout the course of a project, including receptionists, researchers, graphics people, and so on. Irrespective of their role, all employees must project the same enthusiasm for the client that I do, and they do, because that is an ingrained part of our company culture. Look at your own company; you may be surprised at how many members of your team come in contact with the customer. Do they all share your customer values? If not, your business is at risk.

A significant number of companies have restructured over the past five years, resulting in a loss of many middle-management positions. One of the major reasons for this change in the management structure is many companies' realization that they must pay more attention to the customer. They are beginning to realize that everything begins and ends with the customer, and that customers must be an intrinsic focus of the company. Every action must add value to the customer and everyone must focus on customer benefits. We need to work with customers and empower our staff to solve their issues, whether they are in research and development, sales, management, marketing, reception, or a delivery driver.

One of the reasons that online retailer Amazon.com has achieved exceptional brand equity is because it has empowered its customer service representatives to do anything to satisfy the customer. They can even buy books at the corner bookstore to satisfy a customer! One afternoon I got a call from a person at Amazon.com at my home in California because someone in Australia had ordered one of my books that was 10 years out of print. I had a copy, so Amazon.com sent it via Federal Express to their customer in Australia. The cost of the Federal Express was almost double what the client had paid for the book. In addition, Amazon.com paid me my wholesale cost.

One of my favorite sayings is that "It is easier to change people, than it is to change people." In other words: Don't employ your team based on hard skills, qualifications, and experience. Instead, hire them for their smiles, customer skills, and attitudes. You can teach technical skills; you cannot, however, train people on how to smile and be nice to others. It's simple enough: Hire people who like and are liked by other people.

> The best customer service is delivered by people who see things as the customers see them, not as the company sees them.

There are two types of customers in any organization: internal and external. In order to maintain a highly cohesive and motivated work force, exceptional service with internal customers is as important as it is with external ones. Coupled with a good environment and a shared vision, quality internal relations influence external customers. If any of your personnel do not have a positive attitude, replace them before the cancer spreads.

The Quality of Service Is a Reflection of the Workplace Environment

There is a direct correlation between the environment in which the staff member operates and the level and quality of service they give to both fellow internal team members and the external customer. We must do three things to maximize the level of service our employees offer. First, we must *create an environment that encourages high morale and enthusiasm*. This relates both to the corporate culture and the physical environment. With regard to corporate culture, there are two aspects to take into account. These are:

1. **Hard**–The product, service, price, and so on.
2. **Soft**–The emotional experience, customer relationships, ambiance, and so on. Both must be managed and integrated.

Many companies have been very progressive when it comes to the physical environment they design. British Airways developed a glass structure premises built around a cobblestone street, complete with coffee shops, stereos, jukeboxes, beer gardens, and barbecue areas. This environment encourages creativity and enhances staff morale. There are companies in our Los Angeles office building that have included recreation space for employees with music lounge areas and poolrooms. An increasing number of companies with 100+ employees are installing coffee shops, dispensing free lattes and cappuccinos during the day, and converting to an after-work bar in the evening.

The second essential point is to make sure that all members of the team understand the company's vision and direction.

> We cannot merely provide information on a need-to-know basis; rather, we must share it freely and empower all personnel to make decisions that positively affect relationships with customers.

Employees who share the vision and feel like stakeholders care more, are more enthusiastic, and give more to customers.

It is the employees' attitude to the job that makes it interesting, not the job itself. I recall the story about two bricklayers working on St. Paul's Cathedral in London. When asked what they did, one said he was a bricklayer. The other replied that he was helping Sir Christopher Wren build a great cathedral. When President Kennedy was touring NASA he stopped to talk to a janitor. The janitor told the President he was proud to be part of the team putting a man on the moon. People with this type of attitude truly go the extra mile.

Listening to your employees and granting them greater autonomy both elevates their self-esteem and produces excellent results. Front line personnel who constantly face criticism for things beyond their control become disillusioned, which inevitably leads to apathy, increased staff turnover, and mounting costs. Therefore, it is vitally important to empower the people who are best able to make decisions about the customers' needs.

Lawn care manufacturer Victa provides an example of how this can help a company. Though the organization had three quality inspectors on their assembly line, it was still facing severe quality-control problems. They fired these three inspectors and gave the 30 existing employees license to inspect the work up to their point in the process. This resulted in significant increases in quality, a reduction in the number of product rejects, and it decreased absenteeism.

The titles that you give your employees can make a substantial difference as well. Doing little things like calling staff customer consultants rather than shop assistants can greatly enhance self-esteem. At Ovations!, a company in Australia that provides motivational and professional speakers, Leanne Christie is the CEO, that is, The Chief of Everything Ovations, Jan Sinclair is the ESP, Extraordinary Service Professional. These girls really live up to their titles, they are interesting, a talking point, and inspiring.

The third thing to do is to reward team members as meaningful contributors, not just doers. Link performance management and rewards to learning, innovation, business process, financial performance, customer service, and satisfaction. Sears department store did this successfully by introducing employee bonuses and incentives into the company. One-third of the bonus was based on the employee attitude, one-third on customer measurements, and one-third came from traditional financial assessments. Other companies provide incentives for a host of initiatives including attending customer-service seminars or providing innovative ideas.

It is also important to reward staff when they engage in behavior beyond their normal duties or performance—such as meeting exceptional deadlines or doing a job well at extremely busy times—by providing additional staff discounts, gift vouchers, or other tokens of appreciation.

A Customer-Centric Company Culture
Begins with Leadership

It is important to realize that developing great customer service in your organization is not as simple as holding a seminar and informing employees, "This is how it is done." It is not about rote learning, or as simple as Step 1.

Smile; Step 2. Ask, "Would you like fries with that"? There must be a culture change before you can begin training. Training without having executives set a genuine example will only be met with cynicism and distrust.

The problem is that most people who attend training get inspired for a short period, and then immediately revert back to their old ways. In order to be effective, we must *continue* training and lead by example.

> People are not born optimistic or pessimistic; they learn either outlook over a period of time.

Habits must be reprogrammed. To that end, it can take years to change an organization's culture.

Too many employees' self-esteem and personal attitude (SEPA) levels—a measure of how they feel about themselves—are often very low. This is reflected in the poor-me syndrome often referred to as learned helplessness. In his book *Learned Optimism,* American psychologist Dr. Martin Seligman claims that "75% of the people in the world are graduates of 'learned helplessness' and pessimism." In order to overcome this state, you need to consistently treat staff the same way that you want them to treat customers.

Creating an arbitrary set of customer-service rules for your organization is nowhere near as effective as leading by your own example. Effective leadership cannot be achieved by command or a thick rulebook. A successful company will define where it is going, why and how it is going to get there. This ethic needs to be instilled from senior management down, and standardized into the culture in a non-negotiable way. We must use positive and empowering language and avoid any negatives. This establishes a set of core values that serves as a benchmark for everyone's performance. These corporate core values bring out the best in the employees' personal values by changing work ethic into a cause. Staff will emulate management that they admire and respect.

There is obviously going to be some element of risk in empowering employees. Managers need to be comfortable with this, and not feel threatened by a loss of control.

> The most successful leaders always employ people that have more skills in specific areas than they do.

The more these managers encourage, nurture, and develop their employees' talent—and the more empowered employees feel—the more cumulative power goes back to the leader. He or she will then reap the benefits of a highly motivated team.

One of the reasons that people like the Virgin Group's CEO, Sir Richard Branson, are so admired by their staff is because they will do their employees' jobs. Branson is more than willing to work as a cabin steward or as a baggage handler. He listens to his employees and genuinely understands their roles and challenges.

Chick-Fil-A restaurants' CEO, Don Cathy, is another great example of this. Cathy picks up new personnel at 8:00 A.M. for a full day of driving around and explaining the history of the company. He shows them the first store, and communicates his pride in the company. At the end of the day, he takes the new personnel to his home for dinner—and Cathy employs 80 new people each year!

One of our clients, the manager of a Walmart store, was asked to deal with an irate woman who was returning five gallons of paint. She complained, "We had made all of the arrangements to paint our home this weekend, and your staff mixed the wrong color." She then demanded a refund of $110.

"Certainly, Madam," answers our client. "We will refund you the $110, and we will replace the paint with the right color at no cost. But you must promise me that you will always shop at Walmart."

"Why should I?" retorted the woman.

"Because we don't stock this paint. You purchased it up the road at K-Mart." The woman realized her mistake, and Walmart won a customer for life—worth infinitely more than $110.

USAA insurance sent a full refund for the vehicle insurance premiums paid to all their clients who were U.S. servicemen in Afghanistan. This great goodwill gesture not only attracted countless other enlisted clients, it also prompted excellent word of mouth in the greater community.

Outstanding customer service is not an act that can be turned on or off. It is something we must internalize, live, believe, and unconditionally deliver!

How do we know what the customer *really* wants and expects?

Supplying outstanding customer service requires us to constantly exceed the customer's expectations, but how do we know what these are? The current competitive environment makes it absolutely essentially that we conduct thorough customer research to obtain the information needed to gain the competitive edge. This research's objectives should be to identify customers' needs, expectations, and perceptions of service, as well as motivators and inhibitors.

> The key to delivering first-rate customer service is to understand exactly what the customer perceives to be an acceptable level of service—and what they perceive as value.

We find, all too often, that something we regard as excellent service or added value is simply deemed by customers to be their entitlement. At the same time, we may supply something that our customers don't need, expect, or appreciate when an alternative would be more effective in building brand equity. Don't waste time or money on what the customer sees as unnecessary. For example, while some banks have spent a fortune cutting waiting times from five to three minutes, customers didn't even notice the difference. That same money and effort would have been better spent keeping the banks open an extra hour on Saturday—something customers would have *really* appreciated.

Delivering superb service goes hand in hand with another one of today's keystones of successful business: the risk reversal. This simply means that you guarantee that you will deliver what customers expect from your product or service. Some examples of this include supermarkets that give you everything in your basket free if you wait in line for more than five minutes; hotels that give you breakfast for free if it is not delivered to your room within a certain period of time; or a car wash that washes your car again if they haven't done the job 100 percent to your satisfaction. One hospital in the United States even offers 25 percent off your hospital bill if you are not admitted in 20 minutes.

Understanding customer perceptions gives businesses a substantial advantage. There is a famous story about Stew Leonard, founder of the U.S. supermarket chain of the same name. Stew always makes an attempt to form close bonds with both customers and staff. One way in which he does so is by holding weekly breakfast meetings with randomly selected customers. At one of these meetings, one woman made a comment that the supermarket's fish would be better if it was fresh. Though the fish *was* delivered fresh every day, it was then cut and packed in Styrofoam boxes – a step that likely diminished the product's appeal. So, by way of experiment, the supermarket put 50 percent of the fish in the Styrofoam packs and laid the other 50 percent out on beds of ice.

Sales of the fish laid on ice went through the roof. This was clearly a case where listening to a totally incorrect assumption by one customer more than doubled the sales of one brand's product.

Regularly Audit Your Customer Service Performance

Successful companies don't just stop at delivering what their customers want the first time. They regularly conduct extensive research to ensure that their customer service exceeds expectations on an ongoing basis. This research needs to be multipoint and needs to encompass all the contact points between your business and your customers. For example, if you're reviewing your delivery performance, you must speak to the people taking the orders and those making the deliveries, along with your customers.

Research also needs to be ongoing. It was not that long ago that people were happy to know what day the product was being delivered or the repairman was coming. Now they want to know a specific time, and they want it on a day and time that is convenient for them.

Keep Research Totally Independent

Independent feedback—using techniques such as 1-800 numbers, focus groups, mystery shoppers, or customer service surveys—is critical. No matter how well intended they are, in-house personnel are too frequently not as objective as they need to be. They occasionally fail to ask the only question that counts: "Are we totally meeting customer expectations—or are we missing the mark?" The answers to this question will provide a link between your actions and the customer's reaction to those actions.

It is also imperative to conduct regular customer audits. Let's say that you worked in retail. You would review factors such as staff performance, store operation, housekeeping, and customer service. You would also need to analyze staff knowledge, attitude, appearance, phone service, as well as customer greeting and interaction. A store appraisal would include assessing the temperature, ambiance, procedures, and service, as well as checking on housekeeping areas, such as the sales area, windows, lights, dressing rooms, and rest rooms. The customer-service audit itself should take into account every element of your customer contact, such as gift certificates, wrapping, delivery, information provision, VIP service, parking, coffee, phones, baby and children's facilities/services, waiting areas—even coffee table and magazines.

Once you've audited your business, you need to conduct a similar audit of your competitor's customer performance. Upon obtaining this information, you must act on it. The starting point is to hold a frank discussion with everyone who has taken part in the auditing process. You can launch the conversation by reviewing the research and creatively assessing, at every possible encounter with customers, to determine how you can provide exactly what they want and enhance their experiences. There are plenty of opportunities that range from phone calls, to finding parking spaces, the wait at reception, the availability of information, and so on.

Chances are that your customer audit will highlight some weaknesses in your processes and employees. However, this is not a time to criticize staff. Any mistakes they've made simply reflect—consciously or subconsciously—the company culture and management's views.

The more sophisticated your research, the more effective your reaction to the results will be.

> Sadly, only one business in 12 regularly monitors current customer satisfaction.

While a complaint system enables you to see why the very small percentage of those who complain are unhappy, a customer-satisfaction measurement (CSM) program enables the identification of specific problem areas based on statistically sound information and the ability to correct them. You can prioritize improvement based on understanding what the key drivers of your customers' satisfaction levels are. These are the areas that will have the greatest impact on improving the customer's overall perception of your business. You can update customers on your initiatives, thereby sending a strong message to them about your commitment to them through your customer service.

Implement an Ongoing Customer-Management System

Once you have conducted your customer audit and have reviewed every aspect of your business to maximize customer satisfaction, it's time to implement an ongoing customer-management system. This should be in addition to—not a replacement of—your regular customer audit.

Successful customer management requires selecting the right potential customers, acquiring those customers, retaining them, and increasing the value of the relationship, all of which can be achieved by taking the following 10 steps:

1. Review your client base and *rank your customers*—not only in terms of total spending, but also based on ease of doing business and the cost to serve them.

2. *Segment your customers,* not so much by demographics, but *by behavior patterns.*

3. *Get rid of clients who don't fit your customer profile* or who buy from you solely based on price. Do so carefully to avoid negative word of mouth.

4. Listen to your customers and *give them precisely what they want.* Then keep them fully apprised of every element of the transaction—order status, production, and delivery—on an ongoing basis, and advise on the progress of any repairs.

5. *Form an advisory board* of your best customers.

6. Always *look at things from your customer's perspective.* Visit their companies, and make an attempt to truly understand their needs and pressures. Your job is to make them look good to *their* customers, and, therefore, you need to focus on ensuring that your customer's customers are delighted.

7. *Reward better customers with a priority system*—but clearly advise all your customers about how this operates to avoid dissatisfaction.

8. Ensure that your *entire team is customer focused.*

9. *Prevent any breakdown* in customer relations when an order, product, or service *moves from one department to another.*

10. *Fix any problems fast,* and then *overcompensate* the client. Always go the extra mile.

Customer Satisfaction Measures Are Complex

The aim in today's marketplace is not just to produce satisfied customers, since research shows that 62 percent of all customers who are satisfied with a product or service do not repurchase from their original source.

If you want to survive in this increasingly competitive environment, you have to *knock their socks off.*

But wait a minute! Why *don't* these satisfied customers come back?

Customer service is the most measured index in business after net profit. However, the measurements are insufficient more often than not. We need to gauge more than customer satisfaction; we need to assess the customers' experience in terms of emotions like love, anger, excitement, and joy.

The term *dissatisfied customer* can mean different things. One customer may think something like, "I wanted to tell them off—how dare they treat me like that!" This customer is more than dissatisfied; they are angry, and needs to be treated carefully. In some cases—usually when the promise that's been made to the customer is effusive—we want more than to be satisfied; we want to be exhilarated. Therefore, if the experience is inadequate, the letdown is greater!

> For that reason, ascertaining whether a customer is satisfied or not is a very poor indicator of loyalty or customer retention.

A customer is entitled to be satisfied when he or she makes a purchase. The degree of their positive or negative reaction is what is important. For example, if a business advertises immediate service without a delay and customers end up waiting for a half hour, they may not be just dissatisfied; they may be angry, disappointed, frustrated, or even disgusted. The more intense the customer's experience—good *or* bad—the more likely they are to recall and recount it for a long time thereafter.

Customer service generates a fair amount of emotion, the top six of which are:

1. Anger, 30 percent
2. Happy, 21 percent
3. Frustrated, 21 percent
4. Annoyed, 13 percent
5. Disappointed, 10 percent
6. Satisfied, 10 percent

It is telling that only 1 percent of people use the term *dissatisfied* to describe their feelings. It is also interesting that four of the six of these, which account for 74 percent of all responses, are negative. *Happy* is a memorable response that will generate word of mouth and advocates for your businesses, but *satisfied* will not!

Complaints Are an Asset, Not a Liability

The average customer-service level is well below the rank of awesome that is required to maximize success. Additionally, customer satisfaction rates are at an all time low. So why aren't more companies acting on the complaints they receive and making an attempt to improve their game?

The reality is that most companies don't *get* many complaints, which, of course, does not mean their customers or potential customers are satisfied. The number of complaints is frequently more a measure of how easy it is to make complaints and how welcome they are than a measure of actual customer satisfaction. A low percentage of criticism does not signify high satisfaction among customers; in fact, a *Harvard Business Review* study concludes that one of the surest signs of deteriorating customer relations is a *lack* of complaints. Additionally, a recent *Harper's Bazaar* magazine survey showed that only 4 percent of customers with a problem complain; the remaining 96 percent who don't complain simply don't repurchase the product or service!

So why is it that 96 percent don't raise objections? The major reasons are:

- They *believe that it is a waste of time,* and that nothing will change.
- They *fear retaliation.* Even if you make it easy, most people avoid issuing grievances because they're concerned with the consequences. It's no wonder! Think about how we refer to people who complain. We call them fussy, whiners, hard to please, a pain in the butt, unappreciative, and so on.
- Many people also perceive a complaint to be a personal attack and respond accordingly, which *creates an unpleasant situation most customers would prefer to avoid.*

Surprisingly, even with a serious problem with a product or service, only one person in four will complain to the business. However, although they don't complain to the business, they will tell other people—or worse, post it on the Internet. *Harper's Bazaar* also showed that each unhappy customer tells 22 people.

Therefore, every one complaint represents 25 dissatisfied people—
each of whom tells 22 people. This results in a total of *550 people* who
receive negative reports about your company.

What's worse is that these negative stories become increasingly exaggerated every time they're told. In fact, over 70 percent of Fortune 500
companies have disgruntled customers who've established a negative website about them—and www.complaints.com is a constantly growing site. This
kind of exposure is extremely damaging to any business.

The Best Way to Handle a Customer Complaint

Customer-service training is doubtlessly valuable for staff to undergo. This is
especially true in the areas of handling complaints and identifying and
addressing the various emotions a customer might either express or be
feeling. The only proper way to address a personal complaint is by taking
the following steps:

- Use the person's *name*.
- *Thank them* for bringing the problem to your attention, and *explain
  why you appreciate* their advice.
- *Apologize* for the problem.
- Obtain all the information necessary to *make sure you understand the
  problem*.
- Find out what the *customer wants*.
- Begin *to do* something about it *immediately*.
- Create a *positive solution* to *overcompensate* for the frustration your
  customer's encountered.
- Find out *whether the customer is satisfied* with the solution you've
  proposed.
- Take steps to *prevent this kind of problem from occurring again*.

All Is Not Lost When Someone Complains
about Your Product or Service

If you resolve a problem in their favor, 70 percent of complaining customers
will buy from you again, and 95 percent will do so if you resolve a problem on

the spot. If one person handles their problem, 70 percent of customers are satisfied; however, this figure drops to 61 percent when two people are involved.

The interesting thing about complaints is that—when handled correctly and fixed immediately—they lead to a *positive* scenario resulting from what could have been a very negative situation. Research shows that customers who have a problem resolved satisfactorily are much more loyal than those who've never had a problem. For example, charge-card company Diners Club International regards complaints as so important that they established a committee specifically for handling them—for which their managing director serves as chairperson. The committee reviews all written complaints, as well as letters of praise they receive. They identify the problem and resolve all conflicts within 24 hours.

Never cite any internal problems you have as excuses to the customer for unsatisfactory service because, quite frankly, they don't care. They are paying you to get a good product or service; they expect you to solve your problems, and they don't want to experience any negative effects while you do.

Good Service Is Not Difficult to Provide

Once you have a complete understanding of what your customers want and value, you can always exceed their expectations. It is very important not to overpromise, since unfulfilled guarantees lose business. Restaurant chain T. G.I. Friday has a fabulous motto that follows this maxim: "Promise Good, Deliver Great." Disneyland posts signs at various points along their attractions' substantial lines that advise guests of the impending wait. By putting a 40-minute sign at the 30-minute point, they unexpectedly please people when they reach the attraction 10 minutes early, instead of being angry about the time they *did* have to wait. Similarly, my car dealer always gives me an estimate that is $50 to $150 more than the final bill. For that reason, I am always pleasantly surprised at how much money I saved rather than upset about how much I spent.

Little Things Mean a Lot

Actions that don't necessarily require much effort on the part of your employees can mean the world to your customers. For example, it doesn't cost anything for a maître d' or waiter to bid farewell to every customer and open the door for them as they leave. To the customer, this shows appreciation for their business.

My last apartment-building personnel went above and beyond what was required of a typical residence in a variety of ways. They offered 24-hour valet parking, collected children from school, carried shopping bags into the building, provided room service, door-to-door laundry, apartment cleaning, picked up and delivered dry cleaning, got residents tickets to shows, booked flights, washed cars, and much more. Why would anyone want to live anywhere else?

Similarly, stores that have catalogues will often send customers the product they wish to buy in a range of colors, styles, and sizes. This allows buyers to keep the ones they want and send the rest back. These additional touches of friendliness and convenience can make the difference between a one-time purchaser and a customer for life.

Continue to Innovate

No matter how good you think your customer service is, you must continue to improve because customer attitudes can change over time.

> What was once perceived as added value may now be expected.

Organizations that once did the bare minimum now go the extra mile to please customers. For instance, Miami toll-booth collectors have maps showing directions to various landmarks for tourists requiring directions—proving that even government associations and employees can provide good service if they want to.

Every organization must train their staff to chat with customers and listen clearly to their responses, rather than try to pressure them into a sale. Most people are more afraid of being sold to, than of the consequences of buying the wrong item. Case in point: A Japanese company called Kumari manned an auto show, and obtained 211 qualified leads compared with only 25 obtained by the company's top dealer salespeople. The reason for the difference is that conventional auto-sales methods usually put people off. On the other hand, the chat approach encourages a discussion about the customer's requirements more openly. It provides the chance for people to tell you what competition they are considering and other information that can help you close the sale. The staff from Kumari asked questions and explored answers. They also answered questions directly without any sales pitch.

Companies run into trouble when they stop listening to customers and considering what they want. Wrigley's gum had 90 percent of the chewing-gum market until their competitors introduced sugarless gum. Then, Wrigley's market share fell from 90 percent to 33 percent. Had they bothered to find out whether people wanted sugarless gum? Clearly, they hadn't. Similarly, IBM was regarded as the service leader in the computer industry during the 1980s. However, halfway through the decade, they moved their focus to technology and lost 50 percent of their market value.

In 1997, then $20 billion retailer Coles Myer was increasing prices, reducing staff, and pushing suppliers to the limit in order to improve profits through efficiency. They had computers dictating store ranges according to the profit each generated, instead of basing them on consumer preferences. Because of this, customers were becoming upset, so CEO Dennis Eck asked staff members how they would fix the problem. Over 80 percent replied that they would "go back to selling what customers wanted." To that end, Eck set out to give customers what they wanted on a store-by-store basis. For example, a store in a suburb with a large Macedonian population stocked foods popular to that culture and hired a bilingual staff. As a result of these initiatives, earnings increased 15 percent in 12 months. Instead of concentrating solely on profits, the new policy focused on range, price, service, and store environment.

Retailers today face challenges such as the need to reduce check out time to compete with online retailers. New innovations to solve this problem include scanners that check the whole basket instantly instead of one item at a time, and radio-signal smart packaging. These types of modifications are occurring more and more in every industry. The successful companies are the ones that are constantly preparing for the potential innovations in their field.

Your organization should always be trying to come up with new ways to improve your customer service. Progressive Corporation is a great example of exactly how to do so. The company became the fifth biggest motor-vehicle insurance company in the United States, almost overnight, by introducing an exceptional service policy that they referred to as an immediate-response program. Progressive agents arrive at an accident within 30 minutes, console the drivers, inspect the circumstances, and assess the damage. The representative then gets out the laptop and printer, determines the assessment, and issues the driver a check—right there on the spot.

Progressive's 24-hour-a-day, response-within-30-minutes, immediate-settlement policy differentiated it from every other company that has been doing the same paperwork trail system for years. As a result, they ran circles around the opposition.

A study by the 300 companies in the United States insurance industry found that a 1 percent increase in premiums would lead to a 10 percent drop in business. The majority of companies were price focused. Progressive proved that service and quality are both more important than price to over 80 percent of consumers.

This policy was also excellent for Progressive's bottom line, as their quick responses saved money on lot charges and car rental fees. There is also less staff and handling required. The company additionally experienced a major improvement in customer morale. The agents present at accidents developed good relations with both parties present, which led to fewer lawsuits and lawyers' fees. Because they were on the spot, there was less chance to inflate the bill or fake injury—an important point, because up to 30 percent of insurance payouts are fraud. Not only was the program a great marketing tool; it enabled both a decrease in rates and an increase in profits.

In summary: Awesome customer service is simply great business.

It increases loyalty and profits, decreases costs, motivates staff, improves morale, and increases customer feedback, all of which keep you at the cutting edge of change. It also builds brand equity and dramatically increases word of mouth, which we know accounts for four out of every five sales.

Remember: "Instead of seeing a customer in every individual, look for the individual in every customer."

—Jan Carlzon, CEO Scandinavian Airlines

Chapter 12

Add Value to *Every* Transaction

There are two major bodies of water in Israel. Although both are connected to the river Jordan, one, the Sea of Galilee, is rich in sea life, surrounded by fertile, lush growth where colonies of birds' flourish and lots of people play. The other, the Dead Sea, is just that—polluted, stagnant, and supports no life.

Why is there such a difference between two bodies of water fed by the same rich river?

The Sea of Galilee has rich river flowing in and, in turn, rich river flows out equal to what the sea took in. The Dead Sea only has water coming in. What it gets in, it keeps. It takes, but it doesn't give.

The same tends to happen in business and life. I'm sure we all know people who fit into each of these descriptions. Those who don't give become stagnant, whereas those who give and receive thrive. This is a relationship to which we should all pay heed.

It is no secret that today's market place is becoming increasingly sophisticated. People are conscious of quality products and value for money, yet price plays only a minor role in purchase decisions. When a consumer buys a product, they are entitled to expect an excellent product and great service. That is what they are paying for. Receiving excellent service and a great product is a not privilege, it is a right.

As I've cited previously throughout the book, 80 percent of sales for successful companies come as a result of word of mouth. How exactly do you *get* word of mouth? It is not by merely satisfying customers. The only way to get it—and the resultant increased loyalty, proven increased spending, and higher profitability—is by wowing your customers. Just providing satisfaction will not achieve anything except a one-time sale.

There are two elements to giving a customer great value. One is providing awesome customer service, as discussed in previous chapters. The other is adding value to *every single* customer interaction.

Every action you take must do something extra for your customer. Everyone in your organization must focus on providing customer benefits. Every contact you make with customers must result in gaining a little more information about them to enable the building of a profile. You need to work with customers and empower staff to address customer issues.

Customers are not simple and static; they are complex and dynamic. We need to uncover and understand their past behavior to enable a relevant response to current issues. We must integrate all the information we have on the contacts customers make with different parts of a business. In simplistic terms, for example, a bank should incorporate their knowledge of a client's checking account with the branch and loan with the head office.

How Can You Provide Customer Value?

The short answer here is that it requires a combination of people, product, process, and practices. The product alone won't give you a competitive edge in most cases, because if your competition doesn't already have an equivalent product, they soon will. As we know, the actual offering itself has little influence on the customer's ultimate decision-making process. Let's start by establishing some fundamentals.

There are four levels of customer value:

1. **Basic**—Provide a good quality product or service.
2. **Expected**—This includes explanation of benefits and features, good service.
3. **Desired Value**—Provide advice on care, maintenance, additional opportunities.
4. **Unexpected**—This is going the extra mile, service, added value or other benefit.

Employing this last level—unexpected—is the only way to differentiate yourself from your competitors. There are various areas in which you can do so, including:

Environment: Parking, appearance, merchandising, presentation

Sensory elements: Ambiance, atmosphere, music, visual movement

Personal Contact: Empathy, friendly, helpful, good communication

Customer Requirements: Easy to locate products and information

Information: Additional detail when required

Delivery: Presentation, delivery to accommodate customer

Financial: Risk reversal, customer-friendly paperwork

Follow up: After-sale follow up and service

If you take care of your customers, they will come back. If you take care of your product, they won't. It is that simple. A good philosophy to follow is "Never charge a customer for something you would give a friend for free." The best way to impact customers and impress people is by providing great added value. Customers who encounter excellent added value tell their friends; those who receive no more than they expect tell no one; and those who encounter an unpleasant experience tell everyone.

For example, you have been to the ATM hundreds of times to get cash, and it has always given you what you want. Do you tell anyone when the process goes as expected and you get your cash? Of course not! If, however, the machine gobbles up your card and leaves you without the money you need, how many people do you tell? Everyone!

If you merely give your clients value for money in today's market place, you will likely go out of business. You must deliver what you promise and then go the extra mile and add value to every transaction by building heart share with each client. If you don't, you will fail to establish loyalty or brand equity, and a lack of these elements will force you to compete on price and endure the accompanying low margins. You will also depend on high advertising budgets to continually generate new clientele. Wouldn't it be easier to take care of the customers you already have?

Adding Value Differentiates Your Business

Companies are realizing more and more that added value is an element that's critical to differentiating your brand from those of competitors. There is a lot of competition out there offering similar products and services, and very few businesses have something that is not offered anywhere else. That is why, to use the famous saying, "You must sell the sizzle and not the steak. " In other words, you must provide customers with good quality because it is what they deserve and expect. However, you've also got to give them the sizzle, that little something extra that makes your brand stand out. You have to consistently ask, "How can I be a resource for my customer?" Today's buyers are more demanding, more knowledgeable, much more cautious, have many more choices, and are more conscious of perceived value. They are tired of self-interested product pushers.

Every potential customer in the marketplace has a vast and increasing choice of where they buy. Therefore, they will only buy from you if you demonstrate that you really care about satisfying their needs.

You need to care as much about their performance as you do about your own—and they need to see you as such. All that counts is what's important to your customers, not what is important to you.

The importance of added value represents a major change from the past. For example, the corporate focus during the 1970s was on sales. The standard philosophy was to get your foot in the door and do whatever you needed to do to get a sale and make a profit at all costs. Today, more and more customers want *information*. They don't mind being led, but they don't like being sold. This trend has taken hold as the cost of acquiring new customers escalated.

It is also important to add value to the community as a whole. The general marketplace's growing social concerns can be a major benefit to any company. Society has evolved from the many excesses and self-interests of the 1980s and 1990s to reflect people's more basic human nature: the natural instinct to care about the world and the people around them. A mounting number of people are influenced by a company's relationship with a cause that will benefit from their purchase. These changes have, to a large degree, transformed the way we market our products or services from consumer manipulation to consumer involvement.

Putting People First Starts at the Top

Several years ago, President Clinton invited several hundred business leaders to the White House. He spoke to them about the importance of people, their jobs, and society in relation to making a bigger profit at any cost. Public opinion showed very strong support of the President. One of the results of this meeting was that many corporations' became heavily involved in volunteer work in an effort to add value to the community. Companies are developing community programs and giving their staff members time off on full pay to participate in them. Today's public expects companies to be good corporate citizens and contribute to the community, and consumers expect corporations to add value to their transactions. The company that does both has a winning formula.

Although most of us work in order to make money, the marketplace expects more of a goal from big companies. The great thing about giving more is that it helps you grow your business and it makes you feel better about yourself at the same time.

After the self-involved sell-no-matter-what mentality of the 1970s, the 1980s saw a more service-driven culture. Then the added value philosophy was born in the 1990s. Quite simply, this notion dictated that if you gave great service, you would secure more customers. It seemed like almost every seminar and article that you read in business magazines described good service as the panacea for any business. Of course, this was as true then as it is still true today. However, today, there is the additional dimension of adding value.

You Can Add Value in *Any* Business

When I ask clients how they can add value for their customers, I am usually met with either dead silence or an explanation of how their business is different, and it is difficult to add value in what they do.

The first question I frequently receive when discussing this topic with clients or while speaking to a group is this: "I can understand how this approach works in your business, but I am in a totally different industry/field/area. How can we add value to our transactions?" Or put more simply—"How does this work for *my* business?"

After receiving these questions and responses, I then walk my audience through all of the interactions they have with the customer, step by step. I literally make them put themselves in the customers' shoes and consider all the things that could potentially improve their experience at each point in the process. I have begun many seminars with a room of 200 people, none of whom had a single proposal about how to add value for customers. Yet once I got them to really tune into the customers' wavelength, the ideas came thick and fast.

The first thing that business owners need to realize is that value added doesn't have to be a major expense. The old expression that the little things mean a lot is certainly true when it comes to adding value. In fact, little things can mean the difference between success and failure. For example, it doesn't cost a lot for a waiter to provide a complimentary glass of wine with a meal, for a mechanic to deliver your car washed and vacuumed, or a hairdresser to visit an office to see an especially busy client. Value can be added to a customer's experience in countless ways; the bottom line is to always follow these rules:

- *Show you care* about your customer
- Add an *additional* product or service *increment*
- Provide *education or information*
- Work with the client to *customize* a product or service
- Provide exceptional service and *risk reversal*

Let's look at these one at a time in detail.

Show You Really Care about Your Clients

In order to show customers how much they truly care about them, companies must develop a corporate culture that makes customer satisfaction the primary goal. It must permeate all thinking. When this is the case it shows through.

My car dealer is an excellent example of how added value generates repeat business. I have just brought my fourth new car from the same Los Angeles broker in a city in which car showrooms are as commonplace as plastic surgeons. I carefully shopped around several dealers before making my decision, and there's a reason why I made the decision to purchase from the same company over and over again.

I didn't know one dealer from another when I first moved to town. Although I did not purchase my first car from my current dealer, it was the ideal place for servicing since it was just up the road from my office. When I dropped the car off the first time, one of the representatives, Paul, sat down with me and invited me to lunch the following week. Paul and I had a pleasant 45-minute or so lunch during which we spoke about everything but cars. He either had an unbelievable memory or a miniature tape recorder, because that conversation directly led to four new car sales.

Ever since, if there is a mudslide in Malibu Canyon or a fire, earthquake, or any of the other disasters that regularly befall us here in Southern California, Paul is on the phone checking to see if we need any assistance and making sure that all is well. Paul ensured that our mixed-religion household received every Christmas, Hanukkah, Rosh Hashanah, Easter,

New Years, and birthday card on time, often accompanied by small items of vehicle merchandise. My young son always looked forward to getting the matchbox cars that arrived on his birthday. Once, in a period of torrential rain, Paul arrived at my office to double check that my wiper blades were working perfectly. *That* is genuine customer service.

When it came time to make my most recent purchase just two weeks ago, I shopped around, got the best price, and simply asked Paul to match it. Paul sold me another car without having to be a car salesman at all! Though I've never asked him, I'm willing to bet that the reason Paul's is such a successful dealership has a lot to do with their added-value corporate culture.

You don't have to make grand gestures for customers to appreciate it. At some Banana Republic retail stores, they will drive you home if you make $100 worth of purchases. Nordstrom's will give you a personal shopper; you can simply stay home and watch television! Many hotel and supermarket chains actually film their check-in lines now to monitor shoppers' reactions in an attempt to ensure that they're being served before they begin to fidget. Similarly, restaurants are putting cameras in their entrances that are connected to a computer that matches the customer with photographs in the database. The computer then lets the maitre'd know who the customer is and reminds him of the last time they were in the restaurant—as well as the occasion. The, "Good evening Mr. Pritchard, I haven't seen you since you won the Smith account. It's good to have you back" makes a customer feel pretty good—and also impresses the customer's companions.

At a seminar at which I was the keynote speaker, Alan Carter, the owner of a local antique store, told me of the time he approached several radio stations regarding a special promotion for his business. All but one station asked him, "How much are you going to spend with us?" The other station produced two demo spots, with no obligation to buy, and offered him some complimentary spots along with free advertising production. They did all of this without asking Alan how much he planned to spend. Alan then gave his relatively small budget to them. During the promotion, they called him daily to monitor results and even provided a personality to appear at an event he staged. It is no surprise that the station became the cornerstone of all Alan's marketing.

Add an Additional Product

I was fortunate to be friends with the late Peter Korda, one of the world's leading entertainment and sports entrepreneurs, who told me a great story about a company called Hemden shirts. Several years ago, Peter purchased half a dozen custom-made shirts from Eugene Notermans, the company that owns Hemden. A few years after the initial purchase, Peter received a letter from Eugene asking him to send back any shirts that needed new collars and cuffs, and Eugene would replace them for free. Peter later received four shirts with new collars and cuffs plus an additional new shirt at no extra cost, with an accompanying letter that simply asked Peter to consider Hemden whenever he needed new shirts. He did—and guess where he got them! Once I heard about the kind of service they offered, Hemden became *my* shirt supplier as well.

A comparable scenario occurred when our company sold a lot of tickets to the Atlanta Olympics, and included a disposable camera as a gift with each ticket. We didn't advertise beforehand that we were including the camera; it was a surprise. After the games were over, we received literally hundreds of letters of thanks—not for the tickets, but for the cameras. The response was overwhelming. We were thrilled to hear from people who spoke of the wonderful memories our clients had captured; some letters even included copies of photos of their children at the games. We had only slightly cut our margin on the tickets by including the gift. However, these clients have called us each time that they needed tickets for other major events, be it the Super Bowl, World Series, or Masters. We don't have to advertise, and there's little to no chance of our competition poaching our business.

Provide Education and Information

Another highly effective method of establishing a client for life is to provide education and information to your prospect. The material you offer should include existing and evolving knowledge of products, customers, rivals, new technologies, and all new developments in your field. You will find that your customers come to rely on this information, which will add greatly to the value you present.

I gave the keynote address to the Combined Rural Traders Conference, a group that, despite having poor brand awareness in comparison to their competition, was growing at a healthy rate at that time. While researching their address, I discovered that the company was building tremendous relationships in the country regions through their education program. Their experts would assist farmers at no cost on any and all aspects of being on the land. This added great value to the farmer, fostered relationships, and developed brand equity and word of mouth that led to rapidly growing customer share and steadily but securely increasing market share.

Customize Your Product or Service

It is so vital to focus on the customer today that we will continue to see increased customization of products and services for individual clients. It does not matter whether it is a $10 item or a $20,000 item. From noodle shops where you select whether you want Chinese, Thai, or Malaysian and then individualize the ingredients, through to Harley-Davidson where you effectively build your own bike, customization gives the customer added value.

One of our clients is a financial planning company called Associated Planners that has made it second nature to truly tailor their recommendations for each client. They don't just select the best off-the-shelf plan for customers, as many banks and fund managers do. They customize to suit clients' specific needs, interests, and aspirations. As a result, leading professional coaching magazine *Choice* nominated Associated Planners as the second-best financial services company in the country. This has led to a substantial increase in their business.

I have found in my speaking travels that speakers who deliver the same speech at every seminar are finding it harder to get work. On the other hand, those who create speeches that address the client's specific challenges and opportunities enjoy more satisfied clients, which frequently leads to more consulting and other work.

> More importantly, customization is an education process; it enables greater awareness of customer needs and potential community attitude shifts.

Add Value to the Customer's Experience

No matter what business you are in, you must know that you're not selling an apple, a sandwich, or a car; you're selling an *experience*. People will go where there is something to enjoy, where it is fun, and where they are appreciated.

For instance, we did some work with our local children's shoe store. This small shop is in a highly competitive business with slender margins (something that can be hard to believe when you see the price of kid's shoes today!). In fact, this mom and pop store's products are considerably more expensive than the big discount chains. So how could we possibly compel people to shop there instead of the bigger, cheaper guys?

Simple! We changed the store from a boring shoe shop to a unique customer experience.

We filled the shop with sand and set up a sandcastle area and lots of toys. Now people who visit the Yellow Balloon Kids Shoe Store find a play area in the corner of the store with some really neat toys in what appears to be a beachsetting. While proprietor Jan focuses on selling shoes, her colleague David has two roles: he is a shoe salesman, but he is also a clown. He plays with the kids while he is fitting shoes, creates all sorts of balloon shapes for them to take home, and entertains them in the play area. The kids love it. When their moms tell them that it's time to get new shoes, there is a chorus of "Let's go to Yellow Balloon!" This chorus also goes up when they don't need shoes. Only a very brave parent would take their kids anywhere else. What David and Jan have done is add value. They have won the hearts of their clients and their clients' kids, and, therefore, they have won their business.

Provide Exceptional Service

How do you provide exceptional service? First, you figure out what your potential customers want. Then you provide it to them accurately, politely, and enthusiastically. The next step is to go the extra mile and finally, follow up.

Adding value is equally effective in building a large business as it is with a smaller enterprise. When Hyundai cut the prices on its cars by $1,000, Daewoo could have followed suit. However, instead, they released an added-value free-care policy that included free service for three years, free roadside service, and a free replacement car when yours is being serviced. By reducing their price, Hyundai devalued their brand. By adding value, Daewoo enhanced theirs.

Whenever I go for a haircut, I call the salon on my car phone as I approach, and an assistant meets me out front and parks my car for me. They know I'm busy and they don't want me to be inconvenienced by looking for a parking spot. If I have to wait once I arrive, one of the receptionists brings me a cup of tea, coffee, or a cappuccino, offers me a doughnut or a piece of fruit and a choice of the day's newspapers to read. There is also a mobile phone for my convenience if I wish to make a call. I can then make a selection from a range of DVDs. I always select those on business. The last time I was there, I watched part of *The 50 Best Advertisements of All Time*. Very entertaining and educational! The employees encourage me to leave the salon's mobile number with clients or have my calls forwarded so I will not miss out on anything important at work. When I get to the chair, I am offered a glass of Chardonnay, Merlot, or Champagne to sip on while I get my hair cut. Overall, it's a pretty enjoyable experience.

Do they take all the hassles out of me being away from my business? Absolutely.

Do they make me feel welcome? Absolutely.

Do they make me feel comfortable? Absolutely.

Am I likely to take my business elsewhere? No, I'm not, and I am probably going to forgive them if they give me the occasional bad haircut. Do I pay a little more than I would another hairdresser? Perhaps; but because I am fully satisfied, I am not comparing their price with anyone else's. Because they have added value to the transaction, they've consequently removed any concern with price. Giving me a phone to use so that I don't miss valuable calls while I'm away from the office compensates me many times over for any minor increased cost, if there is one.

However, you might wonder, what is the real cost of providing all this added value to the salon? Well, let's see: a couple of minutes to park the car; a drink; newspapers that are offered to every customer during the day; and a coffee and glass of wine that costs just a few dollars. The only risk they're taking is that someone will abuse the phone privilege; but because their clients appreciate it so much, 99 percent of them will only make a call if they have to, and will only redirect calls there if it is important.

Added Value Also Adds to the Bottom Line

Now let's look at how these elements add to the bottom line and serve as an investment rather than an expense. I am just one of a number of customers who—providing their product quality (haircuts) stays good—will remain a customer for life. Every friend or acquaintance that I tell about them also becomes a customer for life. The salon has a full appointment book despite doubling the size of the business in the past couple of years. They no longer have to advertise, which saves the owner, John, over $2,000 a month in newspaper ads. This is more than the cost of his added value and is certainly much more effective. In addition, I suspect that if I checked around, he might have higher profit margins than some of his competitors.

Whether simply a great smile and a warm greeting, a thank you or birthday card, or a small gift for a child, added value is a very powerful marketing tool.

> The great thing about adding value is that it is extremely cost-effective marketing.

To illustrate how powerful adding value is—and how you can actually *save* money on advertising and obtain a much better response—let's look at the following example. Theatre LA was the umbrella organization for 108 live theaters throughout Los Angeles. (The LA Stage Alliance now represents 210 Live Theaters in the LA region.) A few years ago, attendance at member theaters had slumped to 1.3 million a year. To address this drop, the theaters did what most organizations would do: they cut prices, introduced two-for-one ticket offers, and offered a number of other incentives. Yet none of these initiatives hindered the declining ticket sales.

They then hired Marketforce One as their marketing consultant. The first action we recommended was to increase prices back to prior levels. Though this suggestion met with some resistance, we argued that reducing prices simply reduces profitability and makes the organization less competitive. Price cutting will ultimately send you out of business.

Our solution to building attendance was to add value, and the first step was to train the theater staff. It is important to greet *every* patron and make them feel welcome. This warm, effusive attitude to customers is the responsibility of *all* staff, not just the ushers. We held 90-minute added-value seminars for all employees, during which we encouraged their ideas and consequently empowered them to take the initiative.

By introducing a variety of contests and programs in the theaters that required guests to fill out entry forms, the staff was able to generate an extensive database. We used this information to send letters to first-time attendees thanking them for coming and inviting them to come again.

We were also able to invite regular patrons to meet for a cocktail prior to a performance, or to attend small get-togethers with the cast after the show.

These small things were very important to the customers. We created magic moments that were a unique privilege to the theater lovers. The theaters added value and they encouraged people to come back.

When a pregnant woman came to any of the theaters, one of the staff would find out when the baby was due. They kept in contact and sent a congratulatory card and flowers when the baby was born. Children who attended the theater received small gifts as a thank you. Regular customers who requested it in advance would receive priority car parking. If it was wet, people were walked to their cars under umbrellas. When there was mer-chandise connected with a particular production, it was offered to regular patrons at cost price plus a small margin, still much cheaper than retail. In short, regular patrons were made to feel special.

All these added-value initiatives were designed to build attendee loyalty and to thank people for attending. It was all achieved for negligible cost. What was the result? In just 18 months, attendance had jumped from 1.3 to 2.8 million. The theater company achieved this 1.5 million increase without having to run a single inch of additional advertising, and it was accomplished at close to full ticket price—because we added value to every transaction.

You can establish a strong database profile of your own company's customers by asking a series of questions over a period of surveys. This allows you to launch a range of additional value-added benefits. For example, you can send birthday and anniversary cards or give specialized or priority products and services to members of the various database segments that are likely to appreciate them.

Added Value Takes Many Forms

There are many, many ways to add value. For example, *Microsoft* co-founder Paul Allen operates the Experience Music Project (EMP) and Science Fiction Museum and Hall of Fame in Seattle, Washington which are dedicated to the history and exploration of both popular music and science fiction. The Frank Gehry-designed museum building is located on the campus of the Seattle Center, adjacent to the Space Needle and the Seattle Center Monorail, which runs through the building.

The EMP initiative has created a unique and highly profitable added-value program.

Upon entry, guests receive a strap-on electronic guide that enables them to interact with the music-stars memorabilia on display. For example, when you click it at a guitar, it plays the songs made famous by the artist. Every time you interact with an item, the guide alerts the gift shop to your preference. When you arrive at the gift shop on your way out, the CD's you like and the appropriate memorabilia are already laid out for easy selection and purchase.

When The Coca-Cola Company was on an aggressive marketing push into Mexico, they used added value to gain 100 percent distribution in retail stores. Most Mexican retail stores are mom-and-pop shops that cannot afford health insurance. Therefore, The Coca-Cola Company provided storeowners with health insurance in an incentive program based on stock levels and sales. The result was a huge surge in sales.

Loyalty programs are also an excellent way to add value. Customers receive bonus rewards merely by purchasing products or services they would normally buy anyway. Some examples of how powerful these kinds of programs are? Seventy percent of airline customers claim that they would stop using the airline if these initiatives were cut. After joining an added-value loyalty program, people spend 27 percent more with the company than they normally would, and those programs connected to credit cards are shown to increase sales by 46 percent.

Southwest Airlines introduced a fun culture in which staff can dress up or down. Stewards can look like Elvis or Mickey Mouse and are encouraged to be amusing and entertaining. There is also lots of humor from the cockpit. This entire atmosphere has added enjoyment and value to the customer experience, making Southwest Airlines the only U.S. airline to consistently make a profit!

Toyota did a similar thing with motor vehicle sales when they opened Tokyo's Mega Web theme park. This venue is a combination of automotive and entertainment with 140 cars on display, a look at the future world, a traditional driving course, and an e-com electric-vehicle ride. The park attracts over three million visitors a year—something that's really bringing people to the dealership. Again, the result is an enhanced customer experience, and a big boost to car sales.

Great service and added value have become a critical component for countless companies that have introduced customer-relationship management (CRM) programs, and 93 percent of these companies seek enhanced customer loyalty, which, in turn, produces higher revenue, increased profits, and reduced marketing costs. Of all CRM programs, 46 percent are specifically customized for the corporation. You can expect this percentage to grow rapidly as more companies realize the benefits that this level of customer focus brings.

Remember: Forget price, forget location, forget market share. The sure path to success is building heart share, then customer share. Market share and profitability follow. If you provide genuine customer service and add value to every transaction, you will always succeed.

Chapter 13

Building the Brand and First Recall

Often when people see an advertisement, they're not interested in purchasing the item being advertised at that particular point in time. In most cases, the ad simply makes people think of the generic category being promoted. It might remind you that you need to buy razor blades or get a new winter coat, but it doesn't do much for the specific brand being showcased. In order to actually capture a sale, you must make your brand top of mind for potential customers.

To review: as the purchasing process begins in the brain's preconscious, totally emotional segment, you think of the product or service and immediately search for an emotional trigger. You only begin to rationalize purchase options in the conscious mind if no item in that particular category has made an impression on you emotionally.

> Therefore, to achieve a sale, companies must develop the emotional connection between their product or service and the potential customer.

You can accomplish this in two ways. The most powerful and longer-term method is by building a brand the consumer knows and respects. The second method is by creating instantaneous emotional recall. This doesn't mean that the consumer necessarily trusts your brand; it simply means that they remember it. That is usually sufficient for an initial sale, providing your competitors have not positioned themselves as well as you have.

Putting your brand and customer purchasing benefit (CPB) together in front of the consumer everywhere possible will enable you to build brand equity and achieve amazing recall in a very short period of time. For example, if you are a plumber, putting your name and CPB (providing both are effective and proven as discussed earlier in this book) on everything from your advertisements, Yellow Pages, apparel, vehicles, all tools and equipment, all stationary, invoices—really, everywhere possible—will guarantee that you attain high recall after a short period. A retail outlet that includes the name and CPB on everything from the window to the price tags on the shelves will achieve the same result. We have proven literally hundreds of times that this combination will produce extraordinary results if it hits the consumer's hot button.

Emotional connections minimize the likelihood of scrutiny and comparisons. Unless people think of your business first via their preconscious minds, you will usually have to compete with between 5 and 10 competitors on a pragmatic basis. This includes real or perceived measurement yardsticks that encompass quality, reliability, price, service, location, and so on. The law of averages frequently suggests that you will only get a percentage of that business, and that it will most likely be price based. This is not the business you want.

There is a very simple benchmark for judging your performance in this area. If I mentioned your product or service to a randomly selected group of people representing your potential target market, how many people would think of your brand first? If you are not on the short list, you're not in the game. No amount of brochures, advertising, social media, or any form of communication will make you the leader in your field unless they constantly reinforce your name/CPB association, develop your brand equity, and your first recall brand awareness.

However, if you convince the customer that your product is the solution to their requirements, thus satisfying an emotional need, you have a brand with equity and preconscious recall. Why do some brands dominate a category? Why do we pay more for Federal Express to deliver a package than its competitors? Because its CPB—"When it absolutely, positively must be there tomorrow, call FedEx"—made Federal Express the courier of choice. It effectively positioned the company as *the* brand!

Create a great CPB, then use it everywhere you use your name. It will make a big difference to your potential customers' recall—and your business.

A Brand with Equity Is the Only Way to Create a Demand Chain Dynamic

The first question to answer is, 'What is a brand'? A brand is the perception that your company creates through its name, logo, quality, service, price, word of mouth, advertising, community citizenship, and personal experiences. Depending on the quality of those experiences and the value they carry, the brand has equity that influences people to buy it. Since 1980, the average share price in the United States of companies with strong brands has outperformed the market by up to 20 percent. Consumers tend to associate with particular brand profiles, and buy specific brands in order to be a certain type of person.

Brands are the key to competitive advantage. They provide leveragability to both trade and end user, and are the critical weapon in the battle for category leadership. Building a brand can achieve exactly the opposite of using discounted prices and relying on supply chain dynamics to sell product, and establishing brand equity is essential to create demand chain dynamics—the only way to survive in this new age economy. Brands that have equity generate a constantly increasing demand due to word of mouth, all but eliminate churn rates, command price premiums, and, therefore, they increase profits. Yet too many companies today ignore the power of brand equity, and continue to focus instead on sales or pricing policies.

To truly secure your position in business, you must develop a brand for your product that means something to your target audience. One might argue that the reason Japan's top 100 corporations return profits on the order of 1–2 percent compared to their American counterparts' returns of 6–7 percent (despite gross sales of each being on the order of $5 trillion) is branding. United States companies brand *products,* whereas the Japanese have tended to brand *corporations.* Unfortunately, a substantial percentage of the public generally doesn't like or trust most major companies. You can't build equity with advertising; you can only build it through people.

> Advertising doesn't build a brand; people build brands.

You have to mean something substantial to the potential customer. Many major companies have spent the last decade globalizing their brands and creating a uniform positioning in each market—something that can turn out to be a dangerous policy. The consumer's attitudes, perceptions, and cultures vary significantly from country to country. For example the success of L'Oréal cosmetics has been built on promoting different brands in different nations; choosing which to promote was based on views of the local cultures. For people interested in finding the most American product possible, the French company uses the name Maybelline. Those preferring the most French are given the L'Oréal brand. There are even Italian brands for other preferences. All the different lines are sold in all of the markets, but only one is excessively promoted. The result of this is that L'Oréal has been able to maintain double-digit growth for more than a decade. Whether it's selling Italian elegance, New York street smarts, or French beauty through its brands, L'Oréal is expanding out globally to millions of people across a larger range of incomes and cultures. This is what sets L'Oreal apart from one-brand marketers such as The Coca-Cola Company, McDonald's, or Walmart.

On the other hand, possibly no brand has done a better job of global imaging than Korean consumer-electronics manufacturer Samsung Electronics Co. A decade ago, it was a maker of lower-end consumer electronics under a handful of brand names including Wiseview, Tantus, and Yepp, none of which meant much to consumers. Determined to build a stronger identity, the company ditched its other brands to put all its resources behind the Samsung name. Then it focused on building a more upscale image through better quality, design, and innovation.

Beginning in 2001, the newly defined Samsung launched a line of top-notch mobile phones and digital TVs, products that showed off the company's technical prowess. Most people carry their mobile phones with them everywhere, and their TV is the center of the family room. "We wanted the brand in users' presence 24/7," says Peter Weedfald, head of Samsung's North American marketing and consumer electronics unit.

That strategy paid off. Over the past five years, Samsung, previously ranked 20th, has posted the biggest gain in value of any Global 100 brand, with a 186 percent growth. In 2005, Samsung surpassed 28th-ranked Sony, a far more entrenched rival that once owned the electronics category, in overall brand value.

The following cultural blunders are presented in order to illustrate how crucial cultural awareness is in international business today.

- ◆ Managers at an American company were startled when they discovered that the brand name of the cooking oil they were marketing in Latin America translated into Spanish as "Jackass Oil."
- ◆ American Motors tried to market its new car, the "Matador," based on the image of courage and strength. However, in Puerto Rico the name means "killer" and was not popular on the hazardous roads in the country.

♦ A U.S. telephone company tried to market its products and services to Latinos by showing a commercial in which a Latino wife tells her husband to call a friend, telling her they would be late for dinner. The commercial bombed since Latina women do not order their husbands around, and their use of time would not require a call about lateness.

♦ A cologne for men pictured a pastoral scene with a man and his dog. It failed in Islamic countries where dogs are considered unclean.

♦ Procter & Gamble used a television commercial in Japan that was popular in Europe. The ad showed a woman bathing, her husband entering the bathroom and touching her. The Japanese considered this ad an invasion of privacy, inappropriate behavior, and in very poor taste.

♦ One company printed the "okay" finger sign on each page of its catalogue. In many parts of Latin America that is considered an obscene gesture. Six months of work were lost because they had to reprint all the catalogues.

♦ A golf-ball manufacturing company packaged golf balls in packs of four for convenient purchase in Japan. Unfortunately, pronunciation of the word *four* in Japanese sounds like the word *death*, and items packaged in fours are unpopular.

For Long–Term Success Build an Intrinsic Brand

In my experience, there are two kinds of brands. The first are what I call awareness brands. These are well-known names built by sheer weight of media advertising frequency. Though people know the names, they don't really mean much to the consumer. In other words, if the company went out of business tomorrow, no one would miss them. These brands succeed through awareness alone in product categories where none of their competitors have developed superior brand equity. Consequently, this success is usually driven by price. Examples of awareness brands are Circuit City, Saab, Enron, and Netscape.

The second are what I call intrinsic brands. These brands are not built by advertising, but instead they develop equity through the convergence of the company's, employees', and consumers' shared values. They really stand for something in the consumer's mind, and they set the benchmarks by which they judge competitors in the category.

An intrinsic brand is not a name and a logo. Advertising and imagery do not create it and will not motivate the vast majority of consumers to pay more for a product or service.

The intrinsic brand is a reflection of the company, product, or service's personality, integrity, and corporate culture.

It is driven by the passion of people both inside and outside the company. A company's management, staff, and customer relationships foster like attitudes and interests to a degree such that the brand becomes a reflection of the participant's culture as well. For today's customer-centric corporation, this means that everyone in the company, not just the call center reps or those in the field, must be accessible to the customer. They must make information freely available and encourage customers to participate in product development. Apple is an excellent example.

A Disney film will always do better at the box office against even a superior film from Fox, Dreamworks, or another studio, despite the excellent reputations that these studios enjoy. The reason for this is that families trust Disney for children's entertainment; they know they can rely on it. It has brand equity that has certainly been partly crafted by advertising, but the real quality of the brand comes from decades of trust, quality, and service.

How to Build Brand Equity

There are 12 simple rules to building brand equity:

1. **Be focused.** A powerful brand must mean specific things to the customer. If you dilute the brand across a range of products—even single product derivatives or a prestige or budget option—you risk weakening the brand. Even if you introduce a subcategory of a strong brand, it is advisable to create the derivative's own branding; consider Toyota's introduction of "Lexus" as a prestige brand.

2. **Create powerful positioning.** Focus on the most persuasive emotional benefit that your brand offers; for example, *Volvo* cars are the epitome of *safety*.

3. **"Generalize" the category.** Become the generic name for the product category in the way that *"Pass me a Kleenex," "Fix it with Scotch tape," "Google it,"* or *"Make a Xerox"* are.

4. **Be perceived as the first.** If customers see you as the original, then you have the opportunity to build a reputation as the best and develop a powerful brand. Think of Levi Strauss, the original jeans, or Coca-Cola, "the real thing."

5. **Stand for quality.** Is Mercedes Benz the best luxury car? Is Louis Vuitton the best luggage? Does it matter? They are positioned as such, and that is how customers see them.

6. **Have a powerful category-associated name.** The company name creates instant association with the product category. For example, Reliable Office Supplies is a stylized name/logo that not only positions the company, but also says clearly and precisely what it does.

7. **Distinguish between the brand and the company.** This is one element that the Japanese haven't gotten quite right. What is a Sony? Is it a vacuum cleaner, a food blender, a television set, or a stereo system? Which product is a market leader? The brand equity is almost totally dissipated. The consumer simply knows that it is an okay brand. On the other hand, Michelob beer has been distinguished successfully from its parent, Anheuser Busch.

8. **Name and logo.** The company's name and logo must be memorable, easy on the eye, readily identifiable, and relate specifically to the product or service. This significantly assists first recall brand awareness. For example, people associate the name Blockbuster directly to the most successful movies, and, therefore, to the company that provides them.

9. **Color.** A unique color will distinguish you from your competitors. For example, Coca-Cola is red, Pepsi is blue. UPS is brown.

10. **Keep the name universal.** Don't narrow the product or service name's appeal—either for the present or future development—by tying it to a particular locale or little known association. Make the name powerful, applicable, and versatile. Santa Monica Bank became U.S. Bank to broaden its appeal and facilitate expansion.

11. **Keep it consistent.** The name, image, CPB, and product quality must be consistent. If you must change the brand position or image, do it slowly, and clearly explain the changes to your customers in terms that emphasize how the transformation will benefit them. MTV, Walmart, and BP successfully did so; in my view Animal Kingdom and Tropicana failed.

12. **Advertising and publicity.** A brand needs third-party endorsements to build character and reliability, and thus brand equity. This is driven by publicity, which creates awareness of this equity and gives the brand meaning. Advertising reinforces brand equity positioning. For example, Famous Amos Cookies and The Body Shop both generated huge sales through publicity—Famous Amos through his unique success story and The Body Shop through the late Anita Roddick's political activism in support of human and animal rights. Publicity can also have the opposite effect (as evidenced by Nike). Nike's manufacturing (and several other) policies showed that the company did not share the marketplace's values—something that's showed up in their sales performance and stock price as they lost their connection with the community.

It Takes a Village to Build a Brand

Your brand is fashioned, not only by your staff and your product/service's users, but also by opinion leaders, the media, endorsers, and by what you contribute to the community.

> A small group of committed, passionate people can have enormous power in swaying people to their viewpoint.

This creates a chain reaction that is both powerful enough to motivate people and convince them to dismiss any negative information they hear about you.

Brand commitment is very powerful. McDonald's does not have the best burger; Coca-Cola seldom beats Pepsi in taste tests; and most experts argue that Microsoft is not the best operating system. But try to tell that to these brands' devotees.

Be Specific

If you have not yet built strong brand equity, you can begin by doing the following:

- ◆ Objectively review both your own brand and that of your competitors' to understand the strengths, weaknesses, opportunities, threats, and future potential.
- ◆ Create a strategy for implementation and brand building on the basis of emotional and substantive benefits (CPB).
- ◆ Address all obstacles you're facing.
- ◆ Determine how every element of your organization and every person in it will help build the quality of brand.
- ◆ Ensure that all actions, policies, marketing, and advertising contribute to building the brand equity.

The World's Greatest Brands

It always helps to look at the world's top 10 brands and consider why they made the list. Global branding company Interbrand evaluates brands according to four criteria:

WEIGHT—ITS INFLUENCE IN ITS CATEGORY

Length—Its extension outside its category

Breadth—Its franchise in terms of age, consumer types, international appeal

Depth—Its consumer loyalty

The value of a brand to a business can be qualified. Although it's intangible, it is a valuable corporate asset. In the case of Coca-Cola, these intangible assets comprise over 95 percent of its total market capitalization. According to Interbrand, the top 10 brands and their value are shown in Figure 13.1.

BRAND VALUE

The majority of the top 50 global brands have been around for more than 50 years, and each has made a huge investment in marketing their brand during

	2001			2010	
1.	Coca-Cola	$84	1.	Coca-Cola	$70
2.	Microsoft	$57	2.	IBM	$65
3.	IBM	$44	3.	Microsoft	$61
4.	General Electric	$34	4.	Google	$44
5.	Ford	$33	5.	General Electric	$42
6.	Disney	$32	6.	McDonalds	$34
7.	Intel	$30	7.	Intel	$32
8.	McDonalds	$26	8.	Nokia	$29
9.	AT&T	$24	9.	Disney	$28
10.	Marlboro	$21	10.	Hewlett Packard	$27

FIGURE **13.1**

Note: Value in billions of dollars.

that period of time. However, there several brands in the list that have been around only a relatively short time, such as Microsoft and Intel. There are also a number of rapidly rising brands, such as Nokia, that have been around only a decade or so. Such is the power of the Internet and the technology revolution.

Word of Mouth Is a Strong Brand Builder

As mentioned earlier, countless studies have shown that over 60 percent of consumers try new products as a result of word of mouth, compared to the between 5 and 30 percent that do so based on advertising. It's a fact: People love to talk about themselves and their experiences, and people with similar interests are naturally attracted to each other. The Internet, with chat rooms and blogs abounding on all manner of subjects, products, and services, can spread the good or bad word to thousands of people around the world in minutes.

Word of mouth's power is further highlighted by a number of studies that have shown results along similar lines to the following:

- ◆ 90 percent of people trust family members.
- ◆ 80 percent trust their friends.
- ◆ 31 percent trust the media.
- ◆ 13 percent trust corporations.
- ◆ 9 percent trust governments.

This is powerful evidence that the most effective way to build a brand that will withstand the test of time and the rigors of competition is via recommendations of highly delighted customers who become company advocates. This is a huge advantage to a company; frequent users cost less to maintain, create higher margins, attract new users at virtually no cost, and contribute most to the company's short-term profit and long-term wealth.

Building Brand Equity through Consumers, Not Advertising

One company that didn't focus on expensive high-frequency mass media, yet built a powerful brand by leveraging their constituents, is Harley-Davidson.

Harley-Davidson was a tired product in the 1980s, identified with gangs and competing with better and cheaper Japanese products. To counter their negative image, they held town-hall meetings across America in conjunction with bike shows and exhibits of collectibles. They established the Harley Owners Group (HOG) in 1983, a riders' club that gave new buyers access to Harley activities and served as a conduit between owners. The first year's membership was free with the purchase of a bike. Today, the group has more than one million members in more than 1,400 chapters worldwide. The individual HOGs represent a diverse range of interests, from Yuppies to Vietnam Vets to Born Again Christians.

These HOG members transformed the image of motorcycle gangs by holding fundraisers with celebrities. Their national toy-collection drive for the less fortunate is also one of the world's biggest. The giant Harley-Davidson barbecue in Kingman, Arizona, which was supported by the town to the extent that the schools were closed and thousands of residents lined the streets as the riders came to town, demonstrates an example of how the image has changed. In 2003 in Milwaukee, 220,000 Harley-Davidson owners rode from all across North America to celebrate the company's 100th birthday.

Today, Harley-Davidson is the most popular tattoo in the USA; their retail stores and restaurants are both trendy and booming. Scores of top movie and recording stars are Harley-Davidson devotees. The company has encouraged and fostered literally thousands of Harley-Davidson Internet sites. Over the course of just a few years, there has been an extraordinary demand for the product, despite little advertising or promotion. The brand has eliminated the price issue to the degree that quality second-hand bikes sell for more than new list price. Harley-Davidson is now a brand that has true strength, creating not just buyers, but true devotees.

What were the elements that led to Harley-Davidson's fantastic turn-around? The first is that they developed community involvement and shared values that resonated with potential buyers and fostered word of mouth. The second was that they maximized this effect by encouraging this chain reaction. Harley utilized public events to build their market share one satisfied customer and heart share at a time.

> Dialogue, rather than traditional advertising monologue, is the key to building brand equity.

Can Brand Equity Be Transferred Across Product Categories?

Apple's (and formerly Pixar's) Steve Jobs and Virgin's Sir Richard Branson are two motivational leaders who have developed management and staff-driven branding and created a reverence for their brands from both employees and customers alike.

Branson initially developed Virgin into a powerhouse brand by leading by example, securing his people's commitment, and emphasizing the values they shared with the community. Branson's policy of personally working in all aspects of his airline business—being a luggage handler, taking reservations, and even working in the planes' galleys—demonstrated to the staff that he is one of them and he understands each of their roles. This has not only motivated and inspired employees; it also has garnered public admiration that's translated to brand equity and devoted customers.

Virgin clientele are such devotees that they were initially committed to the brand, whatever the product type. However, Branson's entry into a wide range of product and service categories—whether Virgin Airlines, Virgin Records, Virgin Rail, Virgin Bride, Virgin Direct insurance, or any other category, is a unique situation, since it is usually difficult to carry equity into unrelated businesses.

> It is also a risky strategy, because a problem experienced by one business that diminishes the brand equity will affect *all* the businesses.

This has occurred in a number of the Virgin branded businesses, particularly the high-visibility Virgin Railways. Chances are that it will ultimately have a significant effect on the brand equity of all Virgin endeavors, perhaps not before Sir Richard is far less visible.

What Is the Value of Brand Equity?

Creating a brand and developing equity in it involves business planning, human resources, customer service, marketing communication, and product development. It is a longer-term proposition to build a brand one heart share at a time, and it produces the following when it reaches critical mass and the delighted disciples' satisfaction begins to resonate:

- ◆ Intensified loyalty and repeat sales
- ◆ Increased brand credibility
- ◆ Enhanced brand values
- ◆ Reduced discounting
- ◆ Growing word of mouth
- ◆ More publicity opportunities
- ◆ Input for advertising focus
- ◆ Expanded research opportunities
- ◆ Energized staff morale and reduced turnover
- ◆ Stronger links with suppliers

This, in turn, triggers that all-important first recall brand awareness that makes the brand almost bulletproof to competitors.

Remember: A brand is not a name and logo. It is a culture—one that you create by shared values between the corporation, its people, the product, and its customers.

Chapter 14

Where and How Do You Offer Your Product?

Just a few years ago, a single company won the International Automotive Show Advertisement of the Year; winner of the *Time* magazine ad of the year; winner of the *USA Today* award; *Rolling Stone's* ad of the year; and countless other accolades. That company was . . . Nissan!

The result of all these awards and all this recognition? Nissan's sales dropped 3 percent. Their direct competition posted 7 percent gains, and the industry as a whole was up 3 percent. Yet Nissan cut 18 percent of their work force and the company president left to take up a job elsewhere.

A great campaign? It must be if the critics said so—right? Except for one thing: Awards are not worth a damn if the campaign doesn't sell product.

For instance, Pizza Hut paid the Russian Space Agency $1.25 million to put its logo on a Proton rocket taking materials to the Russian Space Station. A great gimmick? Absolutely. Great marketing? Doubtful, depending on how well it was leveraged at retail. The only true measure is whether it resulted directly or indirectly in additional product sales.

In many instances, the quest to simply be different for the sake of it—or to be the pioneer of a new marketing concept—overshadows sound marketing and communication logic. Why is it that marketers increasingly seem to believe they have to go to extremes? Increasing sales is not about increasing brand awareness, whether it is already 99 percent or 9 percent, nor is it about differentiating your advertising. Increasing sales is about differentiating your product, service, good citizenship, and belief system, and it's about providing a great value proposition.

The most significant problem we face is the lack of diligence in selecting the appropriate vehicle and a shortage in the simple skills of effective communication.

Above the Line (ATL), Below the Line (BTL), and Through the Line (TTL)

In business and marketing communications, ATL, BTL, and TTL are advertising techniques. Put simply, ATL promotions are tailored for a mass audience, BTL promotions are targeted at individuals according to their needs or preferences, and TTL is an advertising strategy involving both above and below the line communications.

While ATL promotions can establish brand identity but their performance is difficult to measure, BTL is designed to drive sales enabling marketers' immediate and valuable knowledge on ROI.

Above the line advertising is carried out through mass media, such as television, cinema, radio, print, web banners and web search engines and is primarily, and wrongly in my view, used to promote brands. This is very traditional, is monologue, and is increasingly less effective.

Below the line promotion refers to forms of non-media communication or advertising, using nontraditional strategies, typically focusing on dialogue, through direct means of communication, most commonly direct mail, e-mail, and printed media. BTL has become increasingly important in the communications mix, particularly FMCG (fast moving consumer goods) but also for industrial goods. BTL is an incentive to purchase, usually of short duration. It is efficient and cost-effective for targeting a limited and specific group.

BTL often uses highly targeted lists of names to maximize response rates and often features techniques such as sales personnel deployed at retail stores to generate trials or sales of products. It helps marketers establish one-on-one relationships with consumers where consumer response can be measured. Examples include telemarketing, road shows, promotions, in-shop and shop-front activities, and display units.

Through the line refers to an advertising strategy involving both above and below the line where one form of advertising points the target market to another form of advertising, thereby crossing the "line." In recent years, agencies and clients have switched to integrated communication or through the line approach.

Effective Communication

It is unfortunate that the overwhelming majority of people are bad communicators, especially when the basics of good communication are really quite simple. In my view, the following are a few rules to becoming better listeners and communicating more effectively with one another.

In my view, these are the basic elements:

- ◆ **Listen to what is being said.** This is the most essential element of good communication. Most of us spend too much time formulating our own questions or answers while the other person is still explaining their point.
- ◆ **Stop engaging in automatic listening.** For example, when someone proposes an idea, don't start by immediately judging whether or not you like it, who will complete it, or how it will be done. Ask questions that stimulate creativity and broaden everyone's understanding of the concept and its aims.
- ◆ By taking this approach, we add value to the person with whom we are speaking by making it easy for them to relate.

  In his tape series, *Communication,* British negotiation expert Peter Thompson demonstrates how people don't listen by asking a series of unbelievably simple questions. I ask these same questions in my presentations as well, and I usually receive incorrect answers from roomfuls of highly educated people. Sadly, the majority of people I address are in the marketing and sales business.

  The first question I ask is, "What is 40 divided by $\frac{1}{2}$?" Usually, before I finish the sentence, the answer 20 is yelled from all corners of the auditorium, when the correct answer is of course 80. Another question is, "How many of each species did Moses take on the Ark?" The immediate answer I get is two, despite the fact that Moses didn't go near the Ark! The point that these answers make is the sad fact that we simply don't listen. And we not only miss valuable information by failing to listen; we lose the respect and confidence of our staff and clients.

♦ **Be empathetic.** We need to put ourselves in the other person's emotional position to be able to understand their perspective. Renowned U.S. military figure General George Patton is famous for saying that the key to success is to learn everything possible about the people with whom you're interacting: "I read their accounts, read the same books, listen to the same music. I study their life and their personal battles. Now I know how to predict their moves and how they will react."

♦ **Maintain eye contact.** Doing so demonstrates that we are listening intently and are not distracted. The eyes are the window to the soul and the manner by which we can feel the depth of the other person's feelings or commitment. We also instill confidence in the other person by mimicking their posture and maintaining very open body language.

♦ **Be positive.** We need to send out positive messages when conversing with other people. It has been proven that by couching our requests in negative terms, we greatly enhance the chance that this negativity will occur, because these are the very thoughts we've put in the other person's mind.

♦ **Communicate in the same "language."** Everyone exhibits a predominance of one of the three communication characteristics: auditory, visual, or kinesthetic. Most people display a combination of all three. By developing an understanding of the preferences that each person with whom we are communicating has, we can greatly improve the quality of dialogue and, therefore, make it much more likely that we'll generate a sale.

We are operating in the age of the customer, of maximized one-on-one contact, and of customized products. The critical element in being successful in this environment is the ability to communicate effectively.

Neurolinguistic Programming

People with different characteristics communicate in entirely different ways. How often have you clearly and concisely explained something in detail only to have the other person just not get it? How about passing around photographs to find that, although some people study them, others just pass them on? It is not that the other party is stupid or not interested, it's just that you have different communication preferences. Depending on the purity of the characteristic in each person's makeup, it can almost seem like you're speaking two different languages.

Some 45 percent of people have predominantly the visual characteristic in countries including North America, the United Kingdom, and Australia; they react to visual stimuli. For example, if you point out a view, an object, or show them a photograph, they will show interest. However, if you ask them to listen to the birds or the hum of the engine, the auditory characteristic, they are much less likely to be interested. They will have the same reaction if you ask them to feel the texture of a brick or the quality of the paper sample, actions that would appeal to the kinesthetic characteristic.

People quickly give away their predominant characteristic when speaking with them if you know what signs to look for. A visual person will use phrases such as "I see what you are saying," "Bird's eye view," "Appears to me," "Eye to eye," "See to it," and words like *appear, examine, illustrate, see, notice,* and so on.

Approximately 30 percent of people are kinesthetic, and react to emotion, touch, and feel. Although they may not get enthused over a photo or a view, they prefer to feel and touch things and will really relate to an emotional story. They will use phrases that include "That idea feels terrific," "Come to grips with," "Slipped my mind," "Get in touch with," "Get a handle on it," and words like *feel, emotional, grasp, hunch, sensitive,* and *touch.*

The remaining 25 percent are auditory; they relate to sounds. For example, if you were selling real estate to one of these individuals, you would point out the peace and quiet or the sound of the creek or birds; if selling a car, you would talk about the purr of the motor. Auditory people use phrases like "I hear what you're saying," "Within ear shot," "Clear as a bell," "Express yourself," "Voice your opinion," and words like *announce, divulge, mention, articulate,* and *discuss.*

Neurolinguistic programming (NLP) is an extremely valuable communication tool. It is no coincidence that the top sales people in almost every field of endeavor are all devotees of NLP. Advertising strategies that are crafted to appeal to each of the characteristics will outperform those that are not. When you understand NLP, it enables you to adjust your communication or presentation to suit the other person's "language." This dramatically improves your relationship and interaction with the other person.

Another valuable aspect of NLP is to mirror the physical and speech patterns of the person with whom you are communicating. For example, if the person walks or talks slowly, it will greatly enhance your communication with that person to also walk or talk slowly. People relate better to people that they perceive are "like them" so by mirroring their characteristics, not mimicking them, the rapport between you will be greatly improved.

Once we know what to communicate and how to express it for maximum effect, the question then becomes, 'What vehicles should we use'?

Effect of Media Proliferation, Clutter, and Market Fragmentation

Traditional means of advertising and promotion appear to be increasingly less effective in achieving results and/or cost efficiency these days. It may simply be that we have become more effective at measuring marketing performance, or that businesses simply demand better results and increased cost effectiveness as bottom lines tighten. The overriding question is, "How do we sell more effectively in this new world business order?"

In my view, traditional advertising has really never been very cost-effective. It is just a lot more apparent in this age of increased efficiency, higher productivity, more accurate measurement of results, and a generally more analytical market place. Every available medium—broadcast, print, the Internet, relationship marketing, sponsorship, even signs in bus stops and elevators—all still have their place for a specific target audience. However, because of the increase in channels and proliferation of broadcast vehicles, audiences are becoming much more fragmented. As a result of today's lifestyle, the average consumer has a shortened attention span, increased pressure on their time, and a multiplicity of distractions, all of which are challenges that give marketers much less time to get an effective message across and thereby making communication with prospective clients both more difficult and more expensive.

It is also harder to determine the most effective vehicle to use with the target market and to compare the relative cost effectiveness of the various options. It is more important than ever to select the modes of communication we use much more carefully. To do this, we need to understand the advantages and disadvantages of each as they apply to the particular product or service being marketed. More importantly, we need to know our client, their competition, and their primary and secondary target markets extremely well. We need to have a clear profile of whom and where the potential clients are and the best way to impact and motivate them.

It All Begins with Customer Relations

A thorough knowledge of and focus on your customer is the ideal starting point these days. This familiarity will provide a quality of information on specific and potential customers that enables marketers to select vehicles that maximize impact effectively and cost efficiently. It also aids in determining which specific messages they should communicate.

Nowadays, it is the quality of customer relationships and ability to understand your clients that will determine how effective your customer communications process is. Customer Relationship Management (CRM) is the investigation, understanding, and management of all aspects of consumer contact, including marketing, sales, and service. Unfortunately, the organizational structure in most traditional companies creates barriers to effective CRM. Without drastic change to a more transparent organization, these companies will falter.

The investment required to understand, interact one-on-one with, and develop your products or services in a strategic alliance with your customers represents a fraction of the potential waste in communication costs that will occur without this knowledge. This research makes the marketing investment significantly more profitable.

An organization's position on the chart shown in Figure 14.1 determines the type of communication mediums that it is likely to use. The ability to target more accurately and amplify cost effectiveness increases as the business becomes more progressive. Figure 14.1 indicates that companies today roughly fall into three categories: traditional, transitional, and progressive.

	Traditional	Transitional	Progressive
Business Focus	Products/Sales	Channels/Marketing	Services/Customers
Organization	Product and Channel Management	Promotions and Channel Management	Contact and Customer Management
Business Benchmarks	Product Performance	Customer Revenues	Customer Satisfaction, Value, and Loyalty
Marketing Focus	Advertising, Sales, Promotion	Integrated Marketing Strategy	Niche Marketing, Customer-Specific Marketing
Technology	Transaction Processing, Data Maintenance	Data Access and Warehousing	Customer Involvement, Data Mining

Figure 14.1

Target the Right Message to the Right Audience

The importance of highly accurate targeting and communication of the right message cannot be emphasized enough. A good example of this is The Plaza Hotel in New York, which, until the late 1990s, focused 90 percent of its advertising budget on selling its rooms, restaurants, and bars. However, an analysis of the hotel's profit centers showed that the most gainful facet of the operation came from the functions held there. This prompted the hotel to begin spending 80 percent of the advertising dollars on attracting weddings and other events, which, in turn, attracted guests to rooms, restaurants, and bars and generated higher profitability.

It is also critical to realize that markets are seldom homogeneous, and research is required to determine your precise catchment area. For example, sales of small cars on the east and west coasts of the United States are more than double that of the inland states.

How Effective Is Television Advertising?

There is no question that TV is powerful; it portrays the color, excitement, and vibrancy of products and brings them to life. Yet the disadvantage of television advertising is that there is huge slippage during commercials to many audiences. Additionally, the majority of programs are less targeted than is required today for the cost-effective performance required for most products and services in this economy. This means that there is no real measure of the effective target market reach or cost per thousand effective impacts. Even though television advertising, which is based on the volume of program viewers, appears to represent cost-effective advertising, the reality is that the cost per advertisement is based on the rating of the program during which the advertisement is aired, not on the rating of the advertisement itself. In fact, research has consistently shown that ads always attract far fewer viewers than the program during which they're showcased. For example, the second ad in a break in a program that rates 30 may rate as low as 3.

In these situations, advertisers are essentially paying *10 times* the rate per impact that they think they are—the amount of slippage varies for men and women by time slot. On weekday evenings before 8:30 P.M., women (particularly those who work)—now 50.7 percent of the adult population—are busy doing various household chores that range from cooking, washing dishes, doing laundry, and putting kids to bed. They usually complete these tasks during ad breaks. On the other hand, advertisers who are trying to catch dad on weekends during sporting events are faced with the challenge that he is likely to channel surf during the ads to catch up with sports and programs on other channels.

Advertisers who buy television time pay dearly for people who are not watching. Although this isn't a recommendation to completely rule out television as an advertising medium, it is a warning to pay close attention to whether it's the most appropriate vehicle for your product or service. This will vary based on the time slots you purchase and the resultant slippage potential. It is often much more effective to buy slots in programs that have a smaller audience than in those that are highly targeted and have less slippage.

You need to pay particular attention to ensure you focus your advertising only on your target audience. Forget about a program's total number of viewers; it is only your specific target audience, narrowed down as much as possible, about which you should be concerned.

It's also vital to consider your catchment area, or the maximum geographic area in which people will realistically be interested in your product or service. Only people in these areas count. For example, there's no point advertising citywide if 90 percent of your potential clients live within five miles of your business. A little homework will tell you where your potential consumer is. Then you can divide your target audience into primary and secondary segments and determine each one's relative importance. When assessing the relative worth of television slots in different programs, you must calculate the value in terms of these primary and secondary audiences. Each of these considerations will take your advertising dollar much further.

One last thing to remember when creating a television ad: Although people *watch* television, they do not necessarily *listen* to it. Therefore, ensure that all important information, such as contact numbers, location, free offers, and so on, is written on the screen, not just spoken by the announcer.

Radio Provides Immediacy, Flexibility, and Frequency

Radio is a popular medium for several reasons. Everyone has a radio, and most people listen to it each day. It is also the ultimate immediacy medium because it is comparatively inexpensive and the message can be constantly changed at little cost. You can urge people to act 'now', particularly with live reads. You can't do that with television, because ads need to be produced and scheduled in advance. Additionally, it is fairly expensive to change a TV ad; with radio, it simply requires a copy change. Another advantage of radio is that people usually listen to particular personalities. When these personalities read advertisements, it can have the effect of an endorsement.

> The major value of radio is that it can create wonderful visual pictures of a product that could be more difficult or expensive to convey on television or in print.

People adapt these images to their own personality, so by using creativity, the ad can bring a new dimension to the product.

A few years ago, our firm won a Clio Award for a radio advertisement for an Australian football game that was being held at the Los Angeles Coliseum. We recorded 30-second spots that sold elements of Australian football that Americans find strange—items like uniforms without padding and skintight shorts. We created some pretty off-the-wall visual images of sensational athletes of Amazonian proportions in skimpy shorts. We sold the fun of a unique day out as the benefit, and the ad was the talk of Los Angeles.

An advertisement's effectiveness may increase exponentially with frequency. It is easier, and less expensive, to obtain this frequency with radio than it is with television. However, you again need to be careful in your time slot choice.

We have all heard the expression that statistics lie, and radio stations seem to have more people working on statistics than any other industry on the planet. You can frequently find 30 radio stations in a market, every one of which will send you a brochure claiming they are "number one" for one reason or another. You need to dissect very carefully all that information and disregard absolutely everything that does not directly impact your target market. It is important to look at audience demographics and costs for specific programs instead of for the station as a whole. After all, it may very well be the bottom-rated station that best achieves your company's objectives. So, although it is tempting to consider only the top stations when doing your evaluation, don't disregard anyone before you carefully evaluate their relationship with your target market.

One downside of radio is that recall of ads is very poor; the average person is usually only able to recall less than 5 percent of ads only one hour after hearing them. And the significant number of people that listen in the car, at work, at the beach, and so on, hardly ever have access to a pen to record information. Another obstacle is the number of people listening to ad-free satellite radio, which is becoming increasingly popular.

Is the Print Media Star Fading?

Although print media is falling from favor in this age of limited time and technology, newspapers and magazines still have their place. However, as with television and radio, you must take several factors into account. First, metropolitan newspapers in particular are incredibly cluttered, and usually contain hundreds of ads and a number of inserts. Second, the majority of people don't have much time to read the whole paper, so they skim through it. Another important point: Newspaper circulation in many markets is often not as homogenous as the publications would have you believe, and sales can fluctuate wildly, depending on that particular day's inserts. Many newspapers also sell much better in some regions of a city than others.

The key to choosing the right publications is to investigate very carefully before placing print advertising. It is important to understand that newspaper advertisements are most effective if they contain information, an offer, or a coupon that needs to be cut out and retained. Aside from broadcast and print, it is critical to consider other options to improve both effectiveness and cost efficiency.

Public Relations Builds Brand Equity

The public relations (PR) element is an incredibly powerful marketing tool. With escalating media costs and increased consumer skepticism, it provides a very credible yet inexpensive form of marketing. Public relations is not just free publicity, though; it needs to be part of a carefully planned mix of above- and below-the-line marketing disciplines. Public relations builds an image in terms of credibility and recognition, and it creates a favorable attitude to the activity, product, or company by means that are not considered to be hard sell. Whereas advertising is self-praise that's expected to be complimentary, PR is third party endorsement and reflects what others are saying and, therefore, carries more weight with both the public and corporations alike. This form of exposure is far more reliable than advertising, which customers tend to view with a great deal of skepticism.

In fact, news stories that are part of a PR campaign generate *seven times* the response of an advertising campaign. The focus in a :30- or :60-second slot must be on a single point in order to be effective, whereas news stories allow discussion of the issues and personnel involved, explain the background, or feature human-interest stories. Put simply, advertising takes a single point and hammers it home, creating short-term awareness of one small component. Public relations communicates a much more complex message explained in detail, usually with an emotional human angle—resulting in a long-term effect of enhanced credibility.

How Do We Communicate Online, the Medium of the Future?

Before you can communicate with potential clients on the web, you first have to attract them to your site. You can do this in two primary ways: online or through traditional media. As with all marketing, there is seldom a single vehicle that can achieve the desired results; instead, it requires a mix of communication vehicles.

There are several online ways to draw surfers to your site. A number of brands attract viewers through use of free offers. Some sites give away $10,000 a day; others offer free PCs, no-cost Internet access, free stock trading, tax preparation—and the list goes on. Though costs for advertising on these sites with a hyperlink are usually high, this can be a valuable source of leads if the sites share demographic or psychographic markets.

The accelerating pace of audiences shifting to the Internet was confirmed in August 2010 when professional-services firm giant Price WaterhouseCoopers released figures predicting that online advertising will attract as much revenue as TV and newspapers by 2014. In 2009, Britain became the first country in which the Internet became the largest advertising medium. Paul Fisher of the Interactive Advertising Bureau has predicted that TV, newspapers, and online advertising would all settle at about 23 percent share of the advertising pie.

Banner ad click-throughs have decreased from eight per hundred to less than two per thousand page hits over the past decade. Although some might argue that it is the quality not the quantity of click-throughs that is important, our studies have shown that it is not cost-effective on either front.

> Few people realize that online advertising is more like direct response
> than almost any other advertising form.

However, advertisers don't treat it like direct response. For the most part,
online advertising isn't treated like advertising at all. It seldom has a customer
product benefit (CPB), added value, or a risk reversal, and often there is no
call to action. It is not surprising it doesn't work!

Maximizing the Extraordinary Personal Reach of Social Media

It is, first of all, critical to create a highly targeted social media strategy with
clear, achievable goals, irrespective of the use to which it is being directed.
This process requires that you take the following four steps:

1. Plan
2. Build
3. Promote
4. Measure

One potentially helpful starting point is the custom Facebook page,
which allows users to evaluate what some of the most creative minds in the
Internet business and most innovative brands in the world have developed.

PLAN

First, you must clearly define your business goals and determine which
elements and resources you can leverage. To do this, evaluate your brand
and objectives, business assets, target customer, and brand equity. Then, aim
to structure each social media endeavor so it is clearly tied back to a business
goal. Identify the right strategic opportunities so that you are best leveraging
your assets and resources to enable you to focus on building meaningful
relationships and growing your social platform effectively.

BUILD

In order to build custom pages and content, promotions, and other related
material, you need a creative team that can design memorable brand
experiences. I have a team that I contract to manage social media for my

clients. As with any communication, the images, words, and content will strongly influence the consumer's reaction. You need to build custom Facebook and Twitter pages with applications and promotions that seamlessly integrate with the look, tone, and feel of your brand, while driving interaction. You also need to work on social media 24/7, managing both outbound and inbound activity.

PROMOTE

The way to develop a large and loyal following is by inspiring people to connect to your brand, and the most important element to attracting followers is developing quality content. The content you offer must be inspiring and informative and coupled with incentives to encourage frequent visits to the site. You also need to leverage technologies that will grow your message organically.

MEASURE

A great advantage of social media is the ability to measure its impact. You need to track both positive and negative feedback, along with any changes in volume or sentiment. This allows you to readily see the impact your brand has on the social platform. If you don't tune in to what consumers are saying about your brand, industry, product, and competitors, you are missing the point of engaging in social-media promotion.

The following are some critical facts to know about the most popular and widely used forms of social media today.

- ◆ **BLOG**–Fresh, interesting, and sticky content. Great for search-engine optimization, building followers, and reputations.
- ◆ **LinkedIn**–15 million visitors per month. Great for business profile, search-engine ranking.
- ◆ **YouTube**–84 million visitors per month. Very effective for viral marketing campaigns.
- ◆ **Twitter**–24 million visitors per month. Hot for microblogging, search-engine ranking, building brand and followers.
- ◆ **Facebook**–125 million visitors per month. Closed community.
- ◆ **MySpace**–50 million visitors per month. Search-engine ranking.

Five hundred million people are a lot of individuals to be able to have dialogue with, which is precisely why social media is critical in today's marketing mix.

The Majority of Advertising to Direct People to Web Sites Is Offline

Of the three primary media vehicles, print is most successful because the reader can easily retain the domain name and other details about the site. People who are watching television usually have to scramble to find a pen, an endeavor that is more difficult if traveling at 60 mph on the freeway listening to the radio. Newspapers, particularly local ones, also provide the opportunity to have a story published about your site, thereby providing additional information and reinforcement of your domain name and enhancing the likelihood of recall.

You should also list your domain name on everything possible, from stationary to retail windows, on vehicles and packaging, and so on. In my bestselling book, *Complex Marketing Made Simple* (released 15 years ago), I detailed a number of other opportunities that should be considered, such as outdoor, direct mail, piggybacking with other businesses that have a similar target market, cross promotion with your clients and/or suppliers, mailbox drops, and so on.

Of course, getting viewers to our website is only the first challenge. Once they are there, how do we then encourage them to read our material, participate, and get motivated to buy our product or service? The first step is to realize that you have less than ten seconds to catch and hold their attention. It is, therefore, important to minimize downloading time, at least initially. You should also minimize the amount of graphics, but make sure the ones you do use are powerful and effective. The emotional benefits of using your product or service are a much more powerful marketing tool than loads of graphics. Although the Internet is interactive communication and sites need to provide education and entertainment, it is important to keep a balance.

Among the most successful sites on the web are those that involve site visitors in contests and promotions that appeal to the precise mindset of the audience they are trying to reach. A Jupiter Communications Research survey showed that 49 percent of e-commerce shoppers entered and enjoyed these interactions. When Karen Edwards was head of marketing for Yahoo!, she said, "Promotional elements must have a relationship to the product or service you are selling. Don't forget: the Internet is a combination of information and entertainment. It is all about the customer. Your promotion must be fun, entertaining, and challenging."

> Research also shows that it is not the *size* of any incentive offered that is important, but its relevance to the target market.

Companies must change the interaction, competition, or promotion regularly, ask about and engage the customer, be interested and interesting, and provide them advice and help. It is a very unobtrusive way to get psychographic information.

Utilizing testimonials is another way to both increase the site's credibility and enhance potential usage and sales. Companies can use chat groups to build brand equity and sell products by creating online communities and passionate advocates, thereby driving word of mouth.

Hybrid advertising spots that combine the television and Internet technologies are also highly effective. For example, Nike's promotion for the Air-Cross Trainer II included three cliffhanger commercials that put the viewer in the middle of exciting action with a dramatic ending. Viewers then needed to visit www.whatever.nike.com the website and choose between seven potential endings for each commercial. This kind of advertising changes a 30-second one-way spot into a 20-minute interactive experience, and, of course, visitors can also buy the shoe once they visit the website.

Relationship Marketing

Today's highly sophisticated research capabilities enable us to obtain, develop, and sort information on prospective clients very quickly. This has made relationship marketing an extremely effective marketing tool that helps us focus on getting customers rather than market share.

Relationship marketing allows companies to customize offerings for each potential client or client profile, create client-designed interactive devices, target to specific consumers with unique products, and build longer-lasting customer relationships.

I have already introduced the key marketing drivers: color, name, image, selling benefits, CPB, risk reversal, and added value. Relationship marketing allows every one of these elements to be refined for each individual customer—or, at least, for each customer profile—which greatly enhances the potential for success. It addresses the important issues of efficiency and cost effectiveness. Programs are easy to test on a highly defined target audience, easy and inexpensive to modify if necessary, and, therefore, highly flexible and efficient. Because of the refined targeting this approach affords us, the results we obtain are easy to measure.

Direct Mail

One example of the improved results that database development and profiling capabilities has enabled is direct mail's improved effectiveness. As the mounting volume of junk mail that we receive each day testifies, this marketing method is rapidly gaining acceptance.

Equifax Harris polls show that individuals' acceptance of direct mail increased to over 80 percent in the late 1990s, up from a little over 50 percent at the start of the decade. It was estimated, in 2009, that over 68 percent of all American adults—175 million people—bought from direct mail. The primary reason for this is the high degree of targeting and the reduction in spillage.

As business becomes more global, using traditional media as a cost-effective, efficient communication tool becomes increasingly prohibitive, whereas relationship marketing becomes more and more efficient. The data collection, collation, and one-on-one communication nature of the Internet ensures that relationship marketing will be a major channel of future business revenue.

Despite these new efficiencies, your message's ability to motivate people to buy—whether you convey it via print, online, or elsewhere—is still the bottom line. You cannot succeed by presenting a generic look. Consumers need to see their image in whatever marketing piece you send them. The typeface, copy, and photography/graphics must speak to them and make them feel special. Providing that you offer something interesting and that you've thoroughly researched the benefits, CPB, risk reversal, and added-value elements, direct mail is an excellent cost-effective communication alternative. Because consumers receive a number of catalogs and mailing pieces each day, positioning and brand equity is critical. Direct marketers rely on positioning. The consumer looks at each piece for literally seconds before deciding to retain or discard. For instances in which the same product is offered in two different catalogs, they should each be presented in a way that mirrors the particular consumer profile. For example, one may be casual and pragmatic, the other luxurious and elegant.

The effectiveness of highly targeted direct mail is demonstrated by the results generated. For instance, General Motors mailed information about their credit card to 30 million people and received 7 million responses. Over $7 billion was charged to the cards during the program's first six months. Levi's jeans for girls direct mailed girls 7- to 11-years-old in a back-to-school campaign. They received a 7 percent response and doubled brand awareness.

The NFL expansion organization in Baltimore was under pressure to prove that it had the local support they needed to get the franchise. Because the group had only $85,000, they had no funds for mainstream advertising. The direct-mail campaign they launched instead ended up generating $8.5 million—and sold out all the seats and boxes in their proposed but not yet existent stadium. The Baltimore Ravens joined the NFL in 1996.

Permission Marketing

Permission marketing (also called invitational marketing) takes place when consumers authorize marketers to send them certain promotional messages. This is typically done when companies ask consumers to fill out a survey indicating interests when registering for a service. Organizations then match advertising messages with customers' interests, thereby reducing both clutter and search costs for the consumer while improving targeting precision.

Even though brands can implement permission marketing via any direct medium, the tool has come into its own only with the advent of the Internet. There are two primary reasons for this:

1. The cost of marketer-to-consumer communication on the Internet is low (marketers incur similar costs whether they send out 1 million or 10 million e-mails). Additionally, the web has enabled rapid feedback due to instantaneous two-way communication.

2. The failure of direct mail's approach of sending unsolicited promotional messages. Spammers can easily obtain new e-mail addresses from websites and Usenet groups using software programs that troll the Internet. This is frequently a violation of their privacy rights and governments have strongly legislated against spam mail.

Therefore, spam cannot be a legitimate form of marketing communication. Allowing this would lead to an excessive message volume for consumers, thereby weakening brand reputation. Hence, companies see permission marketing as a feasible alternative for Internet marketing communication.

Consumer interest is the key dependent variable that influences the degree of participation. It is positively affected by message relevance and negatively affected by information entry/modification costs, message-processing costs, and privacy costs. Although targeting customers has been a core marketing principle, most targeting today is more of a targeting–on-averages process. Advertisers obtain the average consumer profile and choose a communications vehicle that matches the target most accurately.

However, we have the power to do much better nowadays. Given the growing capability that technology has given us to address each individual, we can now customize the marketing mix according to specific clients' needs. This integral part of CRM takes a long-term relationship approach as opposed to a short-term transactional approach.

> In essence, permission marketing enables marketers to estimate the customer's lifetime value and allocate resources in accordance with these values.

The emphasis is on retaining existing customers rather than on obtaining new ones.

Viral Marketing

Viral marketing is precisely the same as word of mouth, leveraging, network marketing, and creating mass awareness through stunts, the only difference being that it utilizes the Internet. Viral marketing is any strategy that encourages individuals to pass a marketing message on to others, thereby creating the potential for exponential growth in the message's exposure and influence. Like viruses, such strategies take advantage of rapid multiplication to explode the message to tens, then thousands, then millions.

Viral marketing is sometimes used to describe some Internet-based stealth-marketing campaigns—including blogs and seemingly amateur web sites—that aim to create word of mouth for a new product or service. These campaigns often generate media coverage via offbeat stories that provide extensive exposure, often globally and at no cost.

The term *viral advertising* refers to the practice of sharing interesting and entertaining content that's often sponsored by a brand, aiming to build awareness of a product or service. These commercials often take the form of funny video clips, or interactive Flash games, images, and even text.

Viral marketing has become so popular because of the simplicity of executing the marketing campaign, relatively inexpensive (compared to direct mail) and ability to accurately target your market and attain a rapid response rate. Its main advantage is its ability to obtain a large number of interested people at a low cost.

It is difficult for any business to acquire and maintain a large customer base. Through the use of the Internet and e-mail advertising, business-to-consumer (B2C) efforts have a greater impact than many other marketing tools. Viral marketing is a technique that avoids the annoyance of spam mail; instead, it encourages users of a specific product or service to tell a friend about their satisfaction and provide a positive word-of-mouth recommendation.

Because of the Internet's massive global reach—as well as the ability it affords any individual to send an almost unlimited number of messages instantly to their database—an effective viral campaign can create both awareness and sheer weight of numbers very quickly. As evidenced by the AXE feather viral campaign for Unilever (discussed in Chapter 1), other hosts can piggyback and promote these messages, and then use their resources to increase the reach and exposure. AXE feather spread from 30,000 individual e-mails to 50 million viewers in the span of two years—a jump that demonstrates that the right message, placed in the right environment, will grow exponentially. The message or image replicates, again and again, with geometrically increasing power. In a few short generations, a virus population can explode.

There are several types of viral campaigns:

- ◆ **Pass-along**–A message that encourages the user to forward to others. The basic form of this is chain letters that feature a note at the bottom prompting the reader to forward along. Short, funny video clips that people spontaneously pass along tend to be more effective. Many of these, such as Honda's Cog television commercial, began as TV commercials and have since circulated on the web by word of mouth. The number of people reached in this way is often much greater than the amount who viewed the original television advertisment.
- ◆ **Incentivized viral**–In these initiatives, brands offer rewards for either passing a message along or providing someone else's address,

which can dramatically increase referrals. However, this approach is most effective when the offer requires another person to take action. Most online contests offer more chances of winning for each referral given. However, when the person being referred must also participate in order for the first person to obtain that extra chance of winning, there's a greater chance that the referral will participate.

♦ **Undercover**–In these scenarios, a viral message is presented as a cool or unusual page, activity, or piece of news, without obvious incitements or incentives to link or pass along. It is not immediately apparent in undercover marketing that anything is actually being promoted. Companies make a concerted effort to have the item's discovery seem spontaneous and informal, in order to encourage natural memetic behavior. (Memetic is derived from *meme*, which identifies ideas or beliefs that are transmitted from one person or group of people to another.) Outside-world clues, such as graffiti, which appears in cities with key viral words, are often used to direct people to search out the presented mystery. (Graffiti is images or lettering scratched, scrawled, painted, or marked in any manner in public.) Because of the large amount of unusual and entertaining content on the Internet, this can be the hardest type of viral to spot, especially as companies try to imitate the style and content of amateur websites and authentic underground movements.

♦ **Edgy gossip/Buzz marketing** ads or messages create controversy by challenging the borders of taste or appropriateness. The aim is to inspire discussion of the resulting controversy that will generate buzz and word of mouth advertising. For example, prior to releasing a movie, some Hollywood movie stars get married, get divorced, get arrested, or become involved in some scandal that directs conversational attention to them.

♦ **User-managed database**–These sites allow users to create and manage their own lists of contacts using a database provided by an online service provider. By inviting other members to participate in their community, users create a viral, self-propagating chain of contacts that naturally grows and encourages others to sign up as well. Examples of such services include anonymous matching services like eCrush, business contact management services like Plaxo, and other social databases like Evite and Classmates.com.

Hotmail.com, one of the first free web-based e-mail services, is an excellent example of viral marketing. Their strategy is simple:

1. Give away free e-mail addresses and services.
2. Attach a simple tag at the bottom of every free message sent out: "Get your private, free e-mail at www.hotmail.com"
3. People then e-mail to their own network of friends and associates.
4. These people then sign up for their own free e-mail service.
5. The message is broadcast to their own ever-increasing circle of friends and associates.

A carefully designed viral marketing strategy can spread information extremely rapidly. Transmission of viral marketing can occur in various ways:

- ◆ **Web**–Typing into a web-based form that converts that information into an e-mail and sends it to recipients. There are links in an article that encourage readers to send the material to a friend, which then brings them to a web-based form to fill out. This form converts all the information to the recipient in an e-mail.
- ◆ **E-Mail**–A very common type: forwarding e-mails, such as jokes, quizzes, and pictures.
- ◆ **Word of mouth**–Oral communication and the passing of information from person to person.
- ◆ **IM**– Hyperlinks are sent over instant messaging servers such as Jabber, AIM, ICQ, MSN, Yahoo!, or Google Talk. This method is popular with many young people who are arguably more likely to trust a link sent by a friend via IM than a message sent by that same friend through e-mail.
- ◆ **Reward for referrals**–Sometimes, the marketing company offers a reward for referring customers, encouraging them to use any of the above methods.
- ◆ **Bluetooth**–The widespread use of mobile phones that support free Bluetoothing has enabled promotional videos to be distributed virally between handsets.

Despite its many advantages, there are also currently several barriers to viral marketing, including:

- **Size**–If the viral content is a video clip or streaming video, it may be too large for the recipient to receive. However, newer technologies are eliminating this problem, as Internet connections grow faster and e-mail inboxes become more capable of receiving large files.

- **Media format**–A viral marketing campaign will be unsuccessful if the message is in a format that most people cannot use. For example, if particular software is needed that is not widely used, then people will not be able to open or view the message.

- **E-mail attachment**–Many people receive viral marketing messages while at the office, and company anti-virus software or firewalls can prevent people from receiving these attachments.

- **Cumbersome referral mechanism**–In order for a viral marketing campaign to be successful, it must be easy to use. For example, if the promotion is some sort of game or contest, then asking for referrals should be an option immediately after the game, not a condition to play.

- **Sabotage**–Especially in the case of undercover-style marketing campaigns, discovering the marketing nature of a popular campaign may cause the same social networks to inform people of the commercial intent of the meme, and promote a formal or informal boycott of the company or product in question.

Examples of Viral Marketing

The Subservient Chicken was a viral marketing promotion of Burger King's line of chicken sandwiches and their Have-It-Your-Way campaign. The campaign was based on a web site that features a person in a chicken costume who performed a wide range of actions based on a user's input, showing prerecorded footage and appearing like an interactive webcam. The site takes literally the advertising slogan "Get chicken just the way you like it." There are more than 300 commands to which the Subservient Chicken would respond, including Michael Jackson dance moves such as Moonwalk, Riverdance, and Walk Like an Egyptian.

When told to perform any acts that the Subservient Chicken considered offensive, he walked up to the camera and shook a scolding chicken finger in disappointment. When told to eat food from rival fast-food chain

McDonald's, he approached the camera and placed his finger down his throat; he had a more positive response when told to eat Burger King.

Ecko clothing brand Stillfree.com released a video in support of the company's Still Free campaign. The video's success was due in large part to the did-they-or-didn't-they debate the clip generated. The undercover ad made even the United States Air Force publicly question whether the group who shot the clip did, in fact, breach security at Andrews AFB and spray graffiti along the left wing engine of Air Force One. Though the stunt turned out to be a hoax, the debates swirling around the incident transformed the Still Free slogan from a mere tag line into a national news headline.

Pale lager Carlton Draught's big ad was an award-winning advertisement for the brand that used viral marketing techniques before it was released on television. The advertisement showed two armies—one dressed in maroon, the other in yellow—marching toward one another singing "O Fortuna" from Carmina Burana by Carl Orff, but replaced with lyrics such as "It's a big ad/ . . . expensive ad/This ad better sell some bloody beer." A heroic figure on horseback leads the charge. When viewed from the air, those watching can see the armies form a glass of Carlton Draught and a human body. The glass is then lifted to the mouth, and the audience sees the beer (the rushing, ecstatically leaping yellow-clad men) flowing into the figure's stomach. The ad parodies the visual style of epic battle sequences currently in vogue (a la Peter Jackson's *Lord of the Rings* films) complete with sweeping, larger-than-life panoramas of rugged mountain terrain.

Just 24 hours after release, the big ad had been downloaded 162,000 times and had been seen by over one million viewers in 132 countries within two weeks. The viral release of the big ad was so successful that the company reduced their television media budget so as to not overexpose the advertisement.

Philips Bodygroom Man pushed the envelope of decency with their Shave Everywhere site that promoted the new product Bodygroom. The site and its accompanying video advertisement made light of a very uncomfortable topic for men to discuss. The campaign generated millions of views and visits to the Shave Everywhere site and has given the electronics company an unexpectedly "edgy" persona. The Tell a Friend feature on the bottom right-hand corner of the site was particularly useful in prompting the campaign to make the Internet rounds.

Always Remember Who Your Actual Customer Is

You have two objectives if you have a consumer product. One is to get onto supermarket or retail store shelves, and the other is to create a consumer demand for your product.

> Merely getting your product placed in stores *will not* encourage people to buy it.

In our demand-and-supply economy, it is important to both motivate the consumer to demand the product and the retailer to stock it.

The traditional method for softening up buyers is to buy advertising in the retail publications they read, where you emphasize the product's virtues from their perspective. You can then meet the buyers and use all your powers of persuasion, focusing on research that shows customer appeal, likelihood of purchase, and how that translates in sales terms, and, of course, the profit retailers can make. If you have the available funds, you can hold a launch party for the buyers, wine and dine them, and attempt to get them on board. The next step is to cross your fingers and hope that, when you make the presentation, retailers buy your story *and* your product.

Having promoted many retail products, I know that this approach certainly works. However, in my experience, launching a highly targeted initiative works even better.

A few years ago, our firm first tried an idea that we have used many times since with great success. The buyers at all the major supermarkets had, essentially on the basis of an overcrowded category, rejected our client's snack food product. We painstakingly tracked down the home address of the 37 buyers representing every chain we were pitching. We then sampled the product with a full-size pack to every house in every street in which a buyer lived. For cases in which the item was a food product, we found out where the buyers' children went to school and provided a week or two of supplies to each of the schools. The reasoning behind this was that the children would soften up their parents—our buyers—without any pushing coming from us. This technique both increased the product's credibility, and gave buyers an opportunity to try it with their family. After the sampling exercise in the snack food example, we presented to buyers at their businesses and received 100 percent acceptance, in contrast to our client's 100 percent failure rate just a month or so earlier. We stayed away from buying expensive media and relied, instead, on a much less costly form of direct marketing to communicate our message.

Utilize the Inexpensive Benefits of Technology

It is important to keep up with the opportunities that new technology presents. The interactive marketing revolution reflects the shift to direct response. Computers, printers, modems, CD-ROM's, video/audio, online, and interactive capabilities have been a great boost to marketers. Interactive kiosks and high-tech presentation devices enable us to create more effective and efficient communication programs in both local and global markets. The relatively inexpensive graphics software and notebooks allow us to design elaborate multimedia presentations at a fraction of what it would have cost only a few years ago. These simple packages assist in our building excellent graphics, charts, animation, and sound effects into our presentations.

Today's technologies are simple and convenient. For example, once you have the presentation on disc, you can connect your laptop to a television set, allowing your presentations to be made in any boardroom or lounge room anywhere. This new technology also allows users to set up tiny video cameras on the computer to provide live pictures from the originating computer. This enables you to launch simple video demonstrations from your own office. The effectiveness of this enhanced one-on-one communication has led to predictions that between 10 percent and 40 percent of the money annually spent on marketing communication vehicles will be spent on the World Wide Web or other interactive applications within five years. Tablets such as the iPad enable anyone to produce and present excellent presentations to a potential customer in any setting, anytime, and in any place.

The confluence of Internet, television, cable, and telecommunications companies will continue to open up the Internet to people at home. More people inside corporations are becoming dependent on the real-time communication and access to information provided by computer technology. The ability to build detailed profiles on individual consumers through technology and sophisticated data gathering—coupled with the high quality of customized presentation and the ability to deliver online or through CD-ROMs, and such, to one person or a number of people, is a major advance in cost-effective communication.

The Internet enables a business to engage and entertain the consumer and, with interactive applications, keep the consumer returning to the site. It also allows companies to conduct dialogue with the potential consumer, in contrast to traditional advertising monologue. This repeat access and information transfer reinforces the business information message, building brand equity and loyalty.

Interactive communication not only allows the advertiser to learn more about the consumer, it also allows the consumer to learn more about the specific aspects of the company's product in which they are particularly interested. Marketers' success in many industries will depend on how quickly they adapt to interactive technology and focus on building one customer at a time.

Remember: "The difference between a good company and a great company is the ability to communicate with its customers."

—Lee Iacocca

Chapter 15

Internet Commerce and Social Media

The principles required for Internet marketing are the same as for all other forms of marketing. However, I'm hoping that the advice contained within this chapter will prevent some people from making costly mistakes in their quest to capture markets outside their traditional territory.

There are three fundamental elements of Internet commerce: business to business (B2B), business to consumer (B2C), and consumer to consumer (C2C). This chapter will discuss the practice of e-commerce as a global phenomenon, as well as how both individuals and small- to medium-size enterprises can build an effective website to expand their market catchment area. We will also expand on the extraordinary influence that social media has had on today's commercial environment, as discussed in the previous chapter.

E-Commerce Is a Sales Channel, Another Route into the Market Place

Some argue that the Web has caused the third biggest upheaval in retail, after malls in the 1940s and the major discount warehouses of the 1980s. International Data Corporation (IDC) predicts that the global bricks and mortar retail economy will exceed $13.5 trillion in 2010, with the Internet economy representing 6 percent of that. Extraordinarily, the latest study by Discover Small Business Watch showed that, despite spending nearly a trillion dollars on retail on the web in 2009, 55 percent of small businesses still don't have a website, and 57 percent of them claim that they never will!

Traditional business faces three fundamental problems: market fragmentation, increasingly complex processes, and high inventory due to lack of real-time sales knowledge. The Internet provides price, availability, supplier and product-knowledge transparency, all of which ensures price parity, as well as strict inventory control and product selection. Information technology (IT) optimizes supply chains by enabling rapid adjustment to market conditions. For many businesses, e-commerce can provide a faster time to market at lower costs and immediate access to a global marketplace 365 days a year, 24 hours a day. However, it requires a totally different skill set, involves greatly increased competition, and takes place in an environment in which the customer is truly in charge. The e-commerce aspect of most companies is unlikely to succeed as a standalone. Rather, it must be fully integrated with all other aspects of the business.

> The marketing of a successful business today needs to be offline, online, and in line.

For the majority of businesses, this has proven more difficult than it appears. Not only is it time consuming to seamlessly integrate all departments in a complex organization—and usually requires companies to meld a plethora of different systems and requirements into one—but there is often an attitude gap between traditional and IT-focused staff as well. IT personnel tend to be less structured; they demand more flexibility, have less corporate allegiance, and are less likely to accept conventional notions of boundaries and hierarchy. This often requires a completely revamped culture, environment, and decision-making process. Once an organization establishes a sense of teamwork between all company divisions, it can then coordinate and streamline retail store and web prices with logistics and inventory. This also makes it easier to address corporate policies with regard to issues like online purchase pick-ups and returns to retail. Once they've done so, companies can begin analyzing and categorizing previous transactions and customer databases.

It can also be difficult to integrate customers and partners into the system, and determine appropriate access levels and firewalls. The challenge faced by most bricks-and-clicks businesses has been the need to restructure and incorporate—both internally and with partners and customers as well—without destroying internal and external relationships.

Though companies are making a substantial ongoing investment in technology, this does not all relate to e-commerce. We need to differentiate e-commerce from IT and communication development. The continued expansion of corporate Intranets, data stores, data mining, appliances, and peripherals will greatly increase IT spending, but only a fraction of this will relate to e-commerce.

Internet commerce can be regarded as a communication vehicle that utilizes the same marketing principles as the so-called traditional or legacy businesses, except adapted to online applications. Accordingly, the various marketing techniques discussed throughout this book are accompanied by an explanation of how they connect to online applications in the relevant chapter. This chapter provides an overview of e-commerce opportunities.

Business-to-Business: A True Revolution

The Internet hasn't changed demand and supply; however, it has provided people and companies with a tool to create real demand for new innovations. Where the Internet is providing authentic change is in our ability to do everything much faster—which, in turn, increases productivity and spurs economic growth. The Internet also aggregates buying power, volume discounts, reduces off-contract spending, and labor and production efficiencies with savings of 5 to 20 percent. In 2009, 18.76 billion B2B transactions were conducted on the web.

In 2010, AMR Research showed that 87 percent of traditional businesses will sustain or increase Internet-related spending on customer service, 86 percent will do so for supplier management, and 90 percent will at least maintain Internet spending on business-to-business (B2B) initiatives in the next two years. This is a reflection of the results that clearly demonstrate that replacing existing internal processes with web technologies can help companies run more smoothly, keep customers satisfied, and, importantly, reduce costs. The Internet can reduce the time it takes to respond to customers and enable more precise planning, as well as improve inventory, supply chain, and customer-relationship management (CRM). For example, consumer electronics and networking giant Cisco Systems never physically touches over 55 percent of orders. Their e-commerce initiatives have provided $800 million a year in productivity gains arising from supply chain, customer, and procurement benefits.

Technology enables companies to fully and seamlessly connect internally in a transparent way so that they can track all elements of the business—from customer profiling and recording every interaction, through to production, stocking, sales, delivery, and so on—in real time.

> Once the business is internally connected in this way, management can bring all customers, suppliers, retailers, strategic partners, and consumers into appropriate parts of the transparent real-time loop. This is true CRM.

Additionally, organizations can easily construct firewalls to control the level of access for various internal and external parties. This lets you provide the ultimate added value and customer service, gather exceptional feedback, and serves as a powerful barrier to competitors. Data management dashboard technology can advise executives of any deviation from normal operation, in any area of the business, in real time, which enables immediate addressing of any issues that may arise.

The establishment of competitor-to-competitor exchanges—for example, the online joint purchasing group established by Chrysler, Ford, and General Motors—has improved efficiencies in the whole industry ecosystem, not just their own. Companies' departures from their own culture can also allow them to resolve other economic issues and improve operation.

One of the major problems traditionally facing manufacturers and wholesalers/brokers in the retail industry is the provision of appropriate stock levels to the retail warehouse—and being able to get these items onto shelves. For example, in the supermarket industry, 8.2 percent of products are out of stock at any given time—a number that can increase to 15 percent when products are on promotion. In addition, the cost of failing to comply with the terms of products on promotion can be as high as 30 percent. This represents losses of tens of billions of dollars—to both the manufacturer and the retailer.

The primary problem has continued because it can take up to two months to obtain traditional sales reports. However, thanks to the advent of technologies like registers linked to the supplier (thereby allowing every sale to be tracked in real time), as well as handheld devices that provide instant stock levels, SKUs, facing and pricing details—we can correct these problems instantly. It also leads to improved forecasting, stocking, and delivery, thus generating substantial cost savings. In the case of retailing giant Walmart, 97 percent of goods sold in stores do not pass through a warehouse. Radio Shack selects new store locations based on catalog and Internet sales, and segments customers into 52 categories.

These trends are increasingly blurring the boundaries between manufacturer and retailer, and also putting the traditional wholesaler middleman at risk. Many of the services they provide are in one way or another connected to providing information—much of which can be found online.

With regard to online cost savings, although most small business will grow sales very little, thanks to a web presence they can save significantly by diligently participating in online sourcing of all the products they use in their daily business. For example, AA batteries range online from 32 cents to 82 cents, color printer cartridges from $19.00 to $29.00 and so on—often with no tax. At the same time, a new range of middlemen have developed around the collection, analysis, processing, delivery, and billing services, most of whom are outsourced.

Examples of Integrated B2B Solutions

Communication problems in the construction industry create delays, cost overruns, angry subcontractors, and worried clients. According to *Business Week* magazine, a typical $200 million project at Beers Construction Company (now Beers Skanska) in Atlanta can generate more than 150,000 documents, including technical drawings, legal contracts, purchase orders, requests for information, change orders, and schedules. Beers Skanska's managers also need to collaborate with a very dispersed and diversified group of people, such as engineers, contractors, and subcontractors (and *their* subcontractors), surveyors, inspection companies, traffic engineers, building managers, project supervisors, and architects. Additionally, all these individuals are located in different areas of the country, working different shifts.

Beers Skanska sets up a website (e-Builder) for each project that serves as a repository for storing every document, engineering and architectural drawing, e-mail, calendar, and so on. This way, when someone connected with the project wants to check a drawing, find out when a crucial person is available, or see a log of the weather reports at the job site over the last week, they can easily access the information in seconds.

Additionally, subcontractors who find that a construction site doesn't match their expectations can snap digital photos, post them on the site, and resolve problems much more quickly. These steps can keep a project on schedule, and the archived e-mail, contracts, drawings, photos, and other material come in handy when settling disputes.

The site automates and tracks workflow as well. For example, when a subcontractor fills out a request for information, it goes directly to the general contractor, who signs off on it. The request then travels to the architect, then back to the subcontractor. This has helped turnaround time for information requests to go from 21 days to a mere 5. This has improved Beers Skanska's relationship with clients by allowing them to read meeting minutes and obtain up-to-date, accurate information. Since adopting e-Builder, Beers Skanska has always completed jobs on or before schedule and has reduced communication costs by 60 percent.

General Electric is one company that has been widely praised for e-business initiatives, such as getting its suppliers to bid for business over the web. In 2000, GE gained more than $7 billion in online transactions, purchased $6 billion worth of supplies through its online auctions, and saved about $1.5 billion via streamlined internal processes in its first year of operation.

Technology and consulting firm IBM is another example of this. In 1997, the company began to move its procurement activities online—including the purchase of everything from office supplies to computer chips—by constructing a massive private exchange. Today, this system links IBM to more than 25,000 suppliers, up from 800 at the end of 1998. In 2008, IBM's exchange handled about $63 billion worth of transactions and saved the company nearly $677 million compared with the traditional method of negotiating contracts, completing bills of materials, or even ordering paper clips. Five years ago, it took IBM between 9 and 12 months to negotiate and finalize a contract. Now it takes 30 days or less.

Business-to-Consumer . . . An Effective Niche Market?

Worldwide Internet retailing grew significantly from $15.8 billion in 1999 to $33.5 billion in 2000 and $900 billion in 2009. Although this doesn't necessarily mean that e-retailing will ever represent a substantial segment of the total retail market, it *will* be significant, particularly in industries in which it is not critical to touch and see the item being purchased.

Some 500 of the estimated 68,000 major web retailers are profitable. The most successful of these are extensions of the online catalog companies, followed by established brick-and-mortar retailers, while purely online retailers are unable to attain profitability. In fact, the top 1 percent of retailers on the web generated over 70 percent of total retail sales.

Some brands are lucky enough to have a product the customer knows, making online purchasing all the more convenient. Travel is one of these industries. In 1998, only 3 percent of U.S. travel ($1.9 billion) was booked online; however, this grew to 70 percent ($122 billion) in 2009. This is a win-win situation, as the airline processing cost of $9.49 for a paper ticket was reduced to 30 cents for an e-ticket. Now, barcodes on cell phones can act as airline tickets.

There have also been a number of online success stories in the music industry. For example, unknown band Red Delicious made some of their tracks available for free as MP3 files. This not only generated millions of downloads and substantial CD sales, but resulted in the band's exposure in publications as diverse as *Entertainment Weekly* and the *Washington Post.* Thanks to these stories, the band scored an opening gig with Tom Petty and work at such top-tier venues as the Viper Room in Los Angeles.

E-Retailing versus Traditional Retailing

There are both stark differences and similarities between purchasing online and purchasing in the traditional manner.

◆ **Customer focus.** Over 80 percent of consumers who shop at the best retail stores are more concerned with customer service, quality, return policies, and after-sales service than product reliability and price. Retailers who fail to focus on the customer and commoditize their product play right into e-retailers' hands.

Of course, most e-retailers are so product and noncustomer focused that they have neglected to correct even the simplest of issues, despite the fact that these problems can have a devastating effect on their business. For example, a study by Jupiter Media Matrix in 2008 found that some 20 percent of all online shoppers cease the purchase because of high shipping costs. Yet research conclusively shows that if the shipping cost was added to the price of the product and free shipping was included as added value, 86 percent of these terminating customers would continue with the purchase.

The result is that a majority of online retailers offer free shipping. Since e-retailing is generally a razor-thin margin business, execution must be flawless in order to succeed.

> E-retailers have primarily focused on product and price, and because over 90 percent of consumers believe that like products are interchangeable, such a focus cannot build loyal online customers.

As with physical stores, online customers will shop at the best sites. It is likely that both the online and offline retail arena will become more competitive and intertwined and that organizations who survive in both areas will do so because of exceptional customer service.

The key to successful e-retailing is to develop a personal connection with the customer and to use the kind of permission marketing described in Chapter 14. Although broadband technology, which allows staff personalization, visual guides, entertainment, and so on, significantly helps with this, it will take a seismic shift in retailer attitude and site development for this to occur.

- **Why do shoppers buy online?** In order of priority, the 2009 UCLA Internet Report says the relative importance of reasons are:

Convenience	84 percent
Speed	80 percent
Availability of information	78 percent
Ease of finding products	76 percent
Ability to shop 24/7	72 percent
Lack of sales people	70 percent
Ease of comparing prices	64 percent
It's more fun!	46 percent

- **Information.** Customers want more information nowadays, and online shopping provides this far more effectively, efficiently, at less cost, and more quickly than the traditional approach does.
- **Delivery.** In many industries, brick-and-click retailers who are experts at delivering large quantities of stock to stores via warehouses have completely failed at getting these items to homes or businesses. They've experimented extensively with various delivery systems, from in-house specialty companies, dropping off to central locations, such as schools, 7-Eleven stores, gas stations, and so on. 7-Eleven even partnered with NCR and American Express to produce kiosks where people could buy and pick up at their stores. Coffee giant Starbucks took part in a similar program by accepting returns for products bought on Kozmo.com.

Companies need to base their delivery/pick-up/return partners on three things. First, the company should not be in competition. Second, it should have a common customer base and vision, and third, it should focus completely on the customer. To date, the most successful delivery methods have been the post office and major parcel delivery companies such as Federal Express and UPS. Approximately 72 percent of all parcels delivered in 2010 in the United States will originate on the Internet. E-retailers spend 50 percent of their income on distribution compared with 2 percent for traditional retailers.

◆ **Specific product types.** The Internet is best suited to market certain types of products including:
  • Those that don't have to be physically checked
  • Products for which detailed information is important
  • Those with high profit margins, low distribution costs, or both
  • Customized products

◆ **Customer.** Internet customers are usually a highly desired, affluent group with little time on their hands. People with an income level of $50,000 plus and a college degree are twice as likely to buy online as any other segment. Fifty-seven percent of men and 45 percent of women browsers make online purchases. Not surprisingly, the more time people spend online, the more likely they are to make a purchase— and the more likely they are to ignore online advertising and the lower the click-through rate.

◆ **People love shopping.** There is no question that, although there is a very substantial market for Internet retail, it will never replace traditional retail. Despite what the surveys say, people like to shop. How else do you explain Mall of America attracting 42 million people a year, double the attendance of Disneyland?

◆ **Product returns.** Returning goods is a major problem with online-only stores, as customers need to repackage and send the item back. Even with bricks-and-clicks stores' online divisions, problems such as sale identification; warehousing; issuing replacements, credits, or refunds can become significant unless the company's systems are totally integrated.

◆ **Customer management.** The Internet provides tremendous opportunities for customer feedback and the development of excellent customer relations. Technology allows companies to gather and sort contact information, credit card and other financial details, transaction dates, and data from all hits at the site. They can also add data from other vendors, as well as purchases from related sites, traditional stores, and catalogs to build an accurate, individual customer profile.

◆ **Every visit to the site**—in fact, every click—enables organizations to analyze for trends and continue to hone the customer profile. This in turn enables them to personalize each visit, leading to repeat customers who visit more often, stay longer, spend more money, and provide even more information. For instance, when home improvement giant Home Depot launched an online site in 2000 that was totally integrated with its core business systems, Senior Vice President Ron Griffin said, "We are not online to maximize sales; we are online to maximize customer relationships."

◆ **Impulse purchases.** The most popular (and, therefore, low profit) items in a traditional retail environment are stocked at the back of the store, thereby encouraging customers to make impulse buys of high-profit items on their way in and out of the store. For example, a pet-food store's dog food is often a loss leader; however, they make money when people select high-profit collars and toys. Online pet stores fail because people can't browse effectively and efficiently, and, therefore, only buy the loss leader pet food.

◆ **Browsing.** Successful sites allow potential customers to move from room to room, let them shop by item, or hit the browse button and take their time.

◆ **Major deterrents.** Over 90 percent of people are concerned about credit-card security and privacy of the information they provide online, and with good reason. Studies show that up to 87 percent of all sites have been the subjects of hackers. This is not to say that the shop assistant at the local retail store can't run your credit card through twice; however, it is far less likely, and opportunities for fraud are not nearly as plentiful.

Therefore, the potential market for some Internet retailing appears to be relatively limited.

Consumers have quickly learned how to evaluate companies online. San Francisco-based consulting and networking company Sapient identified 28 attributes of online trust and sorted them into six primary components:

1. **Seals of Approval**–These are corporate partners, such as Visa, that have brand equity that provides credibility.

2. **Brand Equity**–Brand recognition, community, service, quality.
3. **Navigation**–Simple, understandable site, appealing layout, easy to find information.
4. **Fulfillment**–Ease of order processing, return policy, problem solving, security of information.
5. **Presentation**– The way meaningful information is conveyed.
6. **Technology**–Speed of loading, functionality.

Each of these relates precisely to the traits required to be successful in traditional businesses. As I mentioned in the opening segment of this chapter, online retailing is simply an extension of the retail chain that began with the mom-and-pop store.

Corporate Integration of CRM Is the Key

As we've already established, customer-relationship management (CRM) is the process of managing customer contacts (sales, service, and marketing), regardless of the channel, as well as all business processes and data that support these interactions. This includes data analysis, personalization, and cross-department data sharing. Customer relationship management provides the ability to deliver unique marketing messages customized to buyers. These messages are equivalent to one-on-one selling, but they still fall into the category of mass marketing.

The problem with most CRM programs is that they are frequently not fully integrated across the company. Companies compartmentalize their departments into marketing, sales, finance, warehousing, delivery, online, service, and so on. Yet the customer can contact staff at the company by phone, fax, walk in, deal with a distributor, talk to a sales representative, or interact online—who all need to respond *quickly*. Moreover, they need to deal with customers in relation to their last contact with the company. Companies must provide enquiries, quotes, orders, status updates, shipping details, and after-sales service. This requires a totally transparent program that instantly provides every user in the system with details of all contact by that customer, their personalities, past behavior, buying habits, and so on.

> Customers expect and are entitled to a fluidity and continuity—even if they change communication channels—with resellers, partners, in-store, or on the web.

Customers should also have their own customized entry point into the company's system whereby they can access a means to solve their problems. Although a totally seamless integration is difficult to achieve, it is extremely worthwhile. According to McKinsey & Company, customers spend 400–500 percent more time with companies with seamless multiple channels than do customers of purely online businesses.

Integrating a seamless CRM program begins with a customer-centric corporate culture and leadership that permeates the whole company. You need to fully integrate the people before you can integrate software in any business.

> CRM is not software, a performance or accounting tool, or technology. It is a customer-centric business strategy.

There needs to be a flawless one-to-one customer interface in both online and traditional retail.

A recent survey by telecommunications supplier Jupiter Communications found 64 percent of retailers could not track their customers across store, online, and catalog channels. 2008 *InformationWeek* research showed 50 percent of American companies had not even begun CRM planning, almost unchanged from five years earlier. Yet viewing data from multiple channels allows companies to create unified pricing and promotion, better allocate merchandise between channels, and improve inventory and fulfillment.

Amazon.com's focus on customer service at any cost is the key to its longevity in an online marketplace where a majority of its peers have fallen by the wayside. Despite being more sophisticated, is what Amazon.com is doing really that different than the individual customer focus of the corner-store proprietor 50 years ago? People have also been ordering by phone for 50 years. So why is online shopping much different? As many dot-coms—including Amazon.com and Yahoo!, for example—have expanded, they have become less virtual and more like traditional firms.

Yahoo! has some 14,700 employees and rises and falls with the advertising business like other big media firms. As eBay expands into products such as cars, it has been forced to enter into joint ventures with bricks-and mortar firms, thereby having to split profits. This is even truer for Amazon.com, which looks more like a bricks-and-mortar company every day. It has built warehouses around the world and has an ever-increasing staff.

Of course, Amazon.com still has clear differences to traditional retailers. Because it holds its entire inventory in centralized warehouses, it turns over stock much faster than physical retailers do. That is a huge advantage when it comes to rapidly depreciating products such as consumer electronics. Low inventory as a percentage of sales also helps the company grow economically, since costs tend to scale with the number of units shipped, not their value. This may allow Amazon.com to make money in categories that are considered to be low margin. Thanks to the Internet, its potential customer base continues to grow at impressive rates.

What's even more impressive is that Amazon.com's excellent customer profiling and data management system allows the company to predict customer preferences, and, therefore, market to its database accordingly. By having its own products—such as e-reader Kindle, which sold over 3 million units in three years—Amazon.com maximizes performance.

Given examples like these, some might argue that e-retailing is simply a case of "the more things change, the more they stay the same."

How Is E-Retail Performing?

Since e-retail's major opportunity is the ability to personalize information, it is surprising that Jupiter Research shows that only 37 percent of websites actually take advantage of this, and only 26 percent measure their personalization efforts. Interestingly, the vast majority of the most successful and profitable retailers on the web are businesses with both an on- and offline presence. This enables companies to establish brand equity and site awareness offline with exceptional one-on-one customer service that enhances customers' comfort in purchasing. Having a presence in both segments also enables pick up and return from physical stores, which provides both the touch and feel and convenience required by consumers.

Retailers who do e-retail right are reaping the rewards. For instance, apparel and accessory retailer Lands End online has an ever-evolving superb level of personalized customer service. In their physical stores, customers walk into a special booth where scanners map their body and create an electronic 3D model on the website. This enables the customers to try on clothes on their own virtual bodies even after they get home. By the end of 2000, over 1.5 million women had been scanned, resulting in $138 million in sales. In 2009, Lands End took the scanners across the country, getting scans of potential customers to facilitate online demonstrations and sales. The company also asks shoppers questions about their preferred color and style. They then match these preferences against the company's 80,000 items and make individual purchase recommendations to each customer. As consumers buy items, Lands End refines their customer profiles with the information they obtain.

> Successful retailers realize that customers online want the same feeling, ambiance, range, selection, and service of the physical store, but they want it via the Internet.

Retailers like Nordstrom, Calvin Klein, and Lands End have the same store design, color scheme, and décor online, off-line, and in their catalogs. Many retailers are installing Internet terminals in their store to complete the loop and demonstrate that this is totally integrated retail.

Despite the obvious opportunities for those companies who get the retail formula correct, the 2009 Servicesoft, Inc. survey showed that:

- 17 percent of retail sites don't offer an e-mail contact.
- 56 percent took more than two days to respond to questions.
- 12 percent took at least a full business day to respond.
- 10 percent didn't provide phone numbers.

This indicates a lack of basic marketing know-how and little knowledge of today's business drivers. These errors would be fatal whether online or in a television, print, or direct-mail campaign.

As the e-retailing marketplace downsizes, many of the initial incentives, such as free shipping, price discounting, and product giveaways are being eliminated. Without a significant increase in customer focus, these changes will further erode the market potential of e-retail. In fact, global business information provider Datamonitor estimates that online retailers lost over $200 billion in sales due to bad service in 2009.

Examples of Integrated B2C Solutions

7-Eleven convenience stores in Japan are an exceptional example of a retailer who utilized e-commerce's benefits to improve sales and profits at a time when its competitors were struggling with the economic downturn. The company created a user-friendly uniform system that provided sound and pictures to its mostly part-time workers with low computer skills, thereby speeding up the transmission of orders, concepts, promotions, feedback, and sales and performance information. This system connects 8,500 stores, suppliers, consultants, and banks through some 80,000 computers. Users all have phone lines as well as satellite dishes. Dual mainframes in the Japanese cities of Tokyo and Osaka prevent any disruptions due to equipment failure or natural disasters, and a direct link to Microsoft in Seattle provides real-time support.

This uniform system, which replaced a plethora of individual cash registers, enabled 7-Eleven to respond to customers' varying requirements in different regions; monitor ongoing shifts in consumer needs; and improve quality control, stock levels and delivery, product development, and pricing. The company has enjoyed savings that exceed 300 million yen per year. This system allows 7-Eleven to serve as a collection point for utility bills, which generated nearly 4 trillion yen ($30 billion) in 2010. The system even monitors the weather five times a day from a range of points across the county to predict likely food/beverage purchases that day. Orders are processed within seven minutes and dispatched to 230 distribution centers that deliver daily.

The uniform multimedia system facilitates staff training and communication to over 100,000 workers who work in shifts 24/7. In 2000, in a country in which 75 percent of Internet shoppers pay and collect from brick-and-mortar stores, 7-Eleven turned its stores into Internet depots. This well-thought-out uniform system has allowed the company to increase profits significantly, despite the economic downturn, as well as to blitz their competitors.

The Future of B2C

High-speed broadband's rapid emergence has the potential to dramatically increase e-retailing's growth. Customers already access video, e-mail, and Internet on mobile phones and PDAs, and they can now receive relevant information as our mobile devices recognize where users are located at any point in time. For example, I was recently walking past a department store in London when my mobile telephone rang. The voice at the other end advised me that there was currently a sale on at the store and I should go in and browse, not just walk past. Considering there are some 1.5 billion mobile phones, this represents a potentially enormous market, not only for goods and services, but also for information such as traffic, weather, restaurants, theaters, and so on. It is an almost endless list. Information providers can either charge the customer for these services or offset the cost by providing advertising or sponsorship.

Web businesses will have to apply all the knowledge from traditional retail, utilize new data mining and one-on-one communication technology to encourage e-commerce through new e-money methods, and overcome deep-seated security concerns.

Consumer-to-Consumer (C2C)

The Internet allows anyone anywhere in the world to list products or services either on their website or through online services such as eBay or Monster. com. These services provide a highly competitive exchange or purchase source with heavy traffic. The problem an individual faces, unless he or she is extremely well known, is attracting customers to their website. The Internet is an increasingly popular way to communicate C2C with interactions increasing by over 10,000 percent since 2000. This has occurred almost exclusively through a middleman who possesses the muscle to build brand equity and drive people to their site.

The Keys to a Great Website

1. Domain Name

    Try to use your business name, but remember that your business name should always say what you do. Overly clever, difficult-to-recall, or to associate names are usually less successful. Also, try to keep it as short as possible; do not use the 67 characters allowed. This will also help with your search-engine results.

2. Professional, Appealing Design

    The first impression is critical. This means that your design needs to be professional, attractive, exciting, and unique. You need to entice people to go past the landing page. Your website should be easy to navigate and must display quickly on all browsers. Ensure you build your website around the needs of your audience. Keyword search and a site map are also must-haves. Having an attention grabber on the first page will work to attract visitors as well.

3. Use Search-Engine Optimization (SEO)

Most people who go to your website find it through a search engine such as Google, Yahoo!, Bing, Ask, Baidu, AOL Search, and many more. Search-engine optimization is the way you position your website so it is easily found on these search engines, thereby increasing your traffic. If you have invested in a website, you must have SEO.

The ways you can improve SEO results are:

Continually update your content.

Use links within the content of each page.

Share your website with social websites such as Twitter, Facebook, Myspace, Bebo, Friendster, and Hi5.

Write articles and share them with EzineArticles.com.

Create a sitemap on every page of your website.

4. Constantly Update

In order to keep people coming back to your site, you must update it constantly. Most people will look at a number of websites and when they need to make a decision on which ones to revisit, new content is very compelling.

5. Encourage Interaction

There are two types of website visitors:

(a) New—they visit, review, and leave. You need to compel them to return.

(b) Returning—they visit, read, and interact. They do this through commenting on your blog, voting in a poll, signing up for new information, entering a contest—the list is endless.

That said, it is vital that you spend time answering all of the comments you receive. This time that you invest is repaid many times over in increased traffic and enhanced relationships.

To have a popular site, you need to include good information, as well as create a site with personality. This can take the shape of giveaways or contests. A popular site doesn't just happen; you need to work at it. When customers buy from you, interact with them so that they are encouraged to revisit your site. You can do this by e-mailing progress reports or updates on any special promotions or new products available.

6. Build Credibility

You need to position yourself as an expert in the space. To do this, make sure to emphasize your credentials, your history, your experience, your client base, awards you have won, and any associations you belong to. Emphasizing any and all accomplishments works to build your credibility.

As in all marketing, testimonials not only work to build credibility, they also serve as a way for possible customers to feel at ease doing business with you. If you include the customers' contact details, it is even more powerful.

7. Easy to Find Contact Details

Make sure you have a Contact-Us link that provides all of your details including an e-mail link. This link should be prominent on every page.

8. Limit the Size and Number of Your Graphics

Web users want to navigate quickly and easily. The more time spent downloading, the more likely you are to lose the potential client.

9. Use Captions with Graphics

Captions are powerful; after headlines, they are the most read copy on a page. The caption should be a selling tool. Don't describe the graphics or photo; instead, say why it is of benefit to the client.

10. Accept Credit Cards

Make sure you have a shopping cart on the site and assure them, through your payment processor, that their funds are safe.

11. Promote Your Website

Promote the site everywhere possible; it's that simple. Promote on e-mails, letterheads, business cards, clothes, invoices, advertisements, vehicles, and so on. The more exposure, the more visits.

Social Media–A Marketing Phenomenon

Social media is a powerful communications medium that reaches over 500 million people a day. So what is social marketing? It is a marketing opportunity that:

◆ Is disseminated via social interaction
◆ Uses highly accessible channels
◆ Published through scalable techniques

Social media marketing is pull, not push.

- Traditional marketing is push marketing and is old school.
- Traditional marketing is expensive.
- Pull marketing is results driven, cost-effective, and measurable.

New techniques such as blogs and SEO are critical.

Top 10 Social Media Tips for Beginners

1. **The time for Twitter, Facebook, and LinkedIn is now.** To maximize your opportunities, you need to be present on the world's most popular social-networking sites.
2. **Be one with Google.** Register your website with Google and Google Maps so customers can find you. Use Google Alerts to see what the media and bloggers are saying about you.
3. **Post every day.** Commit to blogging/updating your social media presence as part of your daily business routine. Get your followers into the habit of looking at your latest blog.
4. **Find followers.** Read blogs and visit websites to seek those interested in what your company has to say.
5. **Engage in conversation.** Comment, post, update your status, and offer content that compels responses.
6. **Be visual.** Utilize video/YouTube to show customers what makes your business different.
7. **Social-media content should not be the same as your advertising message.** Advertising and social-media content are not the same. Provide real insights into your expertise, not a phony brief message.
8. **Find out what your customers think.** Encourage customers to ask questions, report concerns, and give feedback on your service.
9. **Pace yourself.** You can always increase frequency of content but slowing down can be a red flag.
10. **Be patient.** Success requires effort and a willingness to adapt to changes you may face. As *BusinessWeek* recently stated, "Millions of people are creating content for the social web. It is highly likely that your competitors are already there and your customers have been there for a long time."

It is critical that you create a focused plan to leverage social platforms to achieve real business goals. You need to think about your overall business strategy and the role social media might play in achieving these goals.

There are a number of ways to leverage social media:

◆ Public relations
◆ Customer support
◆ Market research
◆ Brand marketing
◆ Promotions
◆ Consumer education
◆ Sales
◆ Product development
◆ Customer relationship management

Let's Look at These One at a Time

PUBLIC RELATIONS

Social media touches over 500 million people a day, being the most direct and immediate channel into the hearts and minds of consumers. This enables brands to find evangelists as well as deserters. That means, it is up to you to craft the message to reinforce or change attitudes.

CUSTOMER SUPPORT

As I suggested earlier, the majority of business lost by companies is not due to competitors but is due to not paying enough attention to customers. Social media enables constant contact and feedback. It maximizes positive brand equity and gives customers the support they seek at very low cost while enabling them to be connected to a large pool of consumers who think like they do. A clear win-win.

MARKET RESEARCH

It is imperative for companies to get high-quality information on clients, competitors, and marketplace changes. Launching new products, new brands, and new target markets requires constant up-to-date knowledge. Although traditional market research has been expensive and slow, social media enables real time analysis of consumer trends, focus groups, and real-time dialogue at a fraction of traditional costs. You need experts to analyze the information, but you can get literally millions of consumers discussing their rational and emotional needs in real time.

BRAND MARKETING

You can play a behavior-support role in the life of your consumers by building a social relationship with the brand. A substantial number of corporations have launched a slew of social tools across platforms from Facebook to the iPhone over recent years. Be careful not to barrage your potential customers with ego-driven how-great-am-I information. Social media is about them, not you.

PROMOTIONS

Social media is the ideal vehicle to craft great promotions. When created thoughtfully, great promotions spread very quickly, continually doubling themselves almost instantaneously (see Chapter 14).

CONSUMER EDUCATION

This follows the old established formula of:

$$\text{Excite} > \text{educate} > \text{motivate} > \text{convert}$$

You need to plan strategically to bring your prospects along the path to the place where they are ready to buy. This takes education and motivation. Brands need to leverage the interactive capabilities within social platforms to educate and motivate customers through discussion boards, videos, and testimonials. Unlike 30-second commercials, social networks enable you to create a dialogue and build a scenario over a long period of time, enabling education on even the most complex solutions.

SALES

Just about any form of transaction and revenue-generating application can be integrated into social platforms. Although their applications can be complex, they are inexpensive and you are always close to the customer.

NEW PRODUCT DEVELOPMENT

Companies are leveraging the collective brainpower of their social-media fans to identify innovative, new-market opportunities and assist with the development of product concepts. Cisco Systems awarded a $250,000 prize to social-media fans that created a new commercial opportunity. By doing this, a company is not limited to the brainpower of people within their four walls.

CUSTOMER-RELATIONSHIPS MANAGEMENT

Social media is the new version, albeit infinitely faster, more fluid, and more interactive, of mailing lists that were vitally important with traditional media. Being able to build millions, even tens of millions of fans very quickly and maintaining a constant dialogue with them enables endless possibilities. Social media is possibly the most exciting development in communication history that will have a profound effect on the world, both commercially and socially.

Remember: In today's global marketplace, if you don't go online there is a possibility that you will fail. However, if you go online and don't manage customers' expectation, you will certainly fail.

Chapter 16

Close the Sale by Reversing the Risk

The most common reason why people are often hesitant to buy a product or service is because, in one way or another, almost every transaction is a risk. "What if the product doesn't work?" "I wonder if the claims are true?" "Perhaps it is a scam." "Can I afford to really buy it now?" "Do I really need it?" These are all thoughts that people have at the point of purchase.

There are a number of reasons why people may discuss or even negotiate the sale with you right up until you think it's a deal, and then they walk away to consult with their spouse, or maybe to just think about it. Of course, once they wander off to think about it, the chances of them coming back to buy are greatly diminished. It is a great opportunity lost.

One way to change this situation is to take away the risk.

Four Kinds of Risk: Emotional, Physical, Financial, and Social

In business, the majority of purchases of goods or services are expensive. It costs a lot of money to buy new equipment, to engage consultants and advisors, or to obtain quality facilities. Whether a company is large or small, the performance of these products or services has the potential to impact the initiator's reputation, the company's performance, and in many cases can make or break them. The results not only affect the people directly involved, but also other staff, suppliers, and even their families.

The first step in reversing the risk is to research the supplier's reputation. If appropriate, contact government, licensing, or consumer bodies as well. Get references from previous clients to gain confidence in the supplier's ability to do the specific job you require.

However, if the purchasing company has limited capital and fails, it becomes a total loss. That is enough doubt to make the majority of small-business owners choose to struggle by delaying the purchase of the product or service until they can better afford it. By that time, however, they could have made a lot of mistakes and wasted much more than the initial investment, and you would have lost the sale.

However, if the supplier reverses the risk, for example, by giving them the guarantee that if there is a problem they will not have to pay, they have no downside. What do they have to lose by making the purchase? Nothing! At Marketforce One, we provide a guarantee that if our marketing advice does not grow our client's business, we will not charge them our fee.

Risk Reversal Works because People Are Honest

The reason risk reversal is so effective in closing sales is because the overwhelming majority of people are honest. They do not want to take advantage; they simply want a fair transaction. Unfortunately, a number of people in business are cynical, and this prevents them from taking advantage of this powerful selling—and closing—tool. We regularly recommend any one of a number of forms of risk reversal to clients, and despite the argument we put up in favor of them, many are afraid to embrace the principle. Their usual argument is based on their fear that people will use the product, return it, and ask for their money back.

In our company, we offer two risk-reversal opportunities. The first one I have just mentioned, which offers to charge clients no fee if we don't improve their business, and the second technique provides a full money-back guarantee on my books, CDs, and videos.

It is interesting that after performing consultancy work for a large number of corporations, from small to large, in a variety of industries, we have never had one single instance in which our fee has not been paid.

Furthermore, despite the thousands of products sold, we have never had even one return, except for the very occasional defective CD.

How easy would it be for people to claim they were dissatisfied and ask for their money back? Very easy! But people don't. The people who use our services are interested in the big picture, not in scams for a few dollars, and this applies to most industries.

There are a number of types of risk reversal. These include:

◆ Money-back guarantee
◆ Match competitive offers
◆ Replace purchase with another item at no cost
◆ Buy one, get one free
◆ Free trial
◆ Testimonials, awards
◆ Quality of information

1. Money-Back Guarantee

A 100 percent money-back guarantee is probably the most popular, but there are many others to consider. Frequently, on television,
you see advertisements that offer a 30-day free trial. This is also a
favorite of telemarketing firms selling memberships, dining-out books,
and so on. If you don't like the product after 30 days, you simply send it
back, no questions asked. If you do decide to keep it, you simply pay
the bill. This takes the risk out of giving a credit-card number to
someone with a mailbox in another state, or sending money to a
company you have never heard of.

2. Match Competitive Offers

This usually takes the form of "Find a cheaper price elsewhere
and we will pay you double or triple the difference." This is very
popular with motor-vehicle dealers and telephone companies. This
offer is really very low risk for the company offering the deal, because
the price differential in a highly competitive market is usually very
small; even if people did claim, three times a small amount is still very
little.

However, the reality is that after most people buy the product, if
they are satisfied with it, they will get on with their lives and not be
bothered checking other prices. We created this risk reversal for a
Toyota dealer in California who has been making this offer for years.
How many refunds has he ever given out? None!

3. Replace Your Purchase with Another Item at No Cost

Rather than give a refund on a particular item, the business will
allow the customer to return the item they are unhappy with and
select some other item of the same value. If the business offers a wide

range of products or services, this will reassure the customer, because there will almost certainly be something else they provide that the customer will really want.

One DVD and game-rental chain, Civic, promotes that, "If you rent a video you don't like, we will give you another rental for free." The cynic will assume that people will return Academy Award winning movies saying they didn't like them, just to get the free-rental offer. The reality is quite different. On releasing the risk reversal, Civic rentals increased by over 174 percent, yet returns were less than .025 percent. Put another way, for every 4,000 rentals, they had one return. Pretty good business!

4. Buy One, Get One Free

The buy-one-get-one-free offer is a form of risk reversal that is very effective, particularly for new product launches. Little Caesars have grown their business on "Pizza, Pizza," two pizzas for the price of one. The consumer is getting twice what they have paid for, and that represents a good deal that is strong enough to overcome the risk in making the purchase.

5. Free Trial

Sales of Thomas the Tank Engine children's beds were slow. People were concerned about things like whether the bed would date and the child would get tired of it, whether it was worth the money to get a bed in the shape of a train, and so on. The company decided to give customers a month's free trial. They would deliver the bed to the home, the child could sleep in it for a month, and at the end of that period, if clients wanted to return it, there were no questions asked; the company would pay all freight. In other words, there were absolutely no costs to the customers if they were unhappy with the purchases.

The result? The bed was back-ordered for months. The returns? None. Have you ever tried taking a child off a bed after they had slept on it for a month?

6. Testimonials, Awards

Potential customers are reassured by the positive experiences of their peers with a particular product or service. On the large scale, the fact that LeBron James and Kobe Bryant both wear Nike gives a potential buyer confidence that it is a good product. On a smaller scale, my car dealer provides potential buyers with the contact information of local people with similar requirements who also purchased the same vehicle from the dealership. This makes the buyer feel confident that the product will deliver the benefits they seek.

People go to award-winning restaurants, award-winning films, or award-winning businesses because the awards are proof the business is good because it has been recognized as such. Promoting the fact that your business was "Established in 1937," or has "10,000 satisfied customers" assures the potential purchaser that you are stable and reliable, and goes a long way to eliminate any purchase fears.

Quality of Information

If you can provide a potential customer with quality information about the product or service and can answer their questions accurately and confidently, this is also an excellent risk reversal. It gives the customer confidence that they are buying the right product for their needs and that expert help is readily available if they require it.

Choose Your Risk-Reversal Technique Carefully

The principle of risk reversal works for everyone. However, we would recommend that before you implement any form of risk reversal, you research your customers or potential customers to determine two things: The first is whether the offer is strong enough to motivate people to commit, and the second is to assess the downside risk. Remember, you are implementing risk reversal to grow your business, not go out of business.

Remember: When customers purchase products or services, they are entitled to good quality, reliability, and good service. That is what they are paying for. A good risk reversal is not only an excellent sale closer, it is the customer's right.

Chapter 17

Cut through the Clutter

Mainstream communication is so cluttered today that, in order to differentiate ourselves, we need to get noticed. How often have you wondered how another business, doing the same thing you do, makes 50 times more money? The person running it is nowhere near as smart as you are, and you work much harder. Boy, talk about lucky breaks!

Well, the solution is usually much simpler than that. The more successful company probably used a customer product benefit (CPB), focused on benefits, knew their competition, and thought outside the box more often than you did. This enabled that company to maximize its performance and minimize its marketing and sales costs. Maybe the company realized it didn't have all the answers to what its customers needed. Perhaps it was one of those companies that wasted money on research! Then again, maybe they were just lucky.

We have built our reputation on being different, on thinking outside the box. This is an often-used expression and one that is frequently interpreted as meaning a radical approach in a new direction.

> Often, it is just a minor, but unique, change that creates a huge difference in the performance of a product or business.

For example, over a period of 90 years, Oscar Mayer had developed a position of leadership in the processed-meats business. In 1988, they became part of Kraft Foods and in 1990 Oscar Mayer launched Lunchables for Kids with a CPB of "Making fun of lunch," creating a giant new $500 million food segment almost overnight. How did they do it? They took their traditional processed meats, added juice, candy, and games in a convenient pack for

Mom . . . and a new industry was born. Revolutionary? Maybe not, but certainly thinking outside the box!

Creative Thinking Starts with Research

A few years ago, I conceived and implemented the first private ownership of a major sports team in Australia. At a time when all sports teams were membership based, after a long, tough struggle we changed the structure of Australian sports forever, and became owners of the Sydney football team. This team had struggled in another city and was moved to Sydney in Australia's first team relocation.

In Australia, different codes of football, rugby league, rugby union, soccer, and Australian football have huge differences in levels of popularity in different states. In Sydney, the code of football that our team played was as popular as a scorpion in your pants.

We conducted extensive research across 168 suburbs to obtain answers that would enable a strategic marketing plan to be created. The most worrying of the research results was the fact that less than 1 percent of the under-18 demographic in Sydney knew anything about the team, its players, its colors, or the code of football played. As far as I was concerned, this was a disaster as this demographic represented the team's future. Unless we could get the support of the under-18 market, we could not succeed in the long term.

We asked our advertising agency to devise a strategy to address this problem, and their solution was a $500,000, three-year, highly targeted media campaign. They estimated that we could gain 30 percent awareness among the under-18 age group in just three years. Although, in a traditional sense, this was a good plan, the situation called for a very nontraditional solution. I wasn't interested in waiting three years, or spending $500,000, so our creative team analyzed all of the ways we could impact this target market.

> We believed that the most important thing was the size of the idea, NOT the size of the budget.

After a lot of brainstorming, many heated discussions, and a lot of creative thinking, we determined that music was the common denominator among all the kids who were potential long-term supporters. We would make one of the players a "recording artist." The next step was determining the right player. We took headshots of all of the players, with no indication of who they were, and took these photos to all the high schools, malls, and other popular hangouts for teens.

We held a poll among the under-18s to see who they thought was the sexiest. One player, a good looking, surfer-style kid named Warwick Capper was a clear winner. We approached a songwriter friend of mine to create a song and video that would highlight Warwick as a teenage heartthrob. We needed something that would allow appropriate footage of him in situations that the kids would relate to, interlaced with footage of Warwick as a football player.

The idea was to get the kids to relate to Warwick not only as a peer, but also as a football player to get across the idea of what the game was about, the team colors, and the excitement. When I asked Warwick if he could sing, he told me that if he hadn't been a footballer, he would have been a singer, so we went into the studio. Well, I'm sure Warwick wouldn't mind my saying that, although he was a great football player, he wasn't much of a singer. However, luckily through the marvels of modern technology, we ended up with a pretty good record.

Prior to its media release, we distributed the song and film clip and scheduled a full calendar of appearances for Warwick. On release, we already had a groundswell developed, and because it was a singing football player, the response was phenomenal. Every television program, news channel, sports report, all played the song and the film clip. Radio saturated the airwaves with it, and the print media ran literally hundreds of stories. Within eight weeks, over 80 percent of the under-18 demographic in Sydney knew Warwick, the team, and the colors. In addition, over 5,000 kids who had never seen the game before were coming to the matches to see Warwick.

Remember, the agency said invest $500,000, wait three years, and obtain 30 percent penetration. In eight weeks, we achieved a profit on every record we sold, and obtained awareness of nearly 80 percent. Why? Because we thought outside the box!

This is just one of literally dozens of examples over the years in which we have had phenomenal success without using traditional media, and we enjoyed this success by being different.

Differentiation Produces Results

Aspro Clear was the first launch of a product I was ever involved in, several decades ago now, first to the trade and then to retail. This was the first headache product that dissolved in water. At the time, launching products in hotels was always the way launches were done. Make the presentation from the lectern, wine and dine the buyers, and hope they buy into it.

Well, I've always thought of hotel function rooms as extremely boring little boxes with absolutely tasteless pictures and carpets, and even worse chandeliers. So for Aspro Clear, totally unbeknown to anyone, we built a 1930s speakeasy in a public parking lot. Fully decked out with period furniture, the place was incredible. You really could imagine you were back in the 1930s.

To get into the venue, the buyers had to walk through a 100-foot-long black tunnel with UV lights. Once inside, music was playing, and there was food and drinks everywhere; it was party time!

About an hour into the party, we secretly fixed a raid, Al Capone-style, with guns blazing, and it really caught everyone by surprise. As the guests were being relieved of their wallets and watches, the FBI came bursting through, giving everyone a second heart attack. We then gave everyone an Aspro Clear and a glass of water to relieve their headaches. It was the only mention we made about the product all night. It was a fabulous night. The brokers were blown away. We then direct mailed them with all the benefits of stocking the product. We gained over 400 percent more opening orders than any other pharmaceutical product had ever achieved up until that time. Why? Because we got our message across in a totally different way.

Publicity Is More Powerful than Advertising

Possibly the project that got us more publicity worldwide than anything else we have done was the America's Cup. The America's Cup is the oldest active trophy in international sports and is awarded to the winner of best of seven match races between two yachts. The event attracts challengers from around the world and is held approximately every three years.

One day, Sid Fischer, one of the world's great yachtsmen and a long time America's Cup competitor, walked into my office and asked for our help. He had a yacht called *Sunshine* that had been practicing for two years and no one had ever heard of it; yet everyone had heard of *Kookaburra*, the rival challenger for the Cup. Sid needed to raise $3 million to remain competitive, and he needed to raise it quickly. All of the corporations we spoke to said the time span was too short for that sort of investment. Furthermore, they were reluctant to give money to the cause. We routinely came up against push back such as, "Let me see if I've got this straight. I earn five hundred bucks a week with overtime and you want me to give you money to give to some rich guy to sail his yacht? Is that right?" Well, that kind of logic is pretty hard to beat.

We went back to Sid and told him that this would be more difficult than we thought. We then locked ourselves in our boardroom and began to develop a strategy. The first problem was to identify the yacht with the working man. We needed to do this because the public was the only real source of funds; corporations simply couldn't react that fast. We decided that promoting the name *Sunshine* in just a few weeks was unrealistic; the name was unimaginative and boring. The only solution was to rename the yacht. We needed to brainstorm a name that was nontraditional, one that would cause a ruckus and get the public's support.

Most America's Cup yachts are given either majestic or nationalistic names such as *Stars and Stripes*, *America II*, and *Australia*. We didn't have time for these names to get popular; we needed something that would generate immediate controversy. We decided to call the yacht *Steak and Kidney*. This is Australian workers' rhyming slang for Sydney. We knew instantly that the yacht enthusiasts would hate it and the public would love it. Our research also found that the average person did not have a clue about the size of an America's Cup yacht. They thought a 12-meter yacht was 36 feet long. They did not realize that this related to the water-level measurement. In fact, the yachts are over 65 feet long and are 16 stories tall, including the mast and keel.

We decided that since most yachts were launched in water, we were definitely not going to do that. We would launch it on land. In fact, we would launch it in Martin Plaza in the center of Sydney, with huge foot traffic. The city council put up every obstacle possible. They had lots of questions and I must admit some of them were good ones.

However, our persistence won out, and the yacht went on display. Since, at the time, all of the emphasis was on keels, we put a timber skirt around our keel and emblazoned "Sydney's Secret Weapon" on it. (The keel is the principal structural member of a ship, running lengthwise along the center-line from bow to stern, to which the frames are attached. In recent years the technology developments with the keel have been revolutionary and dramatic.) Just to convince everyone that we really had something, we hired security guards with guns and dogs to march around it. Boy was this impressive! Two weeks prior we announced the launch date at which the new name would be unveiled. In that time, we created as much speculation as we possibly could in the media. We were aware that in addition to exposure and a gimmicky name, we needed credibility in order for people to give us the money we needed. To achieve this, I approached every Australian that had won an Olympic Gold Medal in the past 20 years and invited them to attend the launch and endorse the yacht. The day of the launch was spectacular.

Martin Plaza was full of television crews and satellite dishes, networks attending from all over the world. On the yacht, there were Olympians, a band, cheerleaders, tens of thousands of balloons, celebrities, and streamers.

In the two weeks the yacht was in the mall, over two million people had come to see it. On the day of the launch there were literally tens of thousands waiting to see and hear the name. Martin Plaza was jammed. Then we launched the yacht with the bottle of champagne and unveiled the name. The whole city was abuzz; it was party time—all for a yacht that no one had ever heard of or cared about less than two months before. ESPN broadcast the launch live into America. The major daily newspapers in the three biggest cities in the country ran full-page, full-color photographs. A newspaper poll showed that over 80 percent of the population had heard of the yacht launch. Most importantly, the average person related to the Americas' Cup as "their" yacht.

The results were outstanding. Why? Because it was unique, different, and outside the square.

Grab the Initiative

Thinking outside the box does not always mean doing big things. Recently, I was speaking to nearly 1,000 people at a Hyatt Hotel and I mentioned that I fly almost 300,000 miles each year to all corners of the globe and represent a pretty good account for a travel agency. Yet, the agency I am using, although they make great arrangements, usually on short notice, never calls on my return to see how my trip went. Five minutes later, a guy from the audience walked up from the side of the stage and handed me an envelope. I immediately put the envelope in my pocket. Halfway through a sentence it really threw me off my stride. I couldn't stop thinking about this envelope for the rest of my address.

When I finished the speech, I read the letter. It was from a gentleman, David Alcott, who was a travel agent. He had noted what I had said about adding value and thinking outside the box, and he had decided that, even in front of 1,000 people, he would pitch to be my travel agent. When I asked him why he had chosen the middle of my talk to do it, he reminded me that I had told the group to seize the opportunity when it arises or run the risk of missing out. He promised to install a dedicated 800 phone number for me and assign a full-time person to make sure the travel needs of me and my company were taken care of. David showed initiative, added value, and thought outside the box. He also obtained our business. Although I don't recommend that you interrupt someone in the middle of a speech and give him or her heart failure to obtain his or her business, you should always seize the opportunity.

Here are some other examples for thinking outside the box on a smaller scale.

Once a month, on a random Monday or Tuesday night, an Italian restaurant called Macaroni's gives all its patrons a complimentary meal and a letter inviting them to tell their friends about the restaurant. The result? The restaurant was packed, not only on Mondays and Tuesdays, but every night.

Mercedes Benz buyers will not usually test-drive a Jaguar. To combat this, Jaguar offered owners of 3- to 4-year-old Mercedes Benz's a complimentary two-day test-drive of a new Jaguar in exchange for fully detailing their vehicle. When the Mercedes Benz was brought back to the owners, it was a perfect trade-in on the new Jaguar they were test-driving. Far more sales were garnered than ever would have been with a full-page newspaper advertisement, and at a fraction of the cost.

Thinking Outside the Square Creates a Win–Win from Potential Disaster

Kurt Stevens of Stevens Aviation noticed that Southwest Airlines was using a trademarked slogan "Plane Smart." Kurt called Herb Kelleher, president of Southwest Airlines to ask him to stop using it. Herb suggested they arm wrestle for it. The public relations department of Southwest Airlines worked with NBC news on a feature called "Malice in Dallas—Killer Kurt v. Smokin' Herb." The event was held in an arena, where, in a fully staged production, Kurt jogged in while Herb was carried. Hundreds of employees cheered each team on. Not surprisingly, Kurt won and Herb announced that Stevens Aviation had the right to the slogan. Both companies then donated $15,000 to charity.

What could have been an expensive lawsuit resulted in massive internal and external publicity for both companies. Creativity and innovation turned a potentially bad situation into a win-win. The best part is that thinking outside the box doesn't have to cost much money.

Remember: It's not the size of the budget that counts; it's the size of the idea.

Chapter 18

Persistence and Morality Pay

I live in Los Angeles.

Los Angeles is a great place; they've got race riots, earthquakes, bush fires, landslides, a population greater than the whole of Australia, and, of course, my favorite spot, Disneyland.

When I first moved to the United States over 20 years ago, I began building a business and a reputation from scratch.

In the United States, competition is fierce. What you did yesterday is not good enough tomorrow. People are incredibly innovative, and there are literally hundreds of thousands of great marketers who have spent their lives in this dynamic, competitive economy. At the time, the United States was just beginning a downturn, which led to the severe recession of the late 1980s and early 1990s. Corporations had cut their marketing budgets, so, suffice to say, it was not perfect timing to be opening a business in a new country.

However, outside forces are not an excuse for lack of performance. My first task was to greatly increase my marketing skills and become more innovative.

In the early 1990s, we were going through a particularly tough patch, and we got the opportunity to present on a multimillion-dollar project in New York. We formulated a concept, and I ran the idea past the company's sales and marketing manager over the phone. He liked the idea well enough, but in the financial climate of that time, it was going to be a board decision.

The board was meeting in New York in three weeks, and the sales and marketing manager put our presentation on the agenda. With less than three weeks to prepare a full and detailed presentation, we were all burning the midnight oil. Ten days later, we had the package ready to send out to get the artwork and printing done.

Unfortunately, we delivered the proposal only three days before the jury handed down its findings in the first Rodney King trial. What followed were the riots and the siege of Los Angeles. We didn't find out until the next afternoon that our artwork and printing wasn't being done because the rioters had burned down the factory on that first fateful night.

It was now Tuesday, and after our initial panic, we began to re-source some of the material, reprint the rest, and find a new art department and printer. By Wednesday morning, we had contracted a new company in Hollywood to do the artwork and found a local Santa Monica printer who could fit in our job.

The workload over the previous few days had been pretty heavy, and it had taken its toll. Our then company president, who is a diabetic, collapsed in the office on Wednesday night and was rushed to the hospital.

By Friday afternoon, the artwork with corrections was back, and the whole package was ready for the printers. By Saturday afternoon, a copy was on its way by courier to New York, but we were still adding refinements to the actual presentation we planned to make in person.

By lunchtime on Sunday, we had all had it; we needed a break. There was little more we could do before the Tuesday flight to New York. We were confident we had a great presentation and would close the deal. I told everyone in the office to pack it in for the day, and we wandered down to the beach to have a pizza and a couple of bottles of wine.

Big mistake!

One of the guys in the office had a football that they were tossing around the park. I jumped up to catch the ball, but as I jumped, I felt my knee snap. I had totally severed the patella tendon and as I landed, I shattered my knee; I was lying on the ground in excruciating agony.

The paramedics arrived quickly and rushed me to the UCLA Medical Center where the news just got worse. The doctors told me they had to operate immediately. Apparently, tendons shrink, and the longer I waited, the greater the risk of the damage being inoperable. I asked if I could at least wait until Thursday. The answer was yes, I could wait, but I would spend the rest of my life with a stiff leg.

I chose to have the operation. This meant that both the company president and I were in the hospital. By Tuesday, I was out of the operating room, coming out of a morphine-induced trance thinking, I'm about to be out of business.

We were in severe financial trouble. The New York meeting is in 15-hours time, my right-hand person was still in the hospital, I have plaster up to my navel, and I'm full of drugs. I can't reschedule the meeting and the next full board meeting wasn't for another three months.

One of my team members came to the hospital and asked what we were going to do. I felt lousy and pretty depressed and responded that I really didn't know. He suggested a teleconference. Unfortunately, we simply couldn't afford it.

Unknown to me, the staff went ahead with the teleconference idea. They all pitched in, borrowing to get it set up. The board was very sympathetic and understanding and we went through the presentation in about an hour.

Well, guess what happened? They bought the proposal and we went on to establish a successful business.

Why did we succeed? I heard later that the board agreed we presented a sound proposal that they were confident would work. More importantly, they were convinced we believed in the idea so passionately that we were prepared to go to almost any lengths to present the proposal to them and would let nothing stand in our way.

Success Almost Always Takes Time

In 1922, Mary Smith, a U.S. government worker said, "The only place you find success before work is in the dictionary." Nothing has changed.

Most "overnight" successes have usually been working at their profession for many years. For example, Olympic athletes train for years for that one gold medal. History is full of examples of great successes that failed at their first attempt.

- ◆ Walt Disney went to over 200 banks before getting the financing for Disneyland.
- ◆ Colonel Sanders knocked on over 1,000 restaurant doors before he obtained the first customer for his secret herbs and spices.
- ◆ Fred Smith's Yale professor gave him a C for his thesis on overnight delivery service, saying it needed to be feasible to get a better mark. Later he founded Federal Express.
- ◆ Charles Carlson invented photocopying in 1938 but had to wait 21 years until the first Xerox machine was made.
- ◆ Michael Blake, author of *Dances with Wolves*, had 26 years of rejection before the book was published.

- R.H. Macy failed seven times before his department store idea caught on.
- John Creasey received 753 rejection slips before he published the first of his 564 books.
- Thomas Edison left school early because teachers told him he wasn't capable of doing the work.
- Bob Dylan was booed off stage at his first high school talent quest.

If you have done your homework, know there is a need for your product or service, and you keep persisting, you will succeed. Sometimes it just takes a little longer than we had hoped. It is interesting that 96 percent of salespeople stop calling after receiving less than six rejections. A Dartnell Corporation Study showed that most business accounts are won after the prospect has said no eight times.

Morality Pays

Over the years, I have often watched as some people have taken short cuts, ripped people off, and been totally immoral in their business dealings. Some have made deals they knew were bad or they sold goods they knew were faulty, all to chase the fast buck. In every case, after a while their luck ran out; sometimes it was their business, sometimes their personal life, sometimes the law or the IRS got them. It is always better to play it straight, leave some for the next guy. It's more important for you to sleep well at night; have the love, trust, and respect of your partner and kids; enjoy lifelong relationships in business; and have a lot of fun along the way. Life is meant to be enjoyed, not spent ducking and weaving.

> And remember, there are always more opportunities than time to do them.

Fantastic Stories of Inspiration

Many years ago, Al Capone virtually owned Chicago. Capone wasn't famous for anything heroic. He was notorious for enmeshing the windy city in everything from bootlegged booze and prostitution to murder.

Capone had a lawyer nicknamed Easy Eddie. He was Capone's lawyer for a good reason. Eddie was very good! In fact, Eddie's skill at legal maneuvering kept Big Al out of jail for a long time. To show his appreciation, Capone paid him very well. Not only was the money big, but also, Eddie got special dividends. For instance, he and his family occupied a gated mansion with live-in help and all the conveniences of the day. The estate was so large that it filled an entire Chicago city block.

Eddie lived the high life of the Chicago mob and gave little consideration to the atrocities that went on around him. Eddie did have one soft spot, however. He had a son that he loved dearly. Eddie saw to it that his young son had clothes, cars, and a good education. Nothing was withheld. Price was no object. Despite his involvement with organized crime, Eddie even tried to teach him right from wrong. Eddie wanted his son to be a better man than he was. Yet, with all his wealth and influence, there were two things he could not give his son: he could not pass on a good name or a good example.

One day, Easy Eddie reached a difficult decision; he wanted to rectify wrongs he had done. He decided he would go to the authorities and tell the truth about Al "Scarface" Capone, clean up his tarnished name, and offer his son some semblance of integrity.

To do this, he would have to testify against the Mob, and he knew that the cost would be great. So, he testified.

Within the year, Easy Eddie's life ended in a blaze of gunfire on a lonely Chicago street. But in his eyes, he had given his son the greatest gift he had to offer at the greatest price he could ever pay. Police removed from his pockets a rosary, a crucifix, a religious medallion, and a poem clipped from a magazine.

From Zero to Hero

World War II produced many heroes. One such man was Lieutenant Commander Butch O'Hare. He was a fighter pilot assigned to the aircraft carrier *Lexington* in the South Pacific. One day his entire squadron was sent on a mission. After he was airborne, he looked at his fuel gauge and realized that his fuel tank had not been topped off. He would not have enough fuel to complete his mission and get back to his ship. His flight leader told him to return to the carrier.

Reluctantly, he dropped out of formation and headed back to the fleet. As he was returning to the mother ship, he saw something that turned his blood cold: A squadron of Japanese aircraft was speeding its way toward the American fleet. The American fleet was defenseless. He could not reach his squadron and bring them back in time to save the fleet. Nor could he warn the fleet of the approaching danger.

There was only one thing to do. He must somehow divert them from the fleet.

Laying aside all thoughts of personal safety, he dove into the formation of Japanese planes. Wing-mounted 50 calibers blazed as he charged in, attacking one surprised enemy plane and then another. Butch wove in and out of the now-broken formation and fired at as many planes as possible until all his ammunition was spent.

Undaunted, he continued the assault. He dove at the planes, trying to clip a wing or tail in hopes of damaging as many enemy planes as possible and rendering them unfit to fly. Finally, the exasperated Japanese squadron took off in another direction. Deeply relieved, Butch O'Hare and his tattered fighter limped back to the carrier. Upon arrival, he reported in and related the events surrounding his return. The film from the gun-camera mounted on his plane told the tale. It showed the extent of Butch's daring attempt to protect his fleet. He had, in fact, destroyed five enemy aircraft. This took place on February 20, 1942, and for that action Butch became the Navy's first Ace of World War II, and the first Naval aviator to win the Congressional Medal of Honor.

A year later Butch was killed in aerial combat at the age of 29. His hometown would not allow the memory of this World War II hero to fade, and today, O'Hare Airport in Chicago is named in tribute to the courage of this great man. So, the next time you find yourself at O'Hare International, give some thought to visiting Butch's memorial displaying his statue and his Medal of Honor. It is located between Terminals 1 and 2.

So what do these two stories have to do with each other?

Butch O'Hare was Easy Eddie's son.

Remember: If you want the rainbow, you need to put up with the rain.

Conclusion

In today's highly competitive, global, fast-paced, cluttered marketplace, a number of influences are at work, which has had a dramatic effect on commerce. These new developments and technologies have created amazing efficiencies in production, optimizing stock levels, communication, warehousing, and delivery, and has increased productivity accordingly.

> The long-term effect of the Internet on business-to-consumer purchasing patterns is still far from known.

One thing that is for certain is that the consumers' access to detailed information on products and services has been greatly increased. It is my view that the much-hyped revolution in customer purchasing behavior created by the Internet is overemphasized. The overwhelming majority of online business has commenced with a product focus, and the product and its price have been the primary drivers of the marketing strategy. In fact, most of these products have not been marketed at all; they have simply been advertised. There are two flaws in this approach.

First, it ignores all but one of the valuable tools that are available in the full marketing armory. Second, it leads to a commoditization of products, and competitive advantage relies on price. This is disastrous for all but the largest of companies. Success in business comes about from differentiating your product from those of your competitors and selling product at a premium, increasing ROI and, therefore, competitiveness.

Being product driven, these companies had not realized that there is no correlation between brand awareness and sales—until their demise.

This poor marketing strategy occurred at a time of increasingly sophisticated consumers, those who are discerning, who will only buy products that meet their emotional needs in which value is added and there is no purchase risk. The products had to do no harm to the environment, not exploit people or animals, and the company had to share the core beliefs of these consumers.

To be purchased, a business, product, or service needs brand equity. Sure, some businesses, primarily in essential services like gasoline, get through the radar, but consumer sentiment is rapidly changing, as is evidenced by the BP oil spill in the Gulf of Mexico.

In my view, effective marketing today is no different than it always has been. You just need to follow a few simple rules that I have described in this book.

> Marketing is not rocket science; it comes down to knowledge, logic, empathy, and communication.

Follow These Simple Steps to Win:
- Thoroughly understand your product, marketplace, and competitors.
- Understand the customer's emotional need that is fulfilled by your product or service.
- Create a powerful consumer purchasing benefit.
- Add value to every purchase.
- Provide awesome service.
- Understand your catchment areas.
- Differentiate your product or service.
- Educate and empower your team.
- Understand and anticipate change.
- Focus on building equity in your brand.
- Select your communication vehicles wisely.
- Clearly identify your target market.
- Continually push the envelope of your thinking.
- Remember, it's not the size of the budget, but the size of the idea that counts.
- Anticipate and adapt to change.
- Have a clear vision for your business.
- Understand what business you are in.
- Have clear goals that you review regularly.
- Ensure your name and logo clearly reflects your business.
- Remember, the only person that counts is the customer.

- ◆ Remember, price doesn't influence 80 percent of purchases.
- ◆ Be empathetic.
- ◆ Be persistent.

This is an amazing world with extraordinary things to see and do, wonderful cultures to experience, endless fun and enjoyment to be had, and exceptional people to meet. You owe it to yourself to maximize your experience. No matter what your previous history or your current situation, you can achieve it all if you begin today.

You have made a great start by reading this book. Whether you agree or disagree with me, I hope I have got you thinking.

We would be pleased to work with you in a consulting capacity, from a think tank to a business and marketing audit, creation of a full marketing strategy, or taking you to IPO.

Whether on a detailed aspect of marketing to an executive group, motivating and pointing teams in the right direction, or conducting marketing workshops, if I can assist you in any of these ways, please don't hesitate to e-mail me at bob@bobpritchard.com or go to my website www.bobpritchard.com.

Remember: If you are not living on the edge, you are taking up too much room.

About the Author

Bob Pritchard, BSc., CSP., AISMM is Australian born and a 25-year Los Angeles resident who has enjoyed an extraordinary 35-year career. His unique sales, marketing, and motivational ability has taken Bob from sharing an inner-city two-room apartment as a child with three generations of family, to international success as a businessman, marketer, and speaker. His outside-the-box philosophy and focus on ROI and the bottom line has led to Marketforce One Inc. being represented in the United States, Europe, and Australia working with corporations, sports, and entertainment entities.

In 1999, Bob Pritchard won the highly prestigious International Marketer of the Year award. His is an extraordinary journey of courage, motivation, and determination.

Bob's first endeavors—in business and marketing—were in the entertainment arena, staging events that included 38 presentations at the Sydney Opera House. During this period, he created the Australian Pops Orchestra.

For the next decade, Bob became involved in many business ventures, primarily involving the marketing of products, before joining Rupert Murdoch's News Limited. Bob then became marketing director for Australia's richest man, Kerry Packer, at PBL Marketing, focusing on sports, movies, entertainment, television, and magazines. In 1984, Pritchard conceived and engineered the first privatization and stock exchange listing of a sports team in Australia, becoming CEO of the organization that owned both professional football and basketball teams. His achievement in increasing sponsorship, attendance, and media exposure for the football team is the subject of several books and a television documentary.

Following this success, Bob moved to the United States, where Marketforce One, Inc was established.

Pritchard, and Marketforce One, Inc. have created a wide range of media, marketing, sales, and promotion campaigns, both local and international, for both major corporations and small and medium enterprises (companies with less than 500 employees in the United States and with less than 250 employees in Europe—referred to as SMEs) on four continents. Pritchard was appointed as a consultant to Fox Studios for their 260-acre working studios, entertainment, theater, and restaurant theme park. He was also appointed to represent corporate interests at Darling Harbor in Sydney, the fifth largest Summer Olympic Games site in history.

His success in sports is exceptional: marketing of Formula One Motor Racing; Skins Golf with Norman, Nicklaus, Ballesteros, and Watson; seven-nation World Series Cricket; Katarina Witt 18 Olympians Asian Tour; World Champion Heavyweight Evander Holyfield; and Legends Tennis, to name a few.

In 1997, the American Film Industry celebrated its centenary, and Pritchard was selected to develop the program involving all the major studios and television networks. The Los Angeles Philharmonic Orchestra, The Environmental Media Awards featuring Mikael Gorbachev, Disney Chief Michael Eisner, and CNN's Ted Turner, have also numbered among Pritchard's clients.

Bob was selected as the co-host of the 1998 Asia and Pacific region Miss Universe Quest telecast in 56 countries across the world. He also hosted the pilot of the television show *Dreams of Ordinary Men*, which recognized outstanding small business achievement.

Bob devotes a lot of his time pro bono to being the Global Ambassador for Kidney Health and also to The Golden Stave, the entertainment and music industry organization that raises funds for children's charities. Bob is a director and shareholder of several companies in the healthcare, technology, online gaming, and finance industries.

Bob Begins His Speaking Career

In the mid 1990s, Bob began to share his broad international business experience by speaking to corporations and business organizations.

Today, he is one of the most successful business speakers in the world, having spoken in 52 countries on five continents and numbering among his clients 91 of the Fortune 500 companies. He is a regular contributor to television, radio, newspapers, and magazines, and has been featured on *60 Minutes* and other television programs around the world. Pritchard is the author of three internationally bestselling books; he has a daily radio segment on small business tips; he was a director of a company that won four Silver Telly awards in the United States; his success in marketing sports was the subject of several books and a TV documentary; and he has been guest lecturer at universities in the United States, Europe, and Australia.

In 2002, Bob was awarded the prestigious Certified Speaking Professional (CSP) award by his speaking peers.

Pritchard has been described as a genius of vision and a great motivator, communicator, and marketer. As a speaker, he is known for his dynamic delivery, meticulous preparation, and practical take-away value. Bob Pritchard is an extraordinary achiever and has a great story to tell.

"Thanks for helping to make the difference."

—Evander Holyfield

Index